Chicken Soup for the Soul.

for the Soul.

Our 101 BEST STORIES

Woman to Woman

D1007509

Chicken Soup for the Soul® Our 101 Best Stories:
Woman to Woman; Women Sharing Their Stories of Hope, Humor, and Inspiration
by Jack Canfield, Mark Victor Hansen & Amy Newmark

Published by Chicken Soup for the Soul Publishing, LLC   www.chickensoup.com

The publisher gratefully acknowledges the many publishers and individuals who
granted Chicken Soup for the Soul permission to reprint the cited material.

Cover photos courtesy of Randy Faris/Corbis and Jupiter Images/photos.com. Interior
illustration courtesy of iStockPhoto.com/mxtama and Jupiter Images/photos.com.

Cover and Interior Design & Layout by Pneuma Books, LLC
For more info on Pneuma Books, visit www.pneumabooks.com

Distributed to the booktrade by Simon & Schuster. SAN: 200-2442

Publisher's Cataloging-in-Publication Data
(Prepared by The Donohue Group)

Chicken soup for the soul. Selections.

   Chicken soup for the soul : woman to woman : women sharing their stories
of hope, humor, and inspiration / [compiled by] Jack Canfield [and] Mark Victor
Hansen ; [edited by] Amy Newmark.

   p. ; cm. — (Our 101 best stories)

   ISBN-13: 978-1-935096-04-7
   ISBN-10: 1-935096-04-4

1. Women--Literary collections. 2. Women--Conduct of life--Anecdotes. I.
Canfield, Jack, 1944- II. Hansen, Mark Victor. III. Newmark, Amy. IV. Title.
PN6071.W7 C483 2008
810.8/09287   2008930429

PRINTED IN THE UNITED STATES OF AMERICA
on acid∞free paper
16 15 14 13 12 10 09 08   01 02 03 04 05 06 07 08

Chicken Soup for the Soul

Our **101** BEST STORIES

for the Soul.

Woman to Woman

Women Sharing Their Stories of Hope, Humor, and Inspiration

Jack Canfield
Mark Victor Hansen
Amy Newmark

CSS

Chicken Soup for the Soul Publishing, LLC
Cos Cob, CT

Chicken Soup for the Soul

Contents

❸

~Special Moments~

❹

~Motherhood~

❺

~Through the Generations ~

❻

~Inner Strength and Courage~

❼

~The Power of Support~

❽
~ It's All a Matter of Perspective ~

❾
~Overcoming Obstacles ~

❿
~Achieving Your Dream ~

❶❶

~ Taking Time for Yourself ~

❶❷

~ Gratitude ~

Chicken Soup for the Soul

A Special Foreword

by Jack & Mark

For us, 101 has always been a magical number. It was the number of stories in the first *Chicken Soup for the Soul* book, and it is the number of stories and poems we have always aimed for in our books. We love the number 101 because it signifies a beginning, not an end. After 100, we start anew with 101.

We hope that when you finish reading one of our books, it is only a beginning for you too—a new outlook on life, a renewed sense of purpose, a strengthened resolve to deal with an issue that has been bothering you. Perhaps you will pick up the phone and share one of the stories with a friend or a loved one. Perhaps you will turn to your keyboard and express yourself by writing a Chicken Soup story of your own, to share with other readers who are just like you.

This volume contains our 101 best stories and poems for women, from women. We share this with you at a very special time for us, the fifteenth anniversary of our *Chicken Soup for the Soul* series. When we published our first book in 1993, we never dreamed that we had started what has become a publishing phenomenon, one of the best-selling book series in history.

We did not set out to sell more than one hundred million books, or to publish more than 150 titles. We set out to touch the heart of one person at a time, hoping that person would in turn touch another person, and so on down the line. Fifteen years later, we know that it has worked. Your letters and stories have poured in by the hundreds of thousands, affirming our life's work, and inspiring us to continue to make a difference in your lives.

On our fifteenth anniversary, we have new energy, new resolve, and new dreams. We have recommitted to our goal of 101 stories or poems per book, we have refreshed our cover designs and our interior layout, and we have grown the Chicken Soup for the Soul team, with new friends and partners across the country in New England.

Women have always been wonderful sources of inspiration and support for each other. They are willing to lay bare their souls and share their experiences with one another, even with perfect strangers. Put two random women together in a waiting room, on an airplane, in a line at the supermarket, and we are amazed at the sharing that occurs, often at the deepest level.

In this new volume, we have selected our 101 best stories and poems written by women of all ages, for women of all ages. We hope that you will enjoy reading these stories as much as we enjoyed selecting them for you, and that you will share them with your families and friends. We have identified the 27 *Chicken Soup for the Soul* books in which the stories originally appeared, in case you would like to explore our other titles. We hope you will also enjoy the additional books about singles, love, families, pets, sports, and retirement years in "Our 101 Best Stories" series.

With our love, our thanks, and our respect,
~*Jack Canfield and Mark Victor Hansen*

Woman to Woman

Women Making a Difference

Act as if what you do makes a difference. It does.
~William James

The Baby Blanket

A hug is a great gift—one size fits all, and it's easy to exchange.
~Author Unknown

It was a spring Saturday, and though many activities clamored for my attention, I had chosen this time to sit and crochet, an activity I enjoyed but had once thought impossible.

Most of the time I don't mind being a "lefty"—I'm quite proud of it, actually. But I admit, it did cause me a few problems three years ago, when I wanted to help out with a project at church.

We were invited to crochet baby blankets, which would be donated to a local crisis pregnancy center at Christmas. I wanted to participate but I knew nothing about how to crochet, and my left-handedness didn't help. I had trouble "thinking backwards."

I suppose where there is a will, there is a way, because a few of the ladies got together and taught me one stitch. That's all I needed. I learned that granny stitch, and before long I had a blanket made. I was so proud of my little accomplishment and it seemed, inexplicably, so important, that I made quite a few more that same year. I even included in each blanket, as a note of encouragement, a poem I had written that read:

Little girls are sweet in their ruffles all pink.
Little boys in overalls look divine.
But no matter which one the Lord gives to you,
A better "Mom" he never could find.

All of a sudden, my thoughts were interrupted by the ringing of my telephone. I hurried to answer it, and to my surprise and delight, on the other end of the line was Karen Sharp, who had been one of my very best friends ever since elementary school. Karen, her husband, Jim, and their daughter, Kim, had moved away a few years ago. She was calling to say that she was in town for a couple of days and would like to come by. I was thrilled to hear her voice.

At last the doorbell rang. As I flung open the door, we both screamed, as if back in junior high. We hugged each other. Then questions began to fly. Finally, I guided Karen into the kitchen, where I poured a cool glass of tea for both of us and the conversation slowed.

To my delight, Karen seemed to be calm, rested and, most of all, self-assured, which were a few qualities that she had seemed to lose during the last few months before they moved away. I wondered what had caused the positive change.

As we talked and reminisced, Karen began to explain to me the true reasons for her family's move a few years ago. The original reason they had given me was that Jim had a job offer in another city, which they could not afford to pass up. Even though it was Kim's senior year in high school, they still felt it necessary to make the move. Apparently, that had not been the biggest reason.

Karen reached into her purse and pulled out a photograph. When she handed it to me, I saw it was a beautiful little girl — maybe about two or three years old.

"This is my granddaughter, Kayla," Karen said.

I couldn't believe my ears. "You're a grandmother?" I asked. "I don't understand."

"You see," Karen went on, "Kim was a few months pregnant when we moved away. We had just found out, and Kim was having a really rough time dealing with it — she even talked about suicide. We were frantic. So we decided to move away, hoping that she would adjust more easily. When we finally settled in our new home, we hoped that Kim's outlook would begin to improve, but she became more and more depressed. No matter what we said, she felt worthless and like a failure. Then we found a woman named Mrs. Barber, a wonderful pregnancy counselor. She got Kim through some very tough times.

"As the time for delivery came closer, Kim still had not entirely made up her mind about whether to keep the baby or not. Her father and I prayed that she would. We felt prepared to give the baby a loving home—it was, after all, our first grandchild!

"Finally, the day came, and Kim had a six-pound, six-ounce baby girl. Mrs. Barber came to visit her in the hospital. She hugged Kim and told her how proud she was of her. Then she gave Kim a pastel-colored package containing a hand-crocheted baby blanket inside."

At this point, I felt a huge lump come into my throat, and I felt rather limp all over, but I tried not to show my feelings and kept listening to Karen's story.

Karen must have noticed the look on my face. She asked if I was all right. I assured her I was fine and asked her to please continue.

"As I said," she went on, "there was a baby blanket and a little personal note, something about little girls and their ruffles, little boys and their overalls, and a word of encouragement about becoming a new mom.

"We asked who made the blanket, and Mrs. Barber explained that some of the pregnancy centers have people who donate these blankets to new mothers and their babies. Her center was given the surplus from one of the other centers in the state, and she was glad to have one for Kim.

"Kim was so moved by the fact that a total stranger had thought enough to put this much time and effort into a blanket for her baby. She said it made her feel warm all over. She later told her dad and me that the little poem gave her a boost of confidence and helped her to make up her mind to keep little Kayla."

Karen's story had an even happier ending: A year later, Kim was married to a young man who loves both her and Kayla with all his heart. Karen grinned as she told me, then sobered. "My only regret is that I did not feel close enough to our friends here to have been able to lean on you all for support and comfort, instead of turning away.

"We are so thankful for so many things—especially the way

everything turned out; but I think the one thing that we are the most thankful for is that kind person who made that little baby blanket for our daughter and her baby. I just wish I could give her a big hug and tell her how much she is loved and appreciated by our family."

I looked again at the photo of the sweet child in my hands. Then I leaned over to Karen and gave her a big hug.

~Winona Smith
A Second Chicken Soup for the Woman's Soul

The Touch of Kindness

I've seen and met angels wearing the disguise of
ordinary people living ordinary lives.
~Tracy Chapman

"Why do you want to be a nurse, Patricia?"

The two nursing instructors and the dean of nursing sat at their table, squarely facing me as I sat on my hard, straight-backed wooden chair facing them. "Two thousand young people have applied to our program." The dean's voice came from across the room, "and we will select sixty of them. Tell us why we should choose you." She folded her hands and looked up at me from the stack of application forms.

I hesitated a moment, wondering what the other applicants sitting in this same chair had answered. What did they say that was music to the instructors' ears? I tried hard to imagine what they wanted to hear from me.

I thought my reason for wanting to be a nurse sounded simple and silly, so I hesitated and was quiet. It seemed laughable that I should be applying to nursing school at all. During my childhood, I was terrified of doctors, nurses and hospitals. I dreaded every office visit even for an annual checkup! So it was a surprise to many that I now had the desire to become that which I had formerly done my best to avoid. But an incident from my childhood was compelling me, and I drew upon that now.

When I was six years old, my parents were told I needed to be admitted to the hospital for some "tests." They drove me to the children's hospital across town on a cold gray Sunday afternoon. I looked up at the imposing building and then quickly hid my face in my mother's sleeve. I tried to resist going in, but my mother and father were holding my hands and I was whisked along against my will.

We exited the elevator, and my parents led me down a long hallway. When we came to a large room that was divided into cubicles, we stopped. We were directed to one of the cubicles by a stern grayhaired nurse who pointed here and there, showing us where my suitcase should go, where my pajamas and robe should hang, where the button was to press so a nurse would come when we wanted.

My father went downstairs then, and my mother tried to make me feel at home. The gray-haired nurse soon brought a supper tray, but I couldn't eat. Everything here was so different from what I was used to. So my mother picked at the food on my tray while she tried to entertain me. She tried to cheer me by talking about how some of the children there were very sick, and it was nice that I was only there for "tests" and would be able to come home soon.

I wondered why my mother didn't have a suitcase with her. Wouldn't she need some pajamas and a robe, too? After the nurse took the tray away, I learned why. My parents were not allowed to stay with me. They were going home, and I was staying there. They were leaving me, and I'd never been away from them before. As my mother slipped into her coat and prepared to leave, I began to cry.

"No, no, Mama, please don't go, please don't leave me!" I begged. She just smiled slightly and told me she'd be back tomorrow, to be a good girl and do what the nurses told me.

As I listened to her footsteps fade away, I turned over in my bed and curled up in a tight little ball, facing away from the door. I tried to think of something happy. I tried to think of songs I liked to sing. I tried to remember the faces of all my stuffed animals at home. I thought hard, but my thoughts were interrupted by another nurse who said firmly, "Time for bed."

I sat up then, and she removed my robe and pajamas and dressed me in a hospital gown. I lay back down and curled up tighter than ever and wept. The lights were turned out then, and I lay awake in the dark.

Much later, I heard someone enter the room, where I still whimpered in my bed. "You're not asleep yet?" a pleasant, quiet voice asked.

"I can't sleep," I said, trembling.

"Sit up a minute and talk to me," the voice coaxed. I sat up then, and in the dim light I could see it was a nurse, but not one I had seen before.

"I want to go home," I said, sobbing again. The nurse reached forward and held me as I cried. "I think I'm going to be sick," I moaned, and my stomach began to heave.

She held a basin in front of me and wiped my face gently with a damp washcloth. She cradled me then as I calmed down, and I lay limp against her shoulder as she rocked me back and forth.

After what seemed like a very long time, she looked down at me and said, "I have some work to do now, so I can't stay with you." Seeing my dejected look, she added, "But maybe you could come and be with me. Let's see."

In the hallway there were low wooden wagons with mattresses and pillows that the nurses used to take some of the children outside for some fresh air. She brought one of these to my bedside and beckoned for me to get in. As she lifted me down to the wagon, I looked at her shiny name pin and read "Miss White."

Miss White wheeled me out to the nurses' station and parked the wagon by the desk. I watched as she sat and wrote, and every once in a while she'd look over at me and smile. "Want something to drink now?" she asked. I nodded and sipped the apple juice she brought, and soon I drifted off to sleep. Early in the morning she rolled me back to my bed, and I was so tired that I hardly noticed when she told me goodbye.

My mother did come to see me later that day, and the next night was not quite as hard to bear. I had to stay in the hospital for only a few days before my brief ordeal was over. But I never forgot how terrified I felt, and I never forgot Miss White's kindness to a desperately lonely and scared little girl.

This incident ran quickly through my mind, and I thought for a moment before I answered the dean's question. Why did I want to be a nurse? I straightened up in my chair and lifted my chin and said, "Being a patient in a hospital is a frightening thing, for anyone. Some people conceal it better than others, but all patients are afraid. I remember being a frightened child in a hospital when I was only six, and there was a nurse there who was very kind to me. She was the one who made my stay bearable."

The room was quiet as I went on. "I have always remembered her, and I want to be the kind of nurse she was. I want to be the one who cheers up a frightened child, holds the hand of a lonely older person, soothes the anxiety of a nervous patient."

I was accepted to the nursing program and worked hard to learn the skills and techniques necessary to provide the best care for my patients. On graduation night as I stepped up to the stage to accept my diploma, I thought of Miss White and smiled. She would never know what a profound influence she'd had on me. She taught me the most important lessons in nursing. She taught me the significance of empathy for the patient and his or her plight, of compassion in easing the difficulty of another. What she gave to me was now my own to give, the gentle touch of kindness that makes the difference to our patients and to our world.

~Tricia Caliguire
Chicken Soup for the Nurse's Soul

Now I Lay Me Down to Sleep

A mother's arms are made of tenderness and children sleep soundly in them.
~Victor Hugo

Growing up, I wanted to be a doctor, but money was scarce, so I went to nursing school. In 1966, during my senior year, an Army Nurse Corps recruiter came to talk to us. It all sounded so exciting: I would have a chance to travel, it paid well and, most important, I was assured that I wouldn't have to go to Vietnam if I didn't want to—which I didn't.

I signed up. After basic training, I was assigned to Letterman Hospital at the Presidio of San Francisco. During my two years at Letterman, I received orders for Vietnam three times. The first two times, I said no. But the third time, I decided that my two years of experience would probably be a huge asset over there.

We landed in Tan Son Nhut Air Base, and when the airplane door opened, I nearly fell backward, overwhelmed by the heat and the stench. Suddenly, all my experience seemed trivial. Being twenty-three years old seemed very young. I was scared, but there was no turning back.

After our debriefing, I was assigned to the Sixty-seventh Evac Hospital in Qui Nhon. When the helicopter landed on the hospital tarmac, my things were set on the ground. I climbed out, straightening my skirt. The soldiers in the helicopter yelled, "Good luck, Captain" as they took off.

I was in my class A uniform, which meant I was also wearing nylons and high heels. Nothing could have been less appropriate for the surroundings. Miles of barbed wire, topped by concertina wire, encompassed the hospital compound and the large adjoining airfield, along with acres of hot concrete. I squared my shoulders and marched inside the grim cinder block building in front of me. I was told to get some sleep, because I started tomorrow. I gratefully fell into a bed, and in the morning, I donned my hospital uniform—fatigues and Army boots—just like the soldiers.

Because I was a captain, I was made head nurse on the orthopedic ward, which primarily held soldiers with traumatic amputations. I took my role very seriously and had a reputation for strictness.

Being a nurse in the States for two years did not adequately prepare me for Vietnam. I witnessed a tremendous amount of suffering and watched a lot of men die. One of my rules was that nurses were not allowed to cry. The wounded and dying men in our care needed our strength, I told them. We couldn't indulge in the luxury of our own feelings.

On the other hand, I was always straight with the soldiers. I would never say, "Oh, you're going to be just fine," if they were on their way out. I didn't lie.

But I remember one kid who I didn't want to tell. The badly wounded soldier couldn't have been more than eighteen years old. I could see immediately that there was nothing we could do to save him. He never screamed or complained, even though he must have been in a lot of pain.

When he asked me, "Am I going to die?" I said, "Do you feel like you are?"

He said, "Yeah, I do."

"Do you pray?" I asked him.

"I know 'Now I lay me down to sleep.'"

"Good," I said, "that'll work."

When he asked me if I would hold his hand, something in me

snapped. This kid deserved more than just having his hand held. "I'll do better than that," I told him.

I knew I would catch flak from the other nurses and Corpsmen, as well as possible jeers from the patients, but I didn't care. Without a single look around me, I climbed onto the bed with him. I put my arms around him, stroking his face and his hair as he snuggled close to me. I kissed him on the cheek, and together we recited, "Now I lay me down to sleep. I pray the Lord my soul to keep. If I should die before I wake, I pray the Lord my soul to take."

Then he looked at me and said just one more sentence, "I love you, Momma, I love you," before he died in my arms—quietly and peacefully—as if he really were just going to sleep.

After a minute, I slipped off his bed and looked around. I'm sure my face was set in a fierce scowl, daring anyone to give me a hard time. But I needn't have bothered. All the nurses and Corpsmen were breaking my rule and crying silently, tears filling their eyes or rolling down their cheeks.

I thought of the dead soldier's mother. She would receive a telegram informing her that her son had died of "war injuries." But that was all it would say. I thought she might always wonder how it had happened. Had he died out in the field? Had he been with anyone? Did he suffer? If I were his mother, I would need to know.

So later I sat down and wrote her a letter. I thought she'd want to hear that in her son's final moments, he had been thinking of her. But mostly I wanted her to know that her boy hadn't died alone.

~Diana Dwan Poole
Chicken Soup for the Veteran's Soul

One Life at a Time

Some see a hopeless end, while others see an endless hope.
~Author Unknown

As our car slowly made its way through the crowded streets of Dhaka, Bangladesh's capital of 2 million people, I thought I knew what to expect. As leader of the American Voluntary Medical Team (AVMT), I had seen great suffering and devastation in Iraq, Nicaragua and Calcutta. But I wasn't prepared for what I saw in Bangladesh.

I traveled there with a group of AVMT doctors, nurses and other volunteers after a series of devastating cyclones hit the tiny country in 1991. More than 100,000 people had been killed, and now, because flooding had wiped out clean water and sanitation systems, thousands more were dying from diarrhea and dehydration. Children were dying from polio and tetanus, diseases nearly forgotten in the United States.

As we drove to the hospital where we were to set up a clinic, I thought I knew what we were up against: humid, scorching days, heavy rains and crowded conditions. After all, since Bangladesh became independent from Pakistan more than twenty years earlier, some 125 million people lived in an area slightly smaller than the state of Wisconsin.

I glanced out the window at the street teeming with people: men talking in groups, women dressed in bright red and yellow saris, and children chasing each other, darting in between the many carts and rickshaws.

Then I looked more closely. The people were walking through raw sewage. A man stepped over a body in a doorway, just as one of the many body carts pulled up to haul it away. At a busy corner, I saw a woman standing very still, holding a small bundle, a baby. As I watched her face, she pulled her shawl back slightly, and I clearly saw her baby was dead. I suddenly thought of my own healthy children at home, and tears stung my eyes. I'd never seen anything so horrible.

The following day, I decided to ride out to Mother Teresa's orphanage in old Dhaka. A friend had asked me before I left home to visit and see what medical help they needed.

Two of the Little Sisters of the Poor greeted me at the gate and immediately led me to the infant floor. I was astonished to find 160 babies, mostly girls, squalling for attention from the few hardworking sisters.

"There are so many," I said, amazed.

"Some were given up because their parents couldn't feed them," one sister said.

"And others were abandoned because they are girls," said another. She explained that often females are killed at birth because they are considered inferior in the male-dominated culture. What little food there is must go to males.

The irony struck me hard. These baby girls were society's throwaways, yet what had I seen today? Women everywhere: working in the rice fields outside the city, herding children through crowded Dhaka, trying to earn a living by selling trinkets on the street, and here, at the orphanage, caring for the forgotten.

"A couple of the babies have serious medical problems," the sister said. "Would you like to see them?"

I followed her down a row of basket-style cribs to the tiny, sick little girls, both about two months old. One had a heart condition, the other, a severe cleft lip and palate.

"We can't do much more for them," the sister said. "Please help them. Whatever you can do will be a blessing."

I held each baby, stroking each girl's soft, dark hair and gazing into their small faces. How my heart ached for these innocent angels. What kind of a future did they face, if they had a future at all?

"I'll see what we can do," I said.

When I returned to the clinic, hundreds were waiting for treatment and much work needed to be done. I'm not a medical person, so my job was varied: I ran the pharmacy, tracked down medicine when we ran out, negotiated with local officials for equipment or transportation, and scouted the patient line for critical cases.

By day's end, my head was swimming. The helpless babies' cries and the hundreds of faces on the streets and in our clinic all seemed to express the same thing—hopelessness. The thought startled me. These people were without hope. Even Calcutta had not seemed so bleak. Without hope. I repeated the words in my mind, and my heart sank. So much of what AVMT tries to do is give hope.

My inspiration was a woman who had dedicated her life to giving hope to others—my grandmother. We called her Lulu Belle, and she practically ran the Mississippi River town of Cairo, Illinois. She wasn't the mayor or a town official, but if a jobless man came to her back door, she'd call everyone she knew until she found the man work. Once, I came through her kitchen door and was startled to find a table full of strangers eating supper.

"A new family in town, Cindy," she said, as she set the mashed potatoes on the table and headed to the stove for the gravy. "Just tryin' to give 'em a good start." I later learned the man hadn't yet found work, and Lulu Belle was making sure his family had at least one hot meal every day.

Lulu Belle had great faith, and it made her stronger than any woman I knew. Her favorite Bible verse was a simple one: "Do unto others as you would have them do unto you." She believed that if you treated people right, the way you would want to be treated, God would do the rest. So she never worried about where the job or the food would come from—she knew God would provide it.

But God seemed so far away in Bangladesh. I struggled with that thought at our morning meeting. We were set up in a clinic near

Rangpur, in the northern part of the country, and our team had gathered to go over the day's schedule. At the meeting's end I told them what I tell every team: "Remember, we're here to give hope." But the words caught a little in my throat as I wondered how we would do it. Where would hope come from for these people, especially the women, so overwhelmed by disease, poverty and circumstance?

Already, 8,000 people were lined up for treatment. Scouting the line, I noticed something peculiar. All of them were men, many quite healthy. Not until I reached the end of the line did I see any women and children, and most of them looked very sick, some near death. My heart pounded as I realized what was happening. The men expected to be seen first, even if they were perfectly healthy. The women could wait.

I wondered what I should do. I remembered the woman I'd seen on the street, holding her dead baby, perhaps because she couldn't get care quickly enough. I thought of the abandoned babies in the orphanage, and anger and frustration welled up inside me.

Maybe a bit of Lulu Belle was with me as I rushed past the line and back inside the clinic to tell the doctor in charge what was going on. He was as upset as I was.

"Well, what do you think?" he asked. "We can either see all these well men, or we can get the sick women and children up front."

"Let's do it," I said. "Let's do what we came here for."

I ran back outside and asked the interpreter to tell the men at the front to step aside. He did, and immediately I heard a disgruntled murmuring rumble through the crowd. The men were angry and the women were afraid to come forward. The interpreter repeated the announcement, and as we tried to get the crowd to move, a scuffle broke out and soon soldiers appeared, their guns strapped across their chests. They tried to restore order, but several men still pushed to the front of the line.

"Tell them no," I said to the interpreter, gathering all the courage I had. "Tell them we treat the sick women and children first or we fold up the clinic."

The men looked at me for a moment, then backed down and

began letting the women forward. The fear and sadness I'd seen on the women's faces gave way to joy as they rushed to enter the clinic first. They smiled at me, grasping my hands and arms in thanks.

As one woman stretched out her hand to give me a flower, our eyes met, and I saw something incredible: hope. Now I understood. We didn't have to pull off a miracle. It was what my grandmother believed about doing unto others what was right. And out of that simple act, God had brought life-affirming hope.

Our doctors and nurses saved lives that day, and treated thousands during our two weeks in Bangladesh. When it was time to come home, I returned by way of the orphanage, to bring the two sick babies I'd seen back to the United States for treatment. On the plane home, I knew I'd have a surprise for my husband—that we would be adopting one of them, now our beautiful Bridget.

Several months later, I had the privilege of meeting with Mother Teresa about Calcutta's medical needs. In her beautifully simple way, she crystallized what I had felt in Bangladesh.

"How do you deal with the overwhelming needs, the disease, the death?" I asked.

"You look into one face," she said, her voice filled with peace, "and you continue the work." And know that God will do the rest.

~Cindy Hensley McCain as told to Gina Bridgeman
A Second Chicken Soup for the Woman's Soul

A First

I straightened my notebook and pen yet again, making sure the edge of the notebook lined up cleanly with my desk, the pen parallel to the notebook, uncapped and ready to write. But ready to write what...? I glanced around in dismay at the bare conference room. My first day at my first job after graduate school and I was sitting in a conference room instead of an office. The walls were bare. No phone. No shelves. Just a round wooden table and four chairs. Oh, and me.

I glanced at my watch. Five minutes until I would walk down the hall and get my patient. My first real patient. After twelve years of regular school, four years of high school, four years of college and three years of graduate school, I was ready to begin my first day as a psychiatric physician's assistant. I slumped a little in my chair, gnawing on the end of a fingernail.

That morning, I had taken my thirteen-month-old to day care. While she was happy as a clam, racing into the room crowded with toys and games to sit down with "the gang" and eat breakfast, I was still wracked with doubt. Was putting her in day care so I could finish PA school a good decision? Was starting a new job, even though it was part time, the right thing to do? Even though I loved being a mom and while I had friends who were stay-at-home moms and I respected the incredible amount of work they did, there was a part of me that had always known I wanted to have a career.

But instead of appearing immediately after college, like a pot of gold at the end of the rainbow, my career had been elusive, involving jobs in sales, waitressing and reception before landing me in graduate school. As a young girl who dreamed of great wealth and fame, had a strong desire to make a difference in people's lives, and had graduated from an Ivy League school, I hadn't expected to begin my career at this point — in my early thirties with a husband, a mortgage, a thirteen-month-old and thousands of dollars of debt. But here I was. A trickle of ice had been forming in my stomach over the years, growing with every moment of frustration. Now, it had hardened into a large mass of ice, establishing how important this would be.

Christina, my first real patient, was not what I expected. She was petite and dressed in pressed cotton pants and a light blue sweater. She smiled easily at me as I led her to the conference room. I couldn't imagine what she could possibly be here for — she seemed much less nervous than I.

I tried not to cringe as we settled into the conference room chairs. Surely the bare room and lack of a phone, books or diplomas belied my inexperience! If Christina noticed, she didn't let on, and as she began to talk, a story unfolded which belied her composed appearance. For her entire life, she had struggled with violent mood swings, at some moments feeling full of energy and passion, at other moments, depressed and suicidal. Tears poured down her face as she described her anger, which sometimes grew so severe she would scream at her family or even throw things. She couldn't handle stress and would retreat to her room and be unable to cope. Her marriage was rocky due to her volatile moods and her kids were starting to avoid her. She had been treated by other doctors for the depression, but that had only increased her anxiety and irritability. Christina was at the point where she had lost yet another job and was considering leaving her family so that at least their lives could return to normal.

As I questioned her further, it became apparent to me that the young woman in front of me likely had a bipolar disorder, or what is commonly known as manic-depressive illness. People with this illness have periods of depression, but they can also have periods of increased energy, talkativeness, anger or irritability and difficulty concentrating. Despite being treated by several doctors over the years, she had never been diagnosed with or treated for a bipolar illness.

At the conclusion of my questioning, I hesitated. How could I have noticed something that doctors had missed? First real patient, remember? Christina was looking at me expectantly. Waiting. I squelched the tight feeling in my chest and tried to smile reassuringly. Cautiously, I brought up the diagnosis of bipolar disorder and what it meant. We went over the treatments. With a slightly shaky hand, I wrote out a prescription for medication and gave her the name of a good therapist.

Two weeks later, Christina returned to my conference room. As before, she looked well put together in fashionable dark blue jeans and a button-down shirt. We sat down and I spent a moment writing the date in the chart and reviewing the medications I had prescribed. Then came the dreaded moment. It was time to ask the question. I tried to appear calm. "How are things going since your first visit?" I waited for the tears.

Christina looked down for a moment, then her eyes met mine, several tears already welling up at the corners. "You've changed my life," she said simply. She sniffed and pressed a knuckle to her left eye. "I don't know what you gave me, but it was magical. I have been less depressed. I'm not angry anymore. I'm not snapping at my kids. We actually went hiking this weekend and even when a snake almost bit my son on the ankle, I was able to remain calm and handle it. My thoughts aren't racing a mile a minute. I had the first good night's sleep I can ever remember."

I felt a grin forming and tried not to show my amazement. My treatment plan had actually worked! This was not the same woman who had come to me in tears just a few weeks earlier.

"I don't know how I can ever thank you," she sniffed. "You've given me my family back. You've given me my hope back."

As I pressed a tissue into Christina's hands, I tried to hold back my own tears. There was an incredible shift in my stomach. The block of ice I had grown so accustomed to was starting to melt. I could feel the water trickling into my limbs, the cold in my gut replaced by warmth and comfort. Finally, it all clicked. All those years of struggling through jobs I hated, of wondering what my purpose was, of second-guessing my decisions, of dropping my daughter off at day care so I could finish school and start a job. They had led me here to this bare, ugly conference room. And I had changed a woman's life. A woman's entire future—and that of her family's. And she was only my first real patient!

Just think of how many more there were to come!

~Rachel Byrne
Chicken Soup for the Working Woman's Soul

Voice in the Night

How wonderful it is that nobody need wait a single moment before starting to improve the world.
~Anne Frank

When I was nineteen years old, my friend Hanneke Boogaard was studying to become a nurse at Beatrix Hospital in The Netherlands. There, nursing students work during their study, the same as regular personnel. During her work on the night shift, Hanneke was strangely drawn to one patient in particular, a forty-year-old woman in a coma. Because Mrs. Groensma never had visitors, Hanneke remained at her bedside longer than the others. At first she tried not to admit it, since for her all patients should mean the same. But this woman fascinated her.

When Hanneke heard the patient had no living relatives, she spent even more time with her. She'd learned that people in comas could sometimes hear when they were spoken to. This woman had no one to do that for her, so Hanneke talked softly to her every night. Since she didn't know her, she didn't know what to talk about, so she told Mrs. Groensma all about herself. She explained how her parents had died in a car crash when she was young. For hours she shared her many memories of them. That's all she had to cling to now. How she wished she had a specific personal item to remember them by—the golden four-leaf-clover locket her mother always wore. It was lost during the accident and never found, even though relatives searched the crash site and nearby ditch. Night after night, she talked and talked and grew more and more attached to Mrs. Groensma.

She would likely never come out of the coma, and she had no one in the world to care for her. Therefore, the time came for her to be transferred to a nursing home where she would eventually die. When Hanneke objected, she was heavily reprimanded for losing touch with her professional attitude and forbidden to contact the patient in the nursing home. Hanneke saw the logic of her supervisors but could not help thinking about Mrs. Groensma often.

Time went by, and Hanneke became a nurse and found a job in the Beatrix Hospital. One day at work, she was instructing a patient when a lady who was questioning another nurse turned and deliberately walked towards her. It was Mrs. Groensma! They found an empty room where they could speak privately, and Mrs. Groensma explained what she was doing there.

She recalled having been in a dark and lonely place, all alone, until the voice of what she thought must have been an angel started speaking, drawing her attention. Later when that voice stopped talking to her, she longed for the sound so much that she started struggling to get to the place where the voice had come from. She came out of the coma and took a long time to recover. Meanwhile she had questioned the nursing home staff. They eventually told her they had instructions to keep away a certain nurse who had made the mistake of getting too attached to her.

As soon as Mrs. Groensma was able, she came to the hospital to find that nurse. When she heard Hanneke talk to the patient, she recognized the voice that had spoken to her during her coma.

Mrs. Groensma took Hanneke's hand. "I have something I want to give you to thank you. I found it fifteen years ago in a ditch and originally wanted to put pictures of my late husband and me in it and give it to my daughter. When she died, I was all alone and wanted to throw it away, but I never got around to it. I now want you to have it."

Mrs. Groensma handed Hanneke a small box. Inside, sparkling

in the sunlight, lay a golden four-leaf-clover locket. With a pounding heart, Hanneke opened it to see her parents' photos.

Hanneke now wears the locket day and night and visits Mrs. Groensma whenever she wants.

And they talk and talk and grow more and more attached.

~Carin Klabbers
Chicken Soup for the Nurse's Soul

Farewell to the Queen of Hearts

She was only twenty-one years old, a royal rookie on her first visit to Canada, when I met Diana, princess of Wales. Her style at that time was House of Windsor rather than cover-girl glamour. She tended to fold her fingers inward to hide the fact that she bit her nails. But the essence of the woman was as apparent then as it was throughout her public life. She was vulnerable, compassionate, willing to break the rules, take a risk and do what she thought was right.

When I heard the terrible news about her death, and while photos flooded the television screen and commentators serialized her life, I remembered a story about her that I've often shared with family and friends. Although I'd been fortunate enough to meet Diana during royal tours in the 1980s, and later at 24 Sussex Drive in 1991, there was never a story less public or more telling about who this young woman really was. It took place in Halifax in June 1983, just hours after her plane had touched down from England.

The official welcome was being held at the Garrison Grounds, a huge field that on that sunny day was jammed with an estimated 10,000 cheering royal watchers. The crowd was pressed into a U-shape around the edges of the field. The centre was reserved for the trappings of pomp and ceremony. The royal couple was to do a walkabout around the edges of the crowd before proceeding to the centre for the ceremony. I chose a spot near the end of their route and watched what would become a vintage Princess Di walkabout. It turned into a love-in.

Seated near my vantage point were three rows of senior citizens in wheelchairs, who had been positioned to ensure a glimpse of the prince and princess. In the second row, and closest to where I was standing, an elderly gentleman in a pale blue sweater caught my attention. He was watching the princess with enormous pleasure. As the royal couple approached, I thought wistfully, Too bad, old man. You're in the second row. Royalty only stops to speak to people in the first row. As Diana approached, he was straining from his wheelchair so forcefully, I was afraid he might tumble to the ground. Like everyone else on the Garrison Grounds that day, he was transmitting waves of warmth and welcome to the young princess.

Then, as if by telepathy, she saw him and apparently couldn't resist returning the warmth. In a rather unroyal style, she reached her arm in over the heads of the people in the first row to shake his extended hand.

That's when it happened. Suddenly, his arm began to flail. A spasm had overcome the old gentleman. His arm was swinging wildly, to the right and left and over his own head. Everyone was watching the discomfiting scene. For a split second Diana looked stunned and then, when an attendant rushed to the man's side and calmed him, she withdrew her hand and returned to her royal walkabout. My heart ached for the old man. He looked so dejected, so disappointed in himself. Now his head drooped down, his shoulders stooped over. It seemed obvious that he knew he'd missed his chance to greet his princess.

Diana continued along the row but kept looking back at him. Was she concerned? Could this young woman who was just days short of her twenty-second birthday have any idea how he felt? Would she dare to risk embarrassing herself by returning to the man's chair? Surely not. But then there was a space between the wheelchairs and she started moving back toward him. I wondered what she was up to.

You have to imagine the scene: the stiff formality of the entourage, the split-second timing of a walkabout, the royal handlers (aka Royal Canadian Mounted Police officers), the royal household (aka ladies-in-waiting)—all standing around while Diana tiptoes through the uncut grass and takes her royal self to the second row. Although enormously grateful for the bird's-eye view I was getting, even I was bowled over by her decision. The entourage would be held up. The world was watching. It could all go terribly wrong.

When she got to the woman sitting beside the old man she stopped, knelt down and chatted to her for a long time. By now I was certain that she had a plan. The old man was watching her, wringing his hands and still looking distressed. Suddenly, Diana stood up and stepped sideways to his chair. She put her hand on his shoulder, leaned over close to his face and said, "I'm glad to see you. I hope you haven't had to wait too long on this hot day. Maybe they should bring us all some ice cream."

The old man gazed up at her from his chair. Tears were rolling down his cheeks, and his face was wreathed in happiness. She'd touched his heart. And she'd risked a disaster in decorum, not to mention protocol, in the process.

When her life turned upside down in the 1990s, she told a television interviewer she'd never be queen of Britain, but she'd like to be queen of people's hearts. She already was.

~Sally Armstrong
Chicken Soup for the Canadian Soul

Chicken Soup
for the Soul

Women in the Military

The first military women to arrive in Vietnam were nurses, in 1956. As the American presence in Southeast Asia grew, so, too, did the number of young women who served. In all, nearly eight thousand military women were there, along with thousands more who served in the civilian sector.

Eighty-three percent of us were nurses; the rest held positions in special services, supply, air-traffic control, cartography, the USO, American Red Cross and many other jobs in support of our combat troops.

We were all fairly young when we volunteered to serve our country. And many of us were woefully naive in believing our recruiters' promises, mainly that we could be stationed anywhere in the world that we wanted, and that Vietnam was "strictly voluntary."

Still, when our orders arrived sending us to war, most of us believed in our hearts that we were needed, that what we were doing was important, and that it was our duty to go. We did our jobs, facing the perils of enemy fire, horrific heat and humidity, disease, insects, isolation, long work hours and sleepless nights. Then we managed to pull ourselves together, dab some perfume behind our ears and do it all again the next day.

We learned a lot about ourselves. We discovered our strengths and tried to survive our weaknesses. We were ordinary young women trying to function in the most extraordinary of circumstances; dealing in life and death and seeking not just to survive, but to understand.

We did the best we could with who we were and what we had. And daily we collected our memories and stored them away some-place safe, out of our conscious minds where we thought, "I'll deal with this later."

And after a year, we came home, back to "The World." In one plane ride, we went from war to peace. In one year, we had gone from childhood to irrevocable adulthood. We knew we had changed, that our lives would never be the same, and that we could never explain any of it to the folks back home. We couldn't, and we didn't. For as unacceptable as it was for the guys to talk about the war when they came home, no one wanted to acknowledge that young women had been there. Even as the women's movement was making its voice heard, the underlying message was clear: "Nice girls wouldn't have gone to war."

So we came home quietly, went back to our homes, our families, our jobs and never spoke about the war to anybody. Many of us quit nursing and never knew why. Some of us had recurring nightmares, flashbacks, unexplained illnesses, depression, or abused drugs or alcohol. Many women applied themselves with a fury to school, attaining one degree after another, to work, rising to the top leadership positions in their companies, to their church, their social organizations, their families—anything to avoid the memories they had stored away "to think about later." The memories had created a deep, impenetrable wound that needed to be healed.

In 1982, the initial healing ground was laid in the form of the Vietnam Veterans Memorial—The Wall. The women, just like men who had served, were drawn to it. The healing power of that sacred place is evident to all who have been there. We could go to The Wall, and mourn, and cry, and reach out for comfort if we chose, and yet it was so easy to be invisible there.

Women simply weren't recognized as veterans.

Then, on Veterans Day 1993, the Vietnam Women's Memorial was dedicated in Washington, D.C. Thousands of women vets attended, and we were overwhelmed. We lead the parade: the nurses, Red Cross workers, entertainers, women who worked in administration, logistics and intelligence. The streets were lined with people applauding and crying. A vet sat high up in a tree yelling, "Thank you! Thank you!" A man in a flight suit stood for over two hours at attention, saluting as the women passed by. People handed us flowers and hugged us. One G.I. had a picture of his nurse taken "July 1964." He was trying to find her.

We found each other. We know, at last, that we are not alone; that we are not crazy or paranoid, but that we have a lot of work to do in order to heal. We talk to each other and find comfort as well as pain in our words and our tears. Words and tears, that now, finally we share. Now, after so many years, the process has finally begun, and we hold each other close and say, "Welcome home!"

~Janis Nark
Chicken Soup for the Nurse's Soul

Green Ink

I would thank you from the bottom of my heart,
but for you my heart has no bottom.
~Author Unknown

The rush of Christmas was again upon me. I was opening a stack of Christmas cards, glancing quickly at photos of friends' children while listening to my four-year-old daughter rehearse the Little Drummer Boy for her preschool Christmas program. My mind swirled with commitments, cookie recipes and carols, and then it froze.

Staring at the letter in my hand, I couldn't draw oxygen. My ears burned as if I had just come from the December cold into a heated house.

I opened the envelope to find, not a Christmas card, but a letter signed by Helen's four children letting me know of the unfortunate passing of their beloved mother. Forty-seven years had passed since Helen Tibbals walked into my mom's living room. I dropped to my kitchen floor, shaking, while tears flowed down my face for the loss of this angel. And then I smiled. Helen was in heaven where she had always belonged and from where she certainly had come. My mom has told her tale so many times I can still smell the scent of spruce and hear the clang of ornaments in the living room of their house on Hollywood Place:

We heard the sound of someone knocking. Grandma opened

the squeaky front door of her small home, where my three brothers, my sister, my mother and I lived. A slim redheaded woman and her teenage boy stood smiling at us. I watched in awe as the two strangers carried armloads of packages wrapped in red with our names written on white tags in green ink. They also lugged a pine tree, strings of colored lights and glass ornaments, transforming the drab room from black and white to Technicolor. I backed against the threadbare couch to allow her and her son room to unload these treasures. They brought Christmas into our living room.

The woman in the green silk dress introduced herself as Helen Tibbals and her awkward-looking son as Todd Junior. She was a member of First Community Church, the same church we attended, and explained that she had taken a paper gift tag shaped like the star of Bethlehem off the Christmas tree standing in the church vestibule. It had our name on it. She was all lipstick and smiles and smelled like the department store downtown. The sharp scent of peppermint filled my nose as she opened a box of candy canes and invited us to join in decorating the evergreen. All the while, she asked questions about us kids as if we were her own. I had so many questions for her, but was too shy to ask them. Where had this angel and her elf come from, and why did she care so much about my family?

Helen was the gift of Christmas present, not past. A reminder that despite a father who had deserted us, a terminally ill mother and the fact that all five of us lived in a two-bedroom home with my mother and grandmother, God's hope and love lived in the world.

Helen became much more than a Christmas gift; she became a part of Mom's family. Until my mom and her siblings graduated from high school, Helen regularly brought them school supplies, new clothes and chocolates. She even sent them to summer camp each year. When my grandmother struggled with breast cancer, Helen brought candy bars and magazines to the small home as if she were Grandmother's sister. When my mom, aunt and uncles were in college, Helen wrote them faithfully, always using her signature green pen. She attended my grandmother's funeral, my mother's graduation from high school and my parents' wedding.

Helen's generosity expanded to the next generation as she adopted my brother and me as grandchildren, including us in her umbrella of selfless giving. She invited us to her home each summer for a feast and a stroll around her goldfish pond. Every birthday, gifts arrived at our house, our names written across the top in green felt-tip marker. I remember the excitement of seeing an envelope with my name scrawled in Helen's green ink every Easter and Valentine's Day. Poinsettias in December would bear her green signature, and even the place cards at the annual Christmas dinner at her club, where she made sure the waiter kept our Shirley Temples refilled, were written in green ink.

I was still weepy when my husband, Brett, came home from work. I pulled a boiling pot of pasta off the stove, placed it in the sink and scooped up our toddler, Max, whose hands reached to the sky. "Hold, Mama, hold."

I pointed to the tear-spotted letter on the counter.

Brett set his keys down and scanned the note. He turned and wrapped his strong arms around my quaking body. Soon I was able to exhale and push a smile onto my streaked face.

"Honey, can you get an extra name off the Giving Tree at church this year?" I swallowed hard, then continued. "Helen came into my mom's life by picking her name from a tree. I would like to follow her example."

"Of course," he smiled and kissed me on the tip of my nose.

The next day when Brett came home from work, he pulled two yellow pieces of paper cut in the shapes of mittens from the pocket of his parka.

"The directions said to put our name on the half of the tag still hanging on the tree so the church would know who was responsible for that gift," Brett explained while easing his briefcase off his shoulder. "I guess that way no child will go unaccounted for."

I nodded while drying my hands on the holly-embroidered towel by the kitchen sink.

"I wrote B. Smith on this tag, our tag," he said, holding up one of the canary-colored cards. "And on this mitten," my husband's turquoise eyes twinkled, "I wrote 'H. Tibbals'—in green ink."

~Laura Smith
Chicken Soup for the Grandma's Soul

Proud to Be a Nurse

Treat everyone with politeness, even those who are rude to you—
not because they are nice, but because you are.
~Author Unknown

I just saw another television show where the nurse was portrayed as an overly sexed bimbo. It's obvious the image of the nursing profession still needs some good public relations. Once in a while, we have an unexpected opportunity to educate the public as to what nursing is all about.

My chance came on a warm Saturday morning when I had a coveted weekend off from my job in a long-term care facility. My husband and I headed for the Cubs ballpark via the train. Just as the train arrived at the final station, the conductor curtly shouted for all the passengers to immediately leave the car. He hustled us toward the door. On the way, I glimpsed some people huddled around a man lying limply in his seat.

The conductor talked excitedly into his walkie-talkie.

I heard fragments of "emergency" and "ambulance." Surprising myself, I approached him and said, "I'm a nurse. Could I be of any help?"

"I don't need a nurse," he rudely snapped back, loud enough for the crowd to hear. "I need a medic!"

His public put-down to nurses was a punch in the stomach. I was incensed. My adrenaline kicked in, and I abruptly elbowed my way through the crowd, past the insulting conductor and back on the train.

Three men were standing like statues staring at a young man crumpled over in the seat. His face was the color of a ripe plum. Fortunately, the ABCs of cardiopulmonary resuscitation clicked into my brain. The man was obviously obstructing his own airway. I was relieved to find a pulse.

"He had a seizure," one man offered.

"Help me sit him up," I instructed the bystanders, as I loosened his collar and tie. We hoisted him to an upright position, and I quickly did a jaw thrust and tilted his head to the side. Mucous and blood oozed out. With a wadded tissue from my pocket I cleared more thick mucous from his mouth and throat. A thump on the shoulder caused him to take in a big breath of air. Within seconds, his color changed to pink and his eyes opened. His tongue was bruised and cut from biting it, but he was breathing well.

I heard the ambulance siren in the background.

Shaking now, I returned to my husband, praying the man didn't have AIDS and searching for something to wipe my sticky hands on.

"Hey, you did a good job," one of the men who had been a bystander called to me.

"Thanks," I replied with a pleased smile, as I stared directly at the conductor who still clutched his walkie-talkie and looked surprised. He stammered, "I guess a nurse is what I needed after all."

Triumphantly, I marched off, hoping at least one person had a new insight into the capabilities of the nursing profession. Because, at that moment, I was especially proud to be a nurse.

~Barbara A. Brady
Chicken Soup for the Nurse's Soul

11

Abacus

To be upset over what you don't have is to waste what you do have.
~Ken S. Keyes, Jr., Handbook to Higher Consciousness

A lot has been written about what dogs can do for people. Dogs lead the blind, aid the deaf, sniff out illegal substances, give us therapeutic hope and joy, make us laugh with their idiosyncrasies, and give us companionship—to name just a few of their many talents. But what about our duty to dogs—what about their needs, wants, hopes and joys? And what about the ones most people do not want to adopt—the ones who aren't completely healthy or cute? This is a story of just such a dog.

I first learned about Abacus while doing some Internet research on special-needs dogs. I had become interested in special-needs dogs after losing my brother Damon, who was left paraplegic after an accident in 1992 and committed suicide three years later. Damon loved exploring the outdoors and preferred the freedom of driving a truck to working behind a desk all day. Losing those options was difficult enough for him, but the thought that nobody would want him was more than he could deal with. His death made me more aware of the challenges that people—and animals—with disabilities must face.

I knew my husband and I couldn't get a dog because of the no-pets policy at our rental, but I couldn't keep myself from researching them. On www.petfinder.com, there was a listing for a very handsome fellow named Abacus who was staying at Animal Lifeline, a no-kill animal shelter located near Des Moines, Iowa. Abacus had originally been rescued as a stray puppy two years earlier by the kind staff at a veterinary hospital in Nebraska after being hit by a car and subsequently paralyzed. Normally, a stray dog with partial paralysis would have been euthanized because few people want to adopt a dog in that condition. But the veterinarian and his staff saw something special and endearing in Abacus. They took him under their wing and eventually entrusted the shelter in Iowa with his care.

The picture of Abacus on the shelter's web site showed a largish black dog with a rubber ducky in a hydrotherapy tub, enjoying a workout to help improve the muscle tone in his paralyzed hind legs. Through his photograph alone, Abacus cast his spell on me and I was never the same.

I couldn't get the image of Abacus out of my mind and felt compelled to visit him—even though I knew I couldn't adopt him. My husband, John, supportive and understanding as always, drove with me on the nearly two-hour drive to the special-needs animal shelter. When I first saw Abacus in his quarters at the shelter, my breath stopped for a few seconds. It was a little disconcerting to see his atrophied hind legs, the result of his paralysis, but his exuberance and happy-go-lucky attitude quickly masked his physical challenges. I was struck by the sheer joy he radiated. His wide, loving eyes stayed in my mind and heart long after we drove away from the shelter.

Meeting Abacus inspired me to start looking for a house to buy instead of continuing to rent. Soon we found a nice rural home with acreage at an affordable price. I applied to adopt Abacus, and we were able to celebrate his third birthday by bringing him home with us a few weeks later.

Life with Abacus required a few adjustments. I learned daily therapeutic exercises for his hind legs, and how to get his strong, wiggly body into his wheelchair (called a K-9 cart) by myself. His castle, when I am not home, is a special padded room with a comfy mattress and lots of blankets and washable rugs. Often, I wrap his paralyzed legs in gauze bandages to help protect them from the abrasions he gets from dragging them on the floor or from the uncontrollable muscle spasms that occur in his hindquarters.

When Abacus is inside the house but out of his cart, he scoots around using his strong, muscular front legs. At times he can support his hind legs for a while, which looks a bit like a donkey kicking and occasionally causes him to knock things down as he maneuvers around the house. But when he is in his K-9 cart, Abacus can run like the wind. We have to supervise our canine Evel Knievel in his cart, since he can tip it over and get stuck when taking curves too fast.

Even though he requires extra care, I have never thought of Abacus as a burden. Living with him is a privilege. Enthusiastic about everything, he treats strangers like long-lost friends. And as much as he loves food, he loves cuddles even more. His zest for life inspires me, as well as others who meet him. Some people who see him feel pity for his challenges, but I always point out that he is not depressed or daunted by his differentness. I am sure if Abacus could speak, he would say that special-needs dogs can live happy, full lives and can enrich the lives of their adopters as much as—if not more than—a "normal" dog can.

The main reason I adopted Abacus was because I wanted to give him the comfort and security of a forever home, but in addition to that, I felt that he could help me give encouragement to others. A principle I have always lived by was shaped by part of an Emily Dickinson poem I learned as a child:

> If I can ease one life the aching
> Or cool one pain,
> Or help one fainting robin
> Unto his nest again,
> I shall not live in vain.

I only wish my brother could have known Abacus. For although animal-assisted therapy is not a cure-all, I believe a seed of hope can be planted in the heart of a physically, mentally or emotionally challenged child—or adult—when he sees a special-needs animal living a full and happy life in a loving home.

To spread this hope, I worked with Abacus to train him to become a certified therapy dog. After passing an evaluation this year, Abacus has begun visiting a school for special children. My employers at Farm Sanctuary—an organization that understands the mutual healing power that people and animals share—graciously grant me permission to take time off work for these twice-monthly weekday visits. Abacus looks forward to these excursions and always wows the kids (and teachers) with his bouncy "Tigger-like" personality. On occasion, his visiting attire includes his snazzy Super Dog cape that flies behind him as he zooms around in his wheelchair. Abacus always leaves happiness in his wake.

Living with a special-needs animal isn't for everyone, but it is a rare treat for those who choose to take it on. In fact, my experience with Abacus has inspired me to adopt a number of other special-needs animals over the years. All of them have more than repaid my investment of time and energy by being constant positive reminders that life's challenges need not be met with despair and negativity. Their love is healing, their appreciation rewarding, and their quirky personalities add priceless meaning to my life.

~Meghan Beeby
Chicken Soup for the Dog Lover's Soul

12

You Don't Have to Wear a Thong to Belong!

A friend accepts us as we are yet helps us to be what we should.
~Author Unknown

In the winter of 1989, I was thirty-one years old and weighed over three hundred pounds. I spent my days on a couch in front of the TV and suffered every minute, barely able to move or even breathe. I had so much to offer—as a mom, as a wife, as a person—but I felt trapped in my miserable shell. More than anything in the world I wanted help, someone to believe in and to believe in me—a friend to take my hand.

That winter I met Ellen Langley, and my life began to change. She was ten years older and nearly as large, but was calm and self-assured. That fascinated me and drew me into what became a big sister-little sister relationship, a gift of precious friendship.

Because of our friendship, I took the first steps toward actually doing something about my body. It started with a Christmas present from Ellen: a month's membership at one of the hottest fitness clubs in Lake Charles.

"Don't worry," Ellen said as she steered me toward the plate-glass doors. "You're gonna be fine."

I wouldn't have done it if Ellen hadn't come with me. My two little boys had been shocked that morning when their mommy had actually turned off the TV and walked out the door wearing elephant-sized sweatpants and the biggest purple shirt I could find. Now I was amazed as we walked into a room filled with perfect bodies in thongs. Ellen strode in like she owned the place. I was speechless looking at her, as she acted like she was right at home and chatted comfortably with everybody. I, on the other hand, was miserable.

I had already tried the health club scene. Before I'd moved to Lake Charles, I was so lonely and so desperate to find a friendly face that I actually hauled myself to an aerobics studio and signed up for a class. I thought it would be the perfect place to find a friend, but from the minute I slunk into that workout room, the students and instructor alike edged away and averted their eyes. I was so ashamed of my size. I did what I could to keep up, shuffling my feet a little bit and praying for a break, hoping someone would at least say hi.

I had given it my best shot for over a year, only lost a few pounds and was still lonely and ignored. I retreated to food, my source of comfort, love and security. It pushed me past the magic 300-pound mark; it nailed me to the sofa twelve hours a day because I had the lung capacity of a chipmunk. I couldn't even get up to play with my little boys, who had learned not to even bother asking. My emotional fuse was so short that I was snapping at my husband, Keith, and the boys.

Still, there I was at an aerobics studio trying it again. Once the workout began, things got worse. My self-consciousness was displaced by utter despair. The warm-up alone almost killed me. Everyone had their arms up over their heads, stretching, yet I couldn't lift mine past my shoulders. They all bent to touch their toes. I couldn't even see my toes. Then the actual class began—and I just couldn't do it. Two or three minutes of faking it, tapping my toes or whatever, and I had to stop. I felt like a freak. Why was I subjecting myself to this torture?

I looked over at Ellen's strength and told myself, No, you are not going to quit. You're going to stay here if it kills you. And it felt like it would. It felt that way for a long time. I learned to ignore the smirks, sideways glances and looks of pity. The first six months it was Ellen's presence and attitude that kept me going. We had to drive thirty miles each way to the classes, and sometimes we'd just sit in the car before class, having what we called "mini-therapy sessions."

One day, the owner of the club greeted me by name. "Hi, Dee," she said. It was as if the heavens had opened. Words can't describe what that did for my self-esteem. Here was a woman who was tall, thin as a rail, had zero percent body fat and a resting heart rate of 42. And she knew my name.

I made that dinky little "Hi" into a mountain of self-esteem, something I could cling to until another crumb came my way. And they kept coming, those crumbs. A growing number of my classmates began treating me like I belonged, once I showed them I was there to stay. Instructors adjusted my movements to fit the restrictions of my body, and in my own way I began to bloom.

By the end of 1990, I was disappointed that I'd only lost thirty pounds, a mere sliver from my beginning weight of over 300. While it didn't seem like much, I could now do things I hadn't done in years. My mood and energy improved, and I was off the couch. I even ventured outside to play with the boys. I wasn't biting my husband's head off, and I could visit friends, shop, work out and just live.

My eating habits were different; I could stop when full and there were no more midnight refrigerator raids. I learned to enjoy the taste of the food now that I wasn't cramming it in, and I didn't lie about the cookies I ate because I wasn't eating the whole package. The change was happening gradually, naturally. I wasn't super diligent. The place I did my pushing was in the aerobics room, and I let the rest take care of itself.

That aerobics room! Just showing up was a lifesaver. The music, the energy and Ellen—my oasis, the bright spot. Sometimes I'd run out of gas and just stop, wait a while, and then jump back in when I was ready. Sure I felt frustrated, self-conscious and intimidated. Sure I got a little pissed off sometimes. But I persisted... and that made all the difference in the world.

Then all the good fell away when, caught up in the Christmas rush, I stopped working out for three weeks. I regressed, started stuffing myself again, got cranky, began complaining. Finally, my husband even told me to get lost. "You're a nightmare," he said. He was right. I had slipped badly. I realized that my workout wasn't for my body or appearance or how others felt about me. My workout was for how I felt about myself, for how happy I was and how happy that made the people around me, the people I loved. I returned to the club in January with a vengeance. I thought every day about how my life was changing and about how others could be changed.

I thought to myself, How many other heavyweights would want to work out at a hard-body studio if they knew they'd be accepted and not too critically compared with the workout animals around them? How I would have loved people to give me the time of day or feel the instructors reach out. And then I thought, Why not me?

The next day I showed up at the studio to ask the owner: "Why can't I be an instructor?" Her reaction was predictable: partly supportive, partly disbelieving.

She said, "Neat idea, Dee." I actually heard in her tone, Gee, you might be onto something. Some of the staff, however, thought it was beyond ridiculous.

No matter. I enrolled in a National Dance-Exercise Instructor's Training Association (NDEITA) workshop, which included a written exam. The day of the test, I arrived at the Lake Charles YMCA, one of about thirty men and women.

No one was near my size and, of course, I got the usual "good for you, honey" looks. The daylong exam was a snap, and the next morning I was at the owner's office door with a perfect score.

"All right," I said. "Let's go."

She couldn't believe it. Tossing it back in my court, she told me if I could get ten people to sign up for a month, she'd give me a room and a time slot.

So I made up my own flyers and taped them up at every Weight Watchers location, plus-size clothing shop and grocery store in town. They introduced a brand-new, very-low-intensity pre-aerobics workout specifically for overweight people, taught by an overweight instructor.

Twelve prospects signed up—all women. And so, on a Monday morning in April 1991, I walked into the studio and for the first time stepped to the front of the class.

I could see the owner and the staff watching, getting a load of the misfits. I said a silent prayer, popped my tape into the machine, punched the "Play" button... and... kicked... aerobic... butt.

It was like magic. It felt so good to be in front of that class, motivating them, helping them feel accepted, comfortable, like they belonged—because they did. I watched their faces light up and laugh as they moved. It was the most memorable hour of my life, that first class—the hour went by like a minute. It was incredible.

Beyond the inspiration and identification, I gave everyone specialized attention the second she came through that door, assessing her abilities and adjusting techniques to meet her limitations. No one in that room was going to have to bail out and just watch.

Three years after teaching my first class I was awarded Nike's Fitness Innovation Award for the program I created. The New Face of Fitness has been implemented nationally into more than thirty YWCAs through a Nike grant. It has expanded into hospitals, corporations and fitness clubs across the country.

I weigh about 220 pounds and have maintained my hundred-pound loss for years now. I have regular checkups that confirm I've corrected my medical problems, including high blood pressure, elevated blood cholesterol and diabetes.

With all my newfound energy I even wrote a book—*Thin Is Just a Four-Letter Word: Living Fit for All Shapes and Sizes*—that sold far beyond anyone's wildest dreams.

The last thing on my mind fourteen years ago when Ellen helped me find the courage to walk through those doors was that I could actually teach aerobics classes, much less write a book, work on my own video series, and sign up with an agent who negotiated several sports equipment endorsements for me.

The truth is I wouldn't be here if my students hadn't seen a woman their own size in front of those mirrors. They told me so. If I could do that, they said, then by God, so could they.

~Dee Hakala
Chicken Soup to Inspire the Body and Soul

Woman to Woman

True Friends

*A friend drops their plans when you're in trouble,
shares joy in your accomplishments, feels sad when you're in pain.
A friend encourages your dreams and offers advice—
but when you don't follow it, they still respect and love you.*
~Doris W. Helmering

13

A "Dish" with Integrity

When I was twenty-three I graduated from Bowling Green State University with a degree in education. I was aching to work in my field. Visions of standing before my students in a cozy, poster-strewn classroom discussing the nuances of Shakespeare and Sophocles plagued my thoughts. Even the idea of grading piles of essays brought a smile to my lips.

However, the outlook was dim. Already, many of my fellow classmates had taken jobs outside of education because the market was flooded with eager new teachers and jobs were impossible to find.

I searched and searched, taking time off from my minimum-wage job as a hotel clerk to travel the East Coast in the hopes of finding work. A semester passed, and summer was coming to a close; I was beginning to lose hope when a job fair at my alma mater boasted a host of Texas schools in search of teachers. The unemployed flocked to the fair, passing out numerous résumés and interviewing with many a smiling face and Texas drawl. It was there that I interviewed for the job that would introduce me to one of the most dynamic women I have ever met.

Shortly after the fair I was offered a position teaching at an alternative school. I was so anxious to procure work that I did very little research about my new employer and knew only a little about what an "alternative school" in the state of Texas meant. In two weeks my husband and I quit our jobs, bought a new air-conditioned car and drove to Texas. What a risk! We had no idea where the school was and were going on the promise of a contract; we had no actual contract in hand.

On the first day of school, a tall, powder-haired woman with a friendly pink smile and a firm handshake greeted me at the door. She introduced herself to me as Karla Dunn, and she was to be my new principal. It was her first year at the school as well, but not her first year as principal, and I instantly felt at ease in her presence.

I did not know at the time how lucky I was to be in such a small school. There were twenty-five people on staff, and we all took turns telling a little about ourselves and getting to know one another. It was then that I learned that Karla had been a nun for eighteen years! She had left the convent and later married a man who had an affiliation with a Catholic school in Brazil where I had done my student teaching. She knew the school where I had trained, and it was a common ground for us in conversation.

Not everyone thought that Ms. Dunn was the best "man" for the job. The school where I worked was in Houston, Texas and was established to serve expelled and adjudicated students. Young as they were, many of the kids had been arrested for stealing, dealing or abusing drugs, or engaging in gang activity. Many of our students were in foster care or were parents themselves.

We had a hodge-podge of races and opposing gangs that set the stage for a very volatile environment. Because she was an older single woman, and an ex-nun to boot, some of the teachers balked at her authority and the police officers, although compliant, sometimes raised a wary eyebrow. How could such a sweet and classy lady possibly work with such ruffians? Regardless, Ms. Dunn's message was unbending. No matter what the crime, no matter what the circumstances, these kids were still children and they deserved our respect, love and patience.

Despite the pressure, Ms. Dunn was never absent. Every morning when we arrived at school, whether in sheets of rain or numbing cold, there she stood greeting every child and employee with a hearty "Good morning!" and a smile. The students learned quickly to respond to her, and rarely did she have to chase a student down for a reply. She learned their names and took time to talk to them in the hallway. When there was trouble in the classroom she always supported her teachers, but encouraged us to empower ourselves. Her first question when we complained of trouble was, "Have you called the parents yet?" She knew that if we weren't interested in the lives or families of our students they could never be interested in anything we had to say.

And her wisdom was not limited to the students. Her office door was always open, and I drifted in on many occasions to spend a leisurely hour discussing my personal life. I was a new teacher, and had no idea how unusual this relationship with one's principal was; I was also oblivious to how incredibly busy she was and how much of her time I took. Ms. Dunn had a gift for encouragement and listening. She always made me believe I could do anything.

Her greatest gift to me was to make me understand what leadership meant. The staff was so small that daily meetings sometimes turned into "family quarrels" among siblings. Ms. Dunn mediated, listened and carried the weight of us all on her squared shoulders. She was strong in times of conflict but allowed us to feel that we had a say in decisions that were made. She had a gift for diplomacy and a tender heart. More than once I saw her bow her head, eyes filled with tears, and answer a hurt with a firm apology. She was a watcher from the outside, never privy to secrets, knowing she was criticized, but never wavering in her leadership. She had never given birth to a child, but she was a matriarch to us all.

The first year on campus was a hard one for me, as it is for all first-year teachers, and I nearly reconsidered my choice to be a teacher. My marriage was also in turmoil, and these things combined made for trying times. The second year Ms. Dunn wisely paired me with another young teacher who was experienced with troubled youth, and kept her door open to me. My visits became more frequent, but I was guarded in my conversation. My husband and I split, and I moved in with my partner teacher. Before long I began to date a coworker and I knew that in our close-knit school rumors were flying. I saw Ms. Dunn watching, and I could only guess what she thought of me. But her door remained open.

And then one day I decided to rent my own apartment. It was a big move for me and weighed heavily on my mind. I had many bills and had never lived alone before. Somehow, I ended up in Ms. Dunn's office. As always, she encouraged me to follow my heart. I searched for a place within my budget, and found a small but afford-able one-bedroom with a pretty kitchen and a vaulted ceiling in the living room. I bought used furniture from coworkers and yard sales, and crunched numbers in my head. But it was Ms. Dunn's gift that touched me the most.

One day she invited me to her home for lunch, and when I arrived she brought me to the kitchen. Ms. Dunn, now known to me as "Karla," had set out a collection of matching beautiful blue-and-white dishes complete with teacups and serving plates—all in perfect condition. She sat me down at the table, motioned to the dishes and began a story.

"When I first left the convent and was just starting out a woman gave me these dishes because I was in need of them. She gave them to me with one stipulation," Karla began.

"What was that?" I asked.

"That whenever I came across another woman in need, I would pass the dishes on to her. I have passed the dishes on before, and miraculously, God always makes sure they come back to me. These dishes are yours to help you get started, and when you get on your feet, and you no longer need them, I want you to wait for a woman who needs to get started, and pass them on to her. If they should come back into your hands, please continue the tradition."

"Agreed," I smiled. "Thank you so much for thinking of me."

It has been years since Karla gave me that gift, and sealed the gift of our friendship. Karla is still my dear mentor and beloved friend. I see her for lunch from time to time and she listens to my news, although she is more quickly tired from my visits. I still eat from the blue-and-white dishes, but it's time to purchase my own set. Often I wonder about the woman who will inherit these dishes from me. Perhaps in me she will see what I saw in Karla—a kind heart, a spirit that does not cast stones and a firm commitment to integrity. Karla's example is the true nourishment I get every time I eat a meal on these dishes.

~Erin Kilby
Chicken Soup for the Working Woman's Soul

14

The Golden Girls

A friend is one of the nicest things you can have,
and one of the best things you can be.
~Douglas Pagels

Rose and I met when we were in our mid-twenties. I had invited her daughter to my daughter's third birthday party, and Rose came along. We scrutinized each other and assessed the obvious differences. She was a smoker; I wasn't. I dressed conservatively; she didn't. She wore a long, black flowing wig whenever she tired of her short frosted hair; I wore the same "flip" hairstyle for years. But we became best friends.

Despite our differences, we wore a path from my house to hers (sometimes in our fuzzy robes), borrowing sugar, guzzling coffee, sharing baked goods and details of our lives. For twelve years, we went to yard sales, fast-food restaurants, playgrounds and school events together.

Rose and I stayed best friends during tough times, as well. Both of us had turbulent marriages. One summer, both marriages finally fell apart. Coincidentally, Rose's sister Millie ended her marriage about the same time, and so did Rose's childhood friend, Judy.

The four of us became known as The Golden Girls. We discovered a neighborhood club with an outdoor patio, and we spent that summer sipping soda and dancing together to old-time rock and roll.

After that summer, we calmed down a bit. As we created new lives for ourselves, we saw less of each other. Eventually, Rose and I attended each other's weddings, and we visited together at family gatherings and holiday celebrations. Each time, it was as if we'd never been apart.

At my daughter's baby shower, I noticed that Rose's one-of-a-kind laugh seemed hoarse. She told me she'd had a persistent cough for weeks. Soon, diagnostic tests indicated a mass in her lung. Exploratory surgery revealed a large inoperable malignancy. I visited Rose in the intensive care unit afterward.

"I love you," I told my friend, realizing it was the first time I had said the words aloud.

"I love you, too," she said groggily, sealing our bond.

After Rose recovered from surgery, I took her for radiation treatment. We held hands in the waiting room. When our eyes met, they brimmed with tears. On the drive home, we talked about this life and the afterlife. And we talked about a story we'd both read many, many years before, about two friends, one of whom was terminally ill.

"You'll remember that story, won't you?" Rose asked.

"I will," I promised.

The Golden Girls reunited. Millie, Judy and I spent countless hours with Rose. We took her shopping and dining. We humored her when her medication gave her hallucinations. When she became incapacitated, we visited her at home in shifts. I fluffed her pillows, brought her doughnuts, massaged her feet and colored in coloring books with her.

Rose spent the last week of her life in the hospital, heavily sedated, surrounded by loved ones. At fifty-one, her breathing ceased and our mourning began.

A year followed, and I thought of Rose often. One cold November morning, as I left for work, I saw something pink protruding from a drift of decaying leaves. I cleared the debris and gasped in disbelief at a flower bud. During the summer I had planted a tiny, three-inch potted azalea, hoping it would grow into a bush. It hadn't grown at all and had never flowered. But here on this frosty Missouri morning, with the rest of the garden killed by a hard frost, the azalea bloomed.

I thought about Rose all day, and that afternoon, I called her daughter.

"Denise, can you come by after work?" I asked. "I have a surprise from your mom."

When I got home, I checked the azalea again. The tiny pink bud had opened completely and blossomed to the size of a carnation.

That evening, Denise came to my door. She looked just like Rose.

"You're not going to believe this," I said. I told Denise about the conversation Rose and I had had after her radiation therapy.

"Twenty years ago, your mom and I read a story about two best friends. One was terminally ill. She vowed to make a flower bloom in winter to prove there was an afterlife. Your mom and I discussed that story and made a pact that day."

I led Denise to the backyard and showed her my azalea, blooming in winter. Denise and I laughed, embraced, stared in disbelief and cried tears of joy.

"This couldn't have come at a better time," Denise said, wiping her eyes. "It's been almost a year since Mom passed away. You've taken away so much of my sadness. Thank you."

During the next week I watched in amazement as three more flowers bloomed fully. I called Millie and Judy and told them about the plant I nicknamed The Golden Girls, with one blossom for each of us. We rejoiced at the message from our friend. Incredibly, the plant thrived for two weeks, surviving snow, wind and chill. Then, the flowers gradually withered and died, completing the cycle of life. But they left behind a vivid memory and a message for all us Golden Girls that true friendship never dies.

~Linda O'Connell
Chicken Soup for the Gardener's Soul

The Ring I Really Want

*You can't live a perfect day without doing something for someone
who will never be able to repay you.*
~John Wooden

"Oh, I love your diamond," Janet said admiringly as we served lunch to the children in the school gym. "It's beautiful."

"Thanks," I said, and then I confessed. "It's not real; it's just a cubic zirconia."

Her eyes widened. "Wow. I would never have guessed."

I have always had a passion for collecting fine jewelry, but I also own a few quality fake pieces, which generally fool everyone. Janet eyed my large sparkling ring. "I've never owned anything like that," she sighed, looking down at the plain thin wedding band on her hand.

We finished serving the children their Thanksgiving turkey lunch, but Janet's words stayed with me. I knew she and her husband could not afford even the small luxuries of life; they are a Christian family who lives down the street with four boys, and they work hard to make ends meet.

The idea of giving my ring to Janet came to me the next day. I pushed it away immediately. Although the 14-carat gold ring was only a cubic zirconia, I liked it and wore it often with my wedding band. The thought of knocking on Janet's door and presenting her with my ring seemed ridiculous. I try to shrug the notion off, but the thought persisted. It bothered me for a week. I had no peace until finally I prayed: "Lord, if this is something you want me to do, I'll do it, but please go with me and let her be home when I go." I reasoned that if I knocked on the door and Janet wasn't home, which she often wasn't, I would take it as a sign that I didn't have to part with my ring. I felt a little better but was still unenthusiastic about this errand.

The next morning I put the ring in its little blue velvet box, wrapped it up in tissue paper and walked down the street to Janet's house, my heart pounding. She'll think I'm crazy, I thought. What kind of neighbor gives someone a 14-carat gold ring? I don't even know her that well.

I felt like turning around and going home but forced myself to climb the steps to Janet's house. I knocked quietly on the door. No one answered. I stood on her porch, waiting uncomfortably. Knock again, God's spirit prompted. Reluctantly I knocked again. No one answered.

I felt the stirrings of relief. Maybe she was away and I could forget about this whole thing. Just as I stood there contemplating my escape, I heard the doorknob rattle. Janet looked incredibly surprised to see me. "Hi," she greeted me.

"Good morning," I said, struggling not to blush with discomfort. I handed her the small package. "I have something for you."

She looked astounded. "For me?"

I nodded. "The Lord has been telling me all week to give this to you."

She took it and as her fingers closed over the contours of the box, she realized what it was. To my immense surprise, her eyes filled with tears and her hands began to shake. "No," her voice quavered. "I can't accept this. It's too much. I can't accept this."

An immense peace and joy descended upon me there on Janet's front porch. "You're my sister in Christ and I want you to have it," I said, unable to keep the delight from spreading over my face.

Janet unwrapped the ring and cried. I hugged her, my eyes full of tears. She hugged me back. It took a bit of convincing on my part, but she finally agreed to keep the ring. "If you ever change your mind, just tell me and I'll give it back," she promised. It was a few sizes too small for her, so I told her to have it adjusted at the nearby jewelry store, which had extremely reasonable prices.

I thought that was the end of the story, but several weeks later as I was walking past Janet's house, she flew out the door, across the porch and out to the sidewalk.

"I have a present for you," she said breathlessly. She thrust a little package at me.

"Janet, you don't have to do that," I protested.

"Open it," she said, grinning.

I opened it and found a little blue velvet box with my ring in it. I looked up at her, puzzled and slightly disappointed that she had chosen not to keep it.

"I went to the jewelry store you told me about to get it sized," she explained, "but the clerk didn't think it would be good for the claws and setting to enlarge it that many sizes. I was devastated. I finally had something beautiful and I couldn't even wear it."

Janet's smile was incongruent with her story.

"I don't understand," I admitted.

On the sidewalk, in the late afternoon, with the sun slanting through the maple tree in Janet's yard, she told me what had happened. For years, her set of wedding bands had lain in a dresser drawer in her bedroom. She had lost the diamond solitaire, and the rings needed repairs and sizing. It was a gorgeous antique set but she had been unable to wear it. Every Mother's Day, birthday and Christmas, she had quietly gone to that dresser drawer and examined her rings, hoping her husband had surprised her by getting them fixed. And every time she went to the drawer, she was disappointed. Repairing and restoring the rings were simply too expensive. She and her husband had received estimates from jewelers of nearly one thousand dollars for the work. They couldn't afford to spend their money on something so frivolous. My gift had touched her heart, but what she wanted most was to wear her own wedding bands.

On a whim, Janet asked the clerk in the jewelry store about getting her wedding rings fixed. She had given up hope that it would ever happen. It had never occurred to her to consider a synthetic gem — until now. Janet's rings were sized and repaired and the center stone replaced with a cubic zirconia for under $100. She held her hand out to show me. Her rings sparkled in the sunlight. Rows of glittering diamonds encircled a solitaire that flashed with brilliant fire. They were stunning.

"For the first time in seven years, I am wearing my rings again," she said, her voice breaking. "Thank you for your gift. Thank you more than you'll ever know — but these are the only rings I really want."

I walked home in a daze. It took quite a while for the whole extraordinary sequence of events to sink in. I have concluded that God's intricate plans are altogether too incredible to anticipate or comprehend. The next time He wants to entwine my life with another, I will do as He asks — without questions, without doubts — and with trust.

~Rachel Wallace-Oberle
Chicken Soup for the Christian Woman's Soul

16

Birthday Presents

Since there is nothing so well worth having as friends,
never lose a chance to make them.
~Francesco Guicciardini

I clicked my Palm Pilot and flashing words reminded me that I had not completed a task. Staring at the screen, I worried about what in the world I was going to get Colette for her birthday. After almost thirty years of friendship, I was running out of ideas. And it wasn't just for Colette.

I was blessed to have seven incredible lifelong friendships that began in my childhood. Colette, Marcy, Amy and I became steadfast friends while coloring in kindergarten. We added Mary, Kimmie and Rachel to the group in junior high while chasing boys. Claudette joined us in high school while going to football games. With friendships that spanned decades, together we played jump rope, studied, went to dances, fell in and out of love, graduated, traveled, began careers, really fell in love, married and had children. This colorful group of friends had seen each other at our very best and our very worst. No matter what changed in our lives, one thing stayed the same—our friendships.

Here I was, though, staring at my Palm Pilot realizing I was going to be really late with Colette's birthday gift if I did not buy her something today. What could I get her? Last year was a magazine subscription, the year before that candles, before that wineglasses, and before that scrapbook-making kits. Besides, as my friends married and we grew older, we already had just about everything we needed. What could I buy her?

The phone rang and I was happy to escape my unsuccessful pondering. Marcy greeted me cheerfully and began to tell me about last night's girls' dinner. Conversations like this always made me miss my childhood home in Illinois and made it hard to live in Washington, D.C., so far from my friends. Marcy filled me in on the latest gossip. Mary was pregnant with child number four and Amy's son Jake was potty-training. Colette would probably be engaged very soon and Marcy was finalizing her wedding plans. On and on we chatted while laughing about the latest happenings in our lives. Finally, I asked Marcy what she was giving Colette for her birthday. Marcy exclaimed, "Oh, I almost forgot to tell you! Last night we were all talking about our birthdays and how hard it is to buy something unique and useful after all these years of friendship. Also, with everyone having kids, school costs, homes, vacations and basically life, we decided that expensive birthday gifts for our friends really add up. So we decided that this year we're giving each other socks." I laughed and said, "What a great idea!" Marcy continued, "No more than two pairs and they can be any kind of socks. You know, those cute little socks with patterns, or trouser socks, or workout socks. Whatever you want. Next year we're all giving underwear! You should have heard that discussion about who wears thongs, granny underwear or lace! It was hilarious. The year after that we're giving earrings. Isn't this fun?" I quickly agreed and kept smiling. We chatted a few more minutes and hung up.

I tossed my Palm Pilot into my purse and headed to the store. While driving, I couldn't help but think about how smart my friends were. It wasn't the physical gift or the amount of money we spent that was important. What was important was celebrating our friends' birthdays. The inexpensive themes allowed us to be clever, and perhaps even funny, yet it would be low-stress and useful. As I thought of the years ahead, I smiled because from now on birthday buying was going to be so easy and fun. And when you really think about it, regardless of what's inside when we unwrap each other's presents, what we really unwrap is our love.

~Marguerite Murer
Chicken Soup for the Girlfriend's Soul

17

Loving Kelly

"I really like her," my brother told me over the phone.

"Well, tell me all about her," I said. Then I asked all those nosy questions only a sister can get away with asking. What's she like? Where did you meet? Is she "the one?"

I could hear the smile in his voice as he told me about her, and in my mind, I could see that familiar glint in his eyes. For the next twenty minutes, Steve told me all about his new girlfriend. As I continued to listen, I began to know something was not quite right. Then I realized he had not yet told me her name.

"What's her name?" I finally asked, trying to sound lighthearted.

Seconds of silence stretched into an eternity before he quietly, hesitantly, said, "Kelly."

Suddenly, the phone seemed to grow hot in my trembling hand, and I could not speak. Finally, with some effort, I said, "Oh." Then, "I gotta go. I'll call you soon." I sat there for a long time, staring at the phone, remembering another Kelly.

I still remember the first time I saw her. I was seven. I came crashing into the house after school only to be met by the shushing sound escaping around my mother's index finger held firmly against her pursed lips. "Quiet. The baby's sleeping," she whispered.

"Can I see her?" I whispered back, stepping up onto my tiptoes.

"When she wakes up," Mom said firmly.

I looked at Dad. I knew he would help me.

He winked and motioned me over. Ignoring Mom's warning, we sneaked into my bedroom where Kelly, wearing a tiny cornflower-blue gown, lay sleeping. I pressed my face against the rails of her crib. I reached between the bars and touched her cheek. Dad knelt beside me and gently woke her. Kelly opened her blue eyes and looked right into mine.

"My sister, my baby sister," I said in a proud sigh. I loved her from that moment on.

As we grew older and more aware of life, we giggled about boys, and clothes and hairstyles. I answered her questions about periods and love and falling stars. We crossed our hearts and hoped to die should we ever not be best friends.

At night, as we lay in bed with our backs pressed against each other, we shared all our secrets and all our dreams and carefully planned our old age. We would live together and travel the world. We would be "fun old ladies" like the Baldwin Sisters from Walton's Mountain.

When the day came for me to leave for college, Kelly and I clung to each other, and we sobbed into each other's necks for a long time. With Kelly still weeping softly, Mom finally pulled her away and assured me she would be okay. I wasn't sure I would be, though.

When I was twenty-five and Kelly was eighteen, my doctor diagnosed me with a serious illness that left me unable to bear children. Kelly came to me and offered herself as a surrogate to carry a baby for me and my husband, Jeff.

I thought about her offer for a long time. I was more touched than words can say, but not at all surprised. In the end, I decided against it. I loved Kelly so much. I could not, would not, ask her to carry a baby in my stead then give it up to me, even though I knew she would. If only I could have known then what lay ahead just a year later.

Funny, isn't it, how you know when the phone rings it's bad news. It was January 26, 1986, Sunday afternoon, Super Bowl Sunday. We had hamburgers for lunch.

"Yes. When? I see," Jeff said into the phone.

There was no hiding it. I saw the shadow in his eyes. "It's bad, isn't it?" I asked as Jeff slowly replaced the receiver in its cradle.

He held me tightly and gently broke the news. "It's Kelly. She's dead. It seems that carbon monoxide seeped through a crack in an old heater in the hotel room where she was staying last night. She died in her sleep."

My sister, my baby sister. Gone! I couldn't believe it. We had so many plans. It just couldn't be true. It just couldn't.

Three years after Kelly's death, I still found it difficult to talk about her. I could not even speak her name without tears filling my eyes. The thought of Steve dating and possibly marrying someone named Kelly was almost unbearable.

Steve did marry "his Kelly," and I found myriad ways to speak of her without actually saying her name. To Steve—How's your wife? How's she doing? To Mom and Dad—Have you heard from Steve and his wife—from them—from her?

With Steve and Kelly living in Washington, D.C., Jeff and I by then in Alaska, and the lack of travel funds, I did not meet Steve's Kelly until six years after she married him. I did talk with her occasionally on the phone.

She seemed nice, and my brother was certainly happy. I began to look forward to her phone calls but still found myself holding back.

Then, one Christmas everything changed. Steve and Kelly and Jeff and I met at my parents' home in Texas. Kelly and I spent a lot of time talking and really getting to know each other. In spite of my reticence, I found myself liking her more and more. We laughed and giggled and shared secrets, almost like sisters.

"I've always wondered something," Kelly said as we walked through my parents' neighborhood one afternoon.

"What's that?" I asked.

"I wonder if your Kelly would have liked me."

Surprising myself, I answered immediately without hesitating. "Oh, I know she would. She would have scrutinized you closely, but she definitely would have liked you," I said knowingly. "You are beautiful, sweet, adventurous and fun. You like cats. And, most of all, you make her brother happy. And she would have loved your name."

On Christmas Eve, with tears dancing in her eyes, Kelly handed me a small beige and dark green box tied with twine. I pulled the free end of the string and lifted the lid. I gently removed the top layer of cotton. Underneath was a small magnet. Pink and purple pansies surrounded carefully chosen words: "Sisters By Marriage, Friends By Heart."

Tears escaped my control and wetted my cheeks. "Thank you, Kelly," I whispered. Then, I hugged her. "I love you."

Several Christmases have come and gone since that one. Kelly has become one of my very best friends, and another sister whom I love very much. The magnet she gave me still hangs on my refrigerator so that I will see it every day and be reminded of the love we share, that I almost never knew.

~Pamela Haskin
Chicken Soup for the Sister's Soul

Ladies of the Garden Club

Let us be grateful to people who make us happy;
they are the charming gardeners who make our souls blossom.
~Marcel Proust

"Me? Join a garden club?" I asked my boss in amazement. "Why in the world would I do that?"

I was a career-oriented woman in my early thirties. I had no time for a garden. And unless it was a business networking group, I had no interest in clubs.

"As employees of the community health department, our mission is to make the city a healthier place to live," Mrs. Hubbard informed me. I had no idea how joining a garden club would accomplish that. And I had no idea that Mrs. Hubbard's mother was the club president. All I knew was, the boss said "Go"—so I went.

My first meeting was on a Wednesday morning. Looking for the address, I was captivated by the beautiful gardens in this historic Oklahoma City neighborhood. Mature trees formed a canopy blocking the sun's glare, while vibrant purple irises, red and yellow tulips and a sea of white pansies illuminated the yard at Dorothy's home. What a contrast to my new house in the suburbs, where the front flower bed was filled with nothing but pine bark.

Though I was a few minutes late for the meeting, only three others had arrived. The dining room table was set for a full breakfast of quiche, fruit, sausage balls, and poppy seed and banana-nut muffins.

Members slowly trickled in. I was on my third cup of coffee, yet the meeting had not begun. I was a little edgy from the caffeine rush and the thought of all I needed to do at work. Then I learned that the meeting ended at noon and the ladies usually went out to lunch together afterward. I greeted that news with a smile and clenched teeth, and tried to keep from drumming my fingers impatiently.

The members, all past retirement age, introduced themselves. I was the only young person there. But as the meeting began, I found myself relaxing, captivated by the program on native plant species. I was so engrossed in imagining my own bare lawn bursting with plants, that I was caught off guard when President Bonnie announced, "We'd like to hold the meeting at your house next month, Stephanie—if you don't mind."

At the office later that day, I complained to a coworker. "The last thing I want to do is host a dozen women my grandmother's age," I groaned. "The meeting took all morning. And then they wanted me to go out to lunch! I'd been with them two hours already!" But I was stuck.

A month later, on a Wednesday morning, I dashed around my little kitchen. I dumped frozen mini-quiches from a sack and arranged them on a cookie sheet. I whacked two cans of quick-bake cinnamon rolls on the edge of the counter and slapped the doughy blobs on another pan.

This meeting will not be like the last, I thought grimly, looking at my store-bought refreshments. They probably wanted young people in the club just to do all the work!

The doorbell rang.

"I'm a little early, but I thought you could use some help getting ready for your first meeting," announced Dorothy as she entered. "I know you're a busy career gal, so I prepared a casserole and a fruit plate."

Entering the kitchen, she offered to make coffee as I tried to hide evidence of the Pillsbury Doughboy.

"Oh, good! Those cinnamon rolls are my favorites," she confided.

The doorbell rang again. Dorothy suggested she greet members so I could concentrate on being the hostess.

Soon, more than a dozen ladies were assembled. The meeting ran smoothly, and everyone seemed to enjoy the refreshments—even the ones from the frozen-food section.

"Now, since you've been our hostess today, we have a gift for you," said Bonnie. "Open your front door."

When I did, my jaw dropped in surprise. A dozen sacks filled with homegrown plants, potted shrubs and a flat of pansies welcomed me.

"It's your initiation," said Bonnie, laughing heartily. "We brought you something from our own gardens with a note on where to plant it and how to care for it."

"I brought the pansies," whispered Dorothy. "I noticed you admired them at our meeting last month."

Tears blurred my eyes as I thanked them. "I was embarrassed for you all to come out here. My yard is so bare."

"Oh my, no!" exclaimed Bonnie. "It's just a blank canvas waiting for an artist's brush."

Most everyone stayed to help me wash dishes and rearrange chairs.

Two days later, I got a call from Bonnie. "I've separated some coreopsis to plant around your fence," she said. "Say, if you haven't put the plants from Wednesday in the ground, I'll come Saturday morning and help if you want me to. You have been watering them daily, right?"

"Of course," I lied.

That evening I went home and tended the wilting plants, hoping they would revive overnight before Bonnie's arrival.

At seven in the morning, shovels in hand, three members of the Carefree Rose Garden Club arrived. They taught me how to arrange my landscape, and we dug a new twenty-foot flower bed around my front yard. The ladies brought more irises, amaryllis, tulips, hyacinths, coreopsis, pansies, peonies, redbud trees, wisteria, daisies and crepe myrtle bushes. We finished before noon, exhausted.

"It's beautiful," I whooped, as we brushed clumps of dirt and leaves off one another. "I could never have done it without you."

"That's garden club," said Bonnie.

We all staggered over to wash up at the garden hose. Then Dorothy asked me to get a picnic basket and ice chest from her car.

"I thought we'd be too tired to fix lunch, so I made us sandwiches before I came," she said.

Sitting cross-legged on the sidewalk with my newfound elderly friends, I realized I had never been muddier in my adult life. And, I giggled to myself, I couldn't remember having this much fun.

Me? Join a garden club? Where do I sign up?

~Stephanie Welcher Buckley
Chicken Soup for the Gardener's Soul

19

Friendly Reminder

The most wasted of all days is one without laughter.
~e.e. cummings

Friendships are a must for women. If it weren't for friends, women would have to go to the ladies' room alone. And who would offer a truthful assessment about whether an outfit makes your hips look big?

I have a Mustache Pact with my closest friends. If any one of us goes into a coma, the others are bound by our pact to come and wax the mustache of the comatose friend. We women love to share those special moments.

I shared another special moment with friends recently. Several of us were hurrying to a surprise baby shower. We were hurrying because it's tough to surprise the guest of honor when she gets to the party before the guests.

We had pooled our resources to buy "the stroller to end all strollers." It was a collapsible stroller that would stroll the baby, carry the baby, swing the baby—maybe even change the baby—I'm not sure. I thought I heard someone say it sliced, diced and julienned. It was Stroller-ama!

I told the others to run into the house while I got Super Stroller from the trunk. I jerked it into position and started sprinting. Unfortunately, about mid-driveway, Stroller-zilla realized I hadn't fully locked it into place (emphasis on the aforementioned collapsible feature). It collapsed neatly into storage mode.

I probably don't need to give you a science lesson on "momentum," but let me mention that I had a lot of it working for me. The fact that The Stroller-nator stopped on a dime didn't mean much to my little sprinting body, which was immediately airborne.

Please picture a graceful triple axel over the top of the stroller with sort of a one-point, back-end kind of a landing. I finished it off with a lovely flat-on-the-back pose, staring up at the sky for effect. I'd give it a 6.9.

Thankfully, I had my wonderful friends there to rush over and make sure I was okay. Of course, they couldn't actually ask me if I was all right since they were laughing so hard they were about to damage some internal organs! One of them couldn't even stay. She made a bee-line for the house. You know what can happen to laughing women.

That's another thing we love to share: laughter.

This is a little reminder. If it's been a while since you've made time for friends, take the time and share a laugh with a sister. Both are a gift from God. We need each other—there are certain matters that only women understand. Two of those are "mauve" and "taupe." Another is, of course, other women.

Call up your special bud today. While you have her on the line, you might also want to take care of that coma-mustache-pact thing.

~Rhonda Rhea
Chicken Soup for the Sister's Soul

20

Got Tea?

Generosity lies less in giving much than in giving at the right moment.
~Jean La Bruyere

I've known Jenny since the day I started taking piano lessons from her mother. Jenny is blond; I am brunette. All-American Jenny is tall and vivacious. I am petite and quiet. Jenny has a bubbling troupe of siblings; I am an only child. Her favorite flavor is vanilla; I prefer chocolate. Jenny took piano lessons because it was what girls did when they were young, whereas I made music my life.

Our favorite pastime back then was our afternoon tea parties. My first tea set was a Christmas gift the year I was seven. The miniature pieces were decorated with garlands of pink roses and delicate violets. The tea set was accompanied by a charming old trunk filled with all manner of dress-up clothes Mother discovered at the secondhand store. Jenny and I rummaged through the trunk, combining fancy hats, strings of pearls and ecru sweaters with gold buttons until we were pleased with our queenly appearance. We would sit across my child-size table, sipping apple juice and nibbling crackers from the tiny dishes.

Under the Christmas tree every year was a package for the dress-up trunk. Favorite items were kept in the royal collection; others were replaced with new fashion trends. When we were ten, Jenny and I styled each other's hair before foraging through the trunk for high-heeled shoes. With wobbling ankles, we made our way precariously to the kitchen table to pour hot cocoa from Mother's teapot into adult-size mugs, and sample chocolate-chip cookies. And always we talked about our hopes, our dreams and our music.

At thirteen, Jenny and I painted our fingernails with polish and our faces with makeup from the trunk. With a drop of perfume behind each ear, we imagined ourselves as Abigail Adams and Martha Washington discussing the fledgling United States of America, or authors Beatrix Potter and Louisa May Alcott debating book ideas.

For our sixteenth birthdays, Jenny and I pierced our ears. The old trunk held an assortment of brash, dangly earrings we would not wear in public, but which were entirely suitable for tea. Linen napkins across our laps, we savored real tea from Mother's real china tea set, enhanced by slices of banana bread. We made plans to see the world. I would be her bridesmaid, and she promised to be mine.

Eighteen found us on the college rollercoaster. High school graduation flung us at whirlwind speed into the adult world of studies and jobs, cars and insurance, fellows and romance. Jenny's life went one way, mine another. On that vast university campus in fast-paced Southern California, we rarely saw one another.

Except for one special day. We ran into each other on campus and discovered we both had thirty minutes before we needed to be somewhere else. With sudden lightheartedness, we dashed to the nearby café for tea... orange spice for Jenny, raspberry for me. There was so much to talk about. Jenny had met a man with hair as dark as hers was blond. Work at the art gallery and art studies consumed the rest of her time. I was simultaneously pursuing two doctoral degrees in music and squeezing in a few hours of work. And there was a man in my life.

Those precious free minutes turned into a stolen four hours, and we realized with a start that afternoon classes had long since ended. But sitting on the table between us was a teapot our intuitive waitress had discreetly set there before she left to carry on her life away from the café. The bill read, "On the house."

I married that special man in my life. As promised, Jenny was my bridesmaid. My husband and I set up housekeeping in a vintage house near the college, close to family and friends and all that was dear to me. Jenny and I fit in an occasional cup of tea.

Then everything changed. My husband landed an excellent job with a promising future, great benefits and good salary, all in the field he wanted. He was elated. He said, "The move five hundred miles north would be a terrific adventure."

Adventure? I was devastated. All I knew and was familiar with was here. I needed six more months to complete my studies. I didn't know a soul in the new town so far away. I wasn't one who made friends easily. What would I do there?

Moving so far from loved ones proved extremely difficult. I spent the first days crying as I unpacked boxes in our beautiful new home. Everything felt, and looked, gray.

Then came the first knock on my new door. Standing on the front porch was the mailman with a large parcel. I recognized the return address as Jenny's. Dear, lifelong friend Jenny. Those horrible miles between us melted away, as I tore at the wrapping.

The paper parted to reveal a teapot, decorated with garlands of pink roses and delicate violets. Nestled next to the beautiful china piece was a matching set of teacups and saucers along with a box of raspberry tea. Her note read: "I know you will need a close friend in your new home. You have my permission to find a new close friend. Then you will have two close friends."

Sunday, my husband and I visited the nearby church. Renee, an effervescent lady with auburn hair, gave me a hug. "We moved here a year ago, and I know just how lonely you feel."

"Would you come for tea?" I asked.

"I'd be delighted," Renee said with a smile.

Months later, Jenny sent a smaller package, a box of orange spice tea. The enclosed note read, "I'll be there Saturday for tea!" And so Jenny made her first of many visits to our northern home.

When I called Jenny with the news I was expecting our first baby, she sent a package of peppermint tea, to soothe my nauseous tummy.

It's been fifteen years since my husband and I moved north. Renee brought me a beribboned package containing a mug with the picture of an angel and the words, "May your guardian angel keep watch over you when we're apart." Renee and her family were moving out of state.

I sent Renee off with a hug and a package to open on the drive to their new address. The gift bag held a pair of teacups and a note that read: "You will need a close friend in your new home. You have my permission to find one. Then you will have two close friends."

Jenny and I keep in touch mostly by phone. As always, we are startlingly different. Jenny's life takes her to exciting and glamorous places. My world is filled with my three children, carpooling, church and music.

Just last week, Jenny telephoned.

"How wonderful to hear from you," I exclaimed. "But I'm in the middle of giving a piano lesson. Can I call you back?"

"I'm afraid not," she replied with a laugh. "I'm calling from a layover in a New York airport. I'm putting a package in the mail, some delicious herbal teas from a little shop. I thought of you immediately. It's some of those berry flavors you adore...."

~PeggySue Wells
Chicken Soup for the Girlfriend's Soul

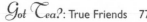

Strengthened by Angels

"Mom, where's my black jacket?" my teenage daughter asked as she joined me in the kitchen while I prepared school lunches.

"I don't know, Jennifer. Wherever you left it," I snapped abruptly, finding it difficult to think about anything but cancer.

Tomorrow! My mastectomy is tomorrow. The thought consumed me as the fear and helplessness that came with this disease roared like a ferocious lion inside me.

My thoughts were interrupted again as my other daughter Melissa exclaimed, "Look at my hair, Mom. My bangs need cutting. I can't go to school looking like this."

She held a pair of scissors in her hand.

"Sit down, Melissa, and give me the scissors," I said halfheartedly.

While trying to focus on cutting her soft blond hair, the thought occurred to me that some day I might not be alive to do this. Tears filled my eyes.

"Are you crying?" she asked. "What's the matter, Mom?"

"It's just that I'm glad to be your mother," I spoke softly. I finished cutting her bangs and took my daughters to school.

When they left the car, I kept thinking about my husband of twenty-three years and our girls. Returning home, I joined my husband for a cup of coffee on the patio before he left for work. "You're going to be all right, honey," he reassured me as his tender arms embraced me like a comforter. "We can bear this. After all, we have the Great Physician with us."

Finally alone, I kept wondering: If I die, who will take our daughters shopping for just the right outfit for their first date? Who will help them learn the importance of friendship, if I am not able to be their friend? Who will support my husband during the tough times, like when he loses a job? And who will help him find the simple things, like mayonnaise in the refrigerator?

Many thoughts paraded through my mind. I had supported friends when cancer had invaded their lives, but now I had to accept the fact that this was not someone else's nightmare—it was mine! For years, God has been my companion, but I'd never been terrified enough to fully "trust in the Lord and be of good courage."

The silence of our home was not a welcomed relief from the demands of my children. I was alone—alone with my thoughts, which kept overflowing like a broken faucet. I curled up in my favorite chair and reached for my King James Bible. I desperately needed solace.

My fingers slowly turned the pages, groping for words of strength and peace. I stopped in Luke and began reading the passage about Christ praying in the garden of Gethsemane: "Father, if You are willing, take this cup from me; yet not my will, but Yours be done." An angel from Heaven appeared to Him and strengthened Him. (Luke 22:42–43) I had read these verses many times but never realized God sent an angel to comfort His son.

"This is what I need," I spoke aloud. "You sent an angel to strengthen Your son. Please give me something to hold on to today. I need an angel."

Routine household chores failed to free my mind from fearful thoughts. I needed a diversion and decided a trip to the market would help. At the store, my grocery list helped me focus. What a relief to think of practical needs like milk, bread and butter. I headed for the cookie aisle to stock up on our daughters' favorite cookies so they would have them while I was in the hospital.

Reaching for the package, I recognized a friend and fellow teacher from years ago.

"Hi, Pat," I tried to sound cheerful.

"Sharon, how are you?" she asked as she steered her cart closer to mine. It was strange how the depth of the question, "How are you?" had changed. It was no longer just a lighthearted social greeting.

"Do you really want to know?" I asked as the knot in the pit of my stomach tightened.

"Of course I do," she replied sincerely.

"They found cancer in my left breast, and I'm going to have a radical mastectomy tomorrow morning. I'm not sure how far the cancer has spread." I fought back tears.

Pat listened intently as I shared my diagnosis and biopsy experience.

"Do you remember Bert Seacat?" she asked while softly touching my shoulder. "She's a teacher, too."

"Yes, I do," I answered. "We taught at the same elementary school. I haven't seen her in twenty years."

"Well," Pat continued, "she had a double mastectomy ten years ago, and she's just as feisty as ever."

I pushed my cart closer to Pat. "She is?" Hope began to flicker within me.

We reminisced for a while and then we both continued shopping. I quietly thanked God for the encouraging news Pat shared about our mutual friend. My heavy burden of anxiety began to lift. I no longer felt limited to my shopping list and began to feel a sense of freedom.

A few minutes later, I made my way to the front of the store and looked down the row of fifteen checkout aisles. I saw Pat again, ready to unload her groceries. I steered my cart behind her.

We started to talk, but my eyes looked beyond her to the woman paying for her groceries. A strange feeling came over me. I looked closer. No, it can't be, I thought, as the woman turned, looked at me and smiled.

"Hi Sharon," she said sympathetically. "Pat was just telling me what's going to happen to you tomorrow morning."

"Bert Seacat," I replied, almost breathless, as tears filled my eyes.

"I'll unpack your groceries, Sharon," Pat offered. "Go and talk with Bert."

Bert put her loving arms around me and my fear began to melt away. "You can do it, Sharon," she encouraged. "You can do it!"

I dried my eyes while she began sharing her experience. "I thought I was going to die. I wondered how my husband and I would be able to accept the loss of part of my body. Many times, I thought my children might be left without a mother to love them. But look at me now!" she exclaimed. "I had both breasts removed. Do you like the ones I had reconstructed?" she chuckled, pulling her shoulders back.

"Your groceries are ready now," Pat interrupted.

"Remember, Sharon," Bert insisted, "you can do it! Call me any-time. I want to help."

After paying my bill, I walked out of the grocery store a much different person than when I had entered. Never before had I ever felt so loved by God. My body was filled with His peace.

Standing by my car, I looked up at the clouds. "Thank you, God, for two special angels. I know I can do it! I can face tomorrow."

~Sharon Wilkins
Chicken Soup for the Christian Woman's Soul

The Church Lady

A friend is the one who comes in when the whole world has gone out.
~Grace Pulpit

Caring for my ailing mother proved quite difficult. I lived 1,700 miles away. My young family also needed attention, so I could only manage to visit her just a week to ten days every month.

Mom's respiratory condition worsened. Oxygen, special medication and a lot of bed rest became her fare of the day, while fatigue, frustration and financial difficulties loomed in my life. Yet, I promised myself I'd try to do what was necessary for as long as it took.

"I can't go shopping."

"I can't visit my neighbors."

"I can't even get to church."

Mom's complaints were unavoidable and valid. Being housebound and isolated from all the activities she so enjoyed caused her to sink rapidly into a state of depression. In a short span of time, it was obvious her mental health deteriorated to the point of worry.

On one visit, I asked, "How are you managing when I'm not here?"

She replied, "Oh, I don't need much these days. But when I do, Gen, the church lady, as you used to call her, comes by and takes care of me."

"What does she do for you?"

"She tidies up, brings me treats, shops for my groceries, makes me a cup of tea and keeps me up-to-date on the latest gossip."

Smiling, I said, "She sounds like quite a friend and a natural caregiver."

Mom's face beamed. "Not only to me but to anyone who needs a helping hand. Look at all she's done for the church over the years. Not only does she cook a few meals for the clergy, she dresses the altar with ceremonial linens and flowers, and keeps the statues and the pews spotless. She washes, waxes and polishes every inch, from floor to ceiling. When you were just a little girl, you always wanted to help her."

I remembered the times I was allowed to go along and do a few small chores.

On another visit, just before Mom was hospitalized, Gen arrived at my mother's door with two home-cooked meals.

"I knew you were coming, and I had a little extra," she said. "Thought you two girls might enjoy not having to cook tonight."

Gen stayed and visited with me after Mom turned in for the night. I got the lowdown on whose children were engaged, getting married, having babies, plus recent deaths and all the new activities at the church. I so appreciated her generosity and company. I thanked her profusely for caring for Mom.

She smiled. "It's my pleasure," she said. "Besides, living right upstairs makes it as easy as can be."

"Mom can be stubborn; I'm surprised she agreed to letting you help her."

"We've been friends a long time, so once we worked out a few problems, everything fell into place. Now it's routine."

My stomach tightened. I asked, "What kind of problems?"

"I guess it started the day the washing machine overflowed," she explained. "I knew she didn't follow directions. And since she doesn't have much laundry, I asked if I could wash a few things of my own in her machine using a special low-suds cleaning product. Catherine was delighted. Now it's a regular routine." Gen added, "We've never had another flood."

"Was there any damage to the house?"

Gen shook her head.

My relief only lasted a few seconds when I saw her brow furrow. "Something else?" I asked.

There was a slight pause.

"Well, there was the afternoon I stopped in for tea." She closed her eyes and made the sign of the cross. "The minute I walked in, I smelled gas. Seems Catherine went to make a cup of tea, couldn't light the burner on the stove and walked away, forgetting to turn the knob back to its off position."

I gasped at the thought of an explosion.

"I opened the windows, aired out the apartment then told her I got a new supply of imported teas from England and hoped she'd help me enjoy them. I promised her I'd come every afternoon. Catherine was thrilled. Now, she waits for me to make the tea. Says I have a special touch." Gen smiled. "And, I've never smelled gas since."

I said a silent prayer.

Gen leaned in close and patted my hand. "Did you know she's not fond of the Meals on Wheels selections?" Before I could answer, she continued. "Catherine took it upon herself to sleep through the delivery time. I told her I loved their food and made a deal to swap it for some of my dishes. We switch all the time now, and she's not losing any more weight."

How I had missed these potential danger signs baffled me. I pointed to Mom's medication containers on the kitchen counter. "Your idea, too?"

A quick nod was followed with, "I convinced her that a different color pillbox for each day makes taking medicine a little more fun. Once we matched a day with a special color, there were no more mistakes."

The more I heard, the more I realized this "church lady" was more than a caregiver; she was an angel. "You're a special person. You've given Mom more than friendship and physical care; you've managed to help her keep her dignity when she needs it most. How can I thank you for your kindness? Can I pay you for your time?"

Shaking her head Gen answered, "Just keep me in your prayers and keep coming as often as you can. I don't think Catherine has much time left."

I promised I would on both accounts and hugged her whole-heartedly. "I worry about her all the time."

"There's no need to worry," Gen told me before she left to go upstairs to her apartment. "I'm here for her, just a few steps away."

Gen was indeed an expert in her field. She washed away my worries and heartaches with her presence and generosity. She waxed my spirit with her unselfish ministry. She polished my faith, hope and charity with her exemplary life.

~Helen Colella
Chicken Soup for the Caregiver's Soul

Woman to Woman

Special Moments

*Love the moment,
and the energy of that moment will spread beyond all boundaries.*
~Sister Corita Kent

Lunch with Helen Keller

My husband and I loved our house in Italy. It sat high on a cliff above Portofino with an extraordinary view of the blue harbor below, and its white beach was surrounded by cypresses. There was, however, a serpent in our paradise: the path up the cliff. The municipal authorities refused to grant us permission to build a proper road in lieu of the mule track. The only vehicle that could climb the narrow path and negotiate the hairpin turns, the steep incline and the potholes, was an old American Army Jeep we had bought in Genoa. It possessed neither springs nor brakes. When you wanted to stop, you had to go into reverse and back up against something. But it was indestructible, and you could rely on it in all weathers.

One day in the summer of 1950, our neighbor, Contessa Margot Besozzi, who of necessity also owned a Jeep, called to say that her cousin had arrived in town with a companion and that her own Jeep had conked out. Would I mind going to fetch the two old ladies in ours? They were at the Hotel Splendido.

"Whom should I ask for at the hotel?" I asked.

"Miss Helen Keller."

"Who?"

"Miss Helen Keller, K-e-l-l...."

"Margot, you don't mean Helen Keller?"

"Of course," she said. "She's my cousin. Didn't you know?"

I ran into the garage, jumped into the Jeep and raced down the mountain.

I had been twelve years old when my father gave me the book about Helen Keller written by Anne Sullivan, the remarkable woman whom fate had chosen to be the teacher of the blind and deaf child. Anne Sullivan had turned the rebellious, brutish little child into a civilized member of society by teaching her to speak. I still remembered vividly her description of the first few months of physical battle with the child, until the glorious moment when she held Helen's left hand under a running water tap and the blind, deaf and up until then mute little girl made history by stammering out an intelligible word:

"Wa-ter."

Over the years I had read about Helen Keller in the newspapers. I knew that Anne Sullivan was no longer with her and that a new companion now accompanied her everywhere. But the few minutes it took me to drive down the hill were not nearly enough to get used to the idea that I was going to meet in person this mythical figure from my early youth.

I backed the Jeep up against a bougainvillea-covered wall and presented myself at the hotel. A tall, buxom, vigorous-looking woman rose from a chair on the hotel terrace to greet me: Polly Thomson, Helen Keller's companion. A second figure rose slowly from the chair beside her and held out her hand. Helen Keller, then in her seventies, was a slight, white-haired woman with wide-open blue eyes and a shy smile.

"How do you do?" she said slowly and a little gutturally.

I took her hand, which she was holding too high because she didn't know how tall I was. She was bound to make this mistake with people she was meeting for the first time, but she never made it twice. Later, when we said goodbye, she put her hand firmly into mine at exactly the right level.

The luggage was loaded into the back of the Jeep, and I helped the jolly Miss Thomson to sit beside it. The hotel porter lifted Helen Keller's fragile body and set it down on the front seat next to me. Only then did it dawn on me that this was going to be a risky undertaking.

The Jeep was open; there was nothing you could hold onto properly. How was I to keep the blind and deaf woman from falling out of the rickety old thing when we took a curve, which had to be done at a fast clip because of the angle and the Jeep's general condition? I turned to her and said, "Miss Keller, I must prepare you—we're going up a very steep hill. Can you hold tight to this piece of metal on the windshield?"

But she continued to look expectantly straight ahead. Behind me, Miss Thomson said patiently, "She can't hear you, dear, nor see you. I know it's hard to get used to it at first."

I was so embarrassed that I stammered like an idiot, trying to explain the problem ahead of us. All the while, Miss Keller never turned her head or seemed puzzled by the delay. She sat motionless, a slight smile on her face, patiently waiting. Miss Thomson knelt across the luggage and reached for her hand. Rapidly she moved Helen's fingers up, down and sideways, telling her in blind-deaf language what I had just said.

"I don't mind," said Helen, laughing. "I'll hold tight."

I took courage, got hold of her hands, and placed them on the piece of metal in front of her. "Okay," she cried gaily, and I switched on the ignition. The Jeep started with a jump and Miss Thomson fell off her seat on top of the luggage. I couldn't stop and help her up because of the steep hill, the dangerous curve ahead and the absence of brakes. We roared upward, my eyes glued to the narrow path, and Miss Thomson helpless as a beetle on its back.

I'd had plenty of passengers in the Jeep, and they'd all complained about the lack of springs. No wonder, with all those boulders and potholes, not to mention the hairpin turns through the olive trees, which only partially obscured the precipitous drop that had unnerved quite a few of our guests. Helen was the first passenger who was oblivious to the danger; she was enchanted by the violent jumps and only laughed when she was thrown against my shoulder. Helen actually began to sing. "This is fun," she warbled happily, bouncing up and down. "Lovely!" she cried.

We tore past our house at breakneck speed—out of the corner

of my eye I saw our gardener, Giuseppe, crossing himself—and continued onward and upward. I had no idea how Miss Thomson was doing, for the Jeep's fearful roar had long ago drowned out her anguished protests. But I knew that Helen was still next to me. Her thin white hair had come undone and fluttered about her face, and she was enjoying the crazy ride like a child riding up and down on a wooden horse on a merry-go-round.

At last we rounded the last curve between two giant fig trees, and I could see Margot and her husband waiting for us at their entrance gate. Helen was lifted out of the Jeep and hugged; the luggage was unloaded, and Miss Thomson upended and dusted off.

I was invited to lunch. While the two old ladies were being shown to their rooms to freshen up, Margot told me about her cousin and her life. Helen was famous the world over, and in every civilized country, the great and the renowned were eager to meet her and do something for her. Heads of state, scholars and artists vied to receive her, and she had traveled all over the world to satisfy her burning curiosity.

"But don't forget," said Margot, "all she really notices is a change of smell. Whether she's here or in New York or in India, she sits in a black, silent hole."

Arm in arm, casually, as if they just happened to be fond of each other, the two old ladies walked through the garden toward the terrace, where we were waiting for them.

"That must be wisteria," said Helen, "and masses of it, too. I recognize the scent."

I went to pick a large bunch of the blossoms, which surrounded the terrace, and laid it in her lap. "I knew it!" she cried happily, touching them.

Of course, Helen's diction was not quite normal. She spoke haltingly, like someone who has had a stroke, and her consonants were slow and labored. She turned to me, looking directly at me because she had sensed where I was sitting. "You know, we're on the way to Florence to see Michelangelo's David. I'm so thrilled; I've always wanted to see it."

Mystified, I looked at Miss Thomson, who nodded.

"It's true," she said. "The Italian government has had a scaffolding erected around the statue so that Helen can climb up and touch it. That's what she calls 'seeing.' We often go to the theater in New York, and I tell her what's going on onstage and describe the actors. Sometimes we go backstage, too, so that she can 'see' the sets and the actors. Then she goes home, feeling that she's really witnessed the performance."

All the time we were talking, Helen sat and waited. Now and then, when our conversation went on too long, I saw her thin fingers take her friend's hand inquiringly, never impatiently.

Luncheon was served on the terrace. Helen was led to her chair, and I watched her "see" her place setting. Quick as lightning, her hands moved over the objects on the table—plate, glass, silverware—memorizing where they were. Never once during the meal did she grope about; she reached out casually and firmly like the rest of us.

After lunch, we stayed on the shady terrace, surrounded by trailing clusters of wisteria like a thick mauve curtain, the sun below us glittering on the sea. Helen sat in the usual way, head raised slightly as though listening to something, her sightless blue eyes wide open. Her face, although an old lady's face, had something of a schoolgirl's innocence. Whatever suffering must have tormented her—and might still torment her, for all I knew—her face showed no trace of it. It was an isolated face, a saintly face.

I asked her, through her friend, what else she wanted to see in Italy. Then she slowly mapped out her Italian journey—all the places she wanted to visit and the people she would meet. Incredibly, she spoke French quite well and could make herself understood in German and Italian. Sculpture was, naturally, her favorite form of art, because she could touch it and experience it firsthand.

"There's still so much I'd like to see," she said, "so much to learn. And death is just around the corner. Not that that worries me. On the contrary."

"Do you believe in life after death?" I asked.

"Most certainly," she said emphatically. "It is no more than passing from one room into another."

We sat in silence.

Suddenly, Helen spoke again. Slowly and very distinctly she said, "But there's a difference for me, you know. Because in that other room, I shall be able to see."

~Lilli Palmer
A Second Chicken Soup for the Woman's Soul

My Blue-Eyed Boy

The soul is the same in all living creatures,
although the body of each is different.
~Hippocrates

My dog, Harry, and I are very close. Harry, an eighty-pound Dalmatian, listens to me when I am upset, comforts me when I am blue and goes everywhere with me. He cares for no other person like he does for me, his beloved mama. Having raised him since he was an eight-week-old pup, I feel the same way about him—he is my blue-eyed boy.

One beautiful Sunday morning, Harry and I went to Central Park. Harry was running off leash on Dog Hill, along with all the other city dogs, while their owners enjoyed a spring day in the park.

I was feeling down because I had been recently laid off from the job I'd held for ten years. Being in the park with Harry was one of the ways I forgot for a while that I was out of work—and that my prospects were not looking good in a tough economy.

I was standing at the bottom of Dog Hill talking to another dog owner, when all of a sudden, we heard someone shout, "He peed on my leg!" I turned to look, and, lo and behold, at the top of the hill I saw a lady gesticulating at my beloved boy, who apparently was the culprit. Horrified, I rushed up the hill. Harry had never done anything remotely like this before.

When I got to where the woman was standing, I reached down

quickly and grabbed hold of Harry's collar in case he decided to do anything else untoward. The woman was bent over, trying to clean up her leg. She was pulling off her shoe because the pee had dribbled down her leg all the way into her shoe.

We straightened up at the same moment, and for a shocked instant, we looked at each other.

"Alexandra!" she said.

"Valerie!" It was my former boss—the one who laid me off three months before.

I apologized to Valerie for Harry's behavior, but all the way home, I laughed and laughed, and gave Harry lots of kisses and hugs. Harry, of course, was thrilled that he clearly had pulled off a winning stunt—though, fortunately, he has never repeated his performance. To this day, when I think about all of Harry's wonderful qualities, his "revenge for mama" still makes me laugh the hardest.

~Alexandra Mandis
Chicken Soup for the Dog Lover's Soul

The Rose Babies

Just living is not enough.
One must have sunshine, freedom, and a little flower.
~Hans Christian Anderson

Most people press a flower in a book when they wish to keep it as a memento. My mother doesn't believe in preserving a memory by hiding it. Her motto is, "Don't press it! When will you look at it again tucked away in a book? Make it grow! Enjoy its beauty as a living flower, not as a withered keepsake."

That's my mother. She can make anything grow.

Recently, Mom received a mixed bouquet of flowers from her sister for her birthday. She is especially fond of roses and was delighted to find two roses in the bouquet. "Oh, look at the lovely roses. I've never seen such a beautiful shade of peach in a rose. I must save it as a souvenir."

I have seen this process many times, but I watch in awe each time. She takes one of the roses and cuts the bottom at an angle with a pair of scissors, wraps the bottom in a dampened paper towel and places the rose in a plastic bag to keep it moist.

Now I know it's my turn. The magic is about to begin. I run to the pantry to get a quart jar, once used for canning peaches.

"Here's the enchanted glass jar," I announce, as I return with it.

We head for her lilac bush. I carry the jar and the plastic bag that contains the rose. She carries warm water in an old coffee can, bent so that it has a spout on each side of it. My mother deliberately keeps her lilac bush overgrown. She trims it in such a way that it becomes fat and dense. The soil beneath it is damp and warm. She easily digs a hole with her hands and places the rose cutting in the hole. I help her carefully pack the dirt around the rose. She places the glass jar over the rose, and firmly twists it into the ground.

Finally, she gives the rose a drink, pointing the spout of the coffee can to the bottom of the glass jar. She whispers, "Oh, little rose, let me warm your toes, this'll keep you safe when the cold wind blows. See you in the spring, little rose."

"Little rose is all ready for her long winter's nap," she explains to me as we walk back to the house.

My mother is shameless when it comes to asking for a rose from someone's front yard or their garden. But no one ever refuses her request. And one time, the giver was especially glad she had shared her bounty.

It was a lovely summer day. My mother and I were walking past our neighbor Dorothy working in her garden. My mother stopped to admire one of Dorothy's roses.

"I've never seen such a beautiful lavender rose, blending into silver at the edge of the petals. Would you mind if I choose one to enjoy?" she asked Dorothy. Proud of her special lavender rosebush, Dorothy was delighted to cut the rose and graciously hand it to my mother. But the lavender rose did not go into a vase, as Dorothy probably assumed. It joined the others under the lilac bush, protected under its very own glass jar.

That Christmas, Dorothy told us that the beautiful lavender rosebush had been stricken by disease in the fall, and it couldn't be saved. "It was my favorite," she said sadly, "and I haven't been able to find another to replace it."

Spring was delayed that year, but finally the fear of frost was gone. My mother was eager to uncover her rose cuttings, each protected under its miniature greenhouse.

"I wonder how many of my rose babies will be ready to begin their new lives?" she mused.

As always, I watched in amazement as my mother uncovered her rose babies. Carefully, she twisted the first glass jar from the warm earth: It was the lavender rose clipping. Would that beautiful rose be reborn? She spied a baby shoot, a tiny leaf peeking its way through the stem. Indeed, the lavender rose was alive.

Mom whispered to me, "Wait until late summer, and I'll have a surprise for Dorothy. I'll nourish our baby, and it'll thrive into a beautiful bush. She'll have her lavender rosebush again. It'll be our secret until then."

And sure enough, late that summer, Dorothy cried for joy as she received her surprise—a healthy new lavender rosebush.

On the card was the following:

Here's a small gift from my garden to you.
It began the day someone gave me a rose, too.
I planted that rose in the good, warm earth,
And I nurtured it—hence its happy rebirth.
After you've planted this gift and it grows,
To keep up the cycle, may I impose?
If I may be bold, do you suppose,
That I might request its very first rose?

~Georgia A. Hubley
Chicken Soup for the Gardener's Soul

The Commanding Secretary

Never say, "oops." Always say, "Ah, interesting."
~Author Unknown

Working as a secretary at an international airport, my sister had an office adjacent to the room where security temporarily holds suspects.

One day security officers were questioning a man when they were suddenly called away on another emergency. To the horror of my sister and her colleagues, the man was left alone in the unlocked room. After a few minutes, the door opened and he began to walk out. Summoning up her courage, one of the secretaries barked, "Get back in there, and don't you come out until you're told!"

The man scuttled back inside and slammed the door. When the security people returned, the women reported what had happened.

Without a word, an officer walked into the room and released one very frightened telephone repairman.

~Russel M. Perman
Chicken Soup for the Working Woman's Soul

Meeting Her Needs

*I*n 1994, our health department began serving as the primary care provider for thousands of patients who had previously only received public-health type services in our clinics. This switch to a "medical model" in our neighborhood clinics was quite a change not only for the patients but also for the staff, who were more accustomed to providing chronic disease follow-up and preventive care, and now were being asked to provide acute care/primary care as well.

Because of this change, I was now a public health nurse in a primary care setting, working with the physician who was trying to meet the women's health needs as best he could. Not having done a lot of women's health previously, he was somewhat disorganized in his visit sequence but usually covered all aspects of care in a thorough, professional manner.

This particular day, the physician was completing a visit with a new, elderly patient. In his usual quiet way, as the patient was preparing to leave the examining room, he said offhandedly, "Oh, Ms. R., would you like to have a Pap smear today?"

Ms. R. appeared surprised and a bit confused because she was already dressed, had received her prescriptions, and thought her appointment was over.

"Why, yes, Doctor, that would be nice," the patient said.

I realized immediately that a communication error had just been made.

"Ms. R., the Doctor is asking if you want your PAP SMEAR done today—your test for cancer of the womb. You would need to get undressed again for that test," I tried to explain.

Ms. R. looked embarrassed and replied, "Oh, Doctor, I'm sorry. I thought you said PABST BEER! No, I don't want a PAP SMEAR today, thank you."

~Judy B. Smith
Chicken Soup for the Nurse's Soul

28

Taking It in Stride

Laughter is the closest thing to the grace of God.
~Karl Barth

As we grow older, life's embarrassing moments don't seem to send us into a tizzy like they did when we were seventeen. Remember how we used to fret and cry over the silliest things? Having a pimple at the end of our nose was a major crisis, charged with great drama and hysteria. Stumbling on the stairs during assembly was enough to keep us home for days, while eye contact with cute boys in the hall could easily send us bumping into walls. Nowadays, let's hope we can simply laugh about those little mishaps and chalk them up to experience.

Take, for example, what recently happened to me at a business conference in Salt Lake City. It's one of "those moments" that I'd like to forget but, unfortunately, is etched in my brain forever.

My flight arrived at the airport just thirty minutes before the first session in the afternoon. Luckily, the shuttle bus was at the curb and got me to the hotel in time to dash into the meeting room. I plopped my suitcase in the corner, grabbed my three-ring binder from it, and began mingling with other attendees as I found my way to a seat.

To my surprise and horror, the entire time I had been circulating around the room, a pair of my purple underpants was hooked onto the end of my notebook, clinging ever so nicely to my forearm for all to see. Let's just say

I'll never be a size two, and my undies aren't lacey little snippets from the Victoria's Secret catalog. No, I get my practical cotton underwear at Sears in the full-figure department next to lawn chairs and power tools.

As I approached the table and noticed my faux pas, my undies did additional damage by falling smack-dab into the teacup of the gentleman seated in the next chair. The weight and bulk of the fabric tipped the cup over, spilling hot water across the tablecloth onto the poor man's lap. What could I do but scoop the panties up and offer him another cup of tea? (I can't remember, but I hope I didn't wring them out — that would have been so tacky.) Meekly, he declined, but to his credit and courage, he stayed right there for the rest of the session, turning out to be a good sport about the entire fiasco.

Everyone had a good laugh, me included. If I had been seventeen, I would have had to drop out of school and move to another town, but at age forty-five I could laugh along with everyone else. What else could I do, especially when many at the conference asked about next year's encore? Perhaps I'll do something in pink!

~Cappy Tosetti
Chicken Soup to Inspire a Woman's Soul

Fresh Sample

You cannot hold back a good laugh any more than you can the tide.
Both are forces of nature.
~William Rotsier

It began as a typical working day. As a registered nurse, I traveled to clients' homes to complete paramedical health assessments for an insurance company.

As I entered this lady's neat, attractive home, I smelled the delicious aroma of pies baking. "Umm, sure smells good in here," I commented.

"I just put a couple of lemon meringue pies in the oven. They're my husband's favorite," my client volunteered.

Returning to the purpose of my visit, we completed the questionnaire quickly. The last section involved collecting a urine sample.

"I collected it earlier and saved it in the refrigerator," she said. "I'll get it for you."

As I emptied the sample into the collection tubes, I noticed the unusual thickness of it. When I tested it with a dip stick, I was shocked at the extremely high protein content.

"Are you sure this is your urine sample?" I questioned. "This almost resembles egg whites."

"Yes, I distinctly remember placing it in the refrigerator in the bottom right-hand corner. Oh! Oh, no!" She wailed. "I've made a terrible mistake. Don't use that. I'll get you a fresh sample."

Not wishing to further embarrass the lady, I asked no more questions. But as I opened the door to leave her home, I heard her removing pies from the oven and the grinding sound of the garbage disposal.

No lemon meringue pie that night!

~Donna McDonnall
Chicken Soup for the Nurse's Soul

30

I'll Plant Anything

Blessed is he who has learned how to laugh at himself,
for he shall never cease to be entertained.
~John Bowell

A good friend of mine was going away on a long trip during the fall. Miriam thought she had given herself plenty of time to do all the things that are required when one goes out of town.

I called her the day before her departure to wish her bon voyage. She was a wreck. She was completely behind on everything she needed to do. "And to top it all off," she lamented, "I bought some wonderful corms to plant for next spring. I'll never get them into the ground now!"

Well, I'll tell you, I can't bear the thought of an unplanted corm, bulb, seed plug, you name it. I always start too many seeds in March and by June I'm tucking them everywhere I can. I just can't bear the thought of a plant not getting a chance to grow. In other words, she was in luck.

"I'll plant them for you," I said.

"Oh, would you? You would do that?" Miriam was elated. She promised to set them out on the porch for me. I knew her garden well, as we have spent many hours together, toiling in each other's gardens. We quickly brainstormed some nice places for them to go. But then she said, "Oh, just put them wherever you think they'll look nice."

I arrived a couple of days later on a chilly autumn morning and spied a frost-covered paper bag on the back steps. With my trowel and bone meal in hand, I set off in search of just the right place to plant.

The corms were weird-looking—not the usual miniature, root-like bulbs. I hadn't asked what kind they were when Miriam and I had last talked, but the two of us were always trying out new varieties of anything we could get our hands on. Being a consummate experimental gardener, there isn't a lot I won't try to plant and coax through our seemingly endless Minnesota winters. So I shrugged my shoulders and went to work. After a lot of digging, arranging, changing my mind, digging some more and rearranging, I finally stood back from the patch of disturbed earth and nodded to myself in satisfaction. They were all planted in the perfect spot.

When Miriam got back a few months later, she and I went out to dinner to celebrate her return. At the restaurant we laughed about what a wreck she had been when she was trying to get out of town. And then she said, "You know, I still can't believe I forgot to put those corms out! What a ditz brain I am!"

I looked at her quizzically. "What do you mean? Of course you put them out. They were sitting on the porch in a paper bag, right where you said they'd be."

"No," she said, "they're still sitting on the counter where I left them."

Then an expression of dawning realization spread across her face. It held an odd combination of amusement and alarm.

"Valerie, I'm so sorry...."

"What?"

"I'm truly sorry...."

"What?!"

She paused as if to prepare me for her news. Then she slowly said, "That was cat poop."

"What?!"

"Cat poop," she repeated. "I'm afraid I cleaned the litter box out before I left and forgot to put it in the garbage. I guess I must have left it on the back steps. You planted cat poop."

News like this doesn't sink in immediately. It sort of bounces around in your head and all you can hear are the echoes. Cat poop... cat poop....

Miriam looked at my face—and did the best she could to keep from laughing. Tears welled up in her eyes, and she pressed her lips tightly together. I usually have a good sense of humor. But I was too busy replaying the images of me picking these hard little corm-like kernels from a brown paper bag and lovingly planting them in Mother Earth's bosom. I took a long drink of my wine. I wasn't sure I could laugh about this.

Miriam managed to pull herself together. She cleared her throat and, sensing my state of shock, politely asked, "So, where did you plant them?"

"Uh, next to the catnip," I replied. The next thing I knew we both had collapsed into a fit of laughter. Much to my surprise, I was laughing. And it felt good. Very good.

Years have passed since then, and both our gardens and our friendship have continued to grow. That story has grown, too—to become one of our dearest bonds. I guess, true to form, I really will try to plant just about anything.

~Valerie Wilcox
Chicken Soup for the Gardener's Soul

31

The Subway Dog

I think we are drawn to dogs because
they are the uninhibited creatures we might be
if we weren't certain we knew better.
~George Bird Evans

I was twenty years old and living away from home for the first time. For companionship, I had a dog named Beaufort, who, although gentle, weighed more than I did and had a mouthful of sharp teeth. I felt safe going anywhere with Beaufort at my side.

In order to be free during the day to enjoy walks in the park and other things I liked to do, I took a job working the four-to-midnight shift in downtown Boston. The only downside of this arrangement was that I had to ride the "T"—the Boston subway—home from work late at night. As time passed, I discovered that keeping to one-self was an important survival mechanism. I avoided making eye contact and carried a book under my arm to read while I rode.

One night, I had finished work and was heading home. Every night, I rode the Red Line from Park Street Station to Andrew where I would get off and walk the six blocks home, knowing Beaufort was waiting patiently.

That night was different.

Park Street Station has a steep flight of stairs leading down to the underground platforms. I was tired as I fumbled for a token to put in the turnstile. I knew I had one—I always did. I rummaged around from pocket to pocket, but found nothing.

"Oh, man," I groaned.

The station was quiet at that time of night with only two or three more trains scheduled before the "T" closed at one in the morning. I walked over to the collector's booth and pulled out a dollar.

"One token, please."

People who ride the "T" often regard the token collectors inside the booths as only one step removed from ticket machines, so it was understandable that I wasn't paying attention to the man behind the booth's thick glass and the metal bars. But he was paying attention to me.

He slid the token and my change under the window. Then he spoke, "Hey, would you like a dog?"

Startled, I looked at him, not sure I had heard him correctly. "Excuse me?"

"Would you like a dog?" he repeated.

He looked down, motioning with his chin. I leaned over and it was only then that I saw the subject of his inquiry.

Inside the booth was a dog—a very small type of terrier with lots of wild, wiry hair. The dog appeared to be trembling but looked at me as if to say, Yeah, and what's your problem?

I was surprised, and as an animal lover, a little troubled. "Where'd he come from?" I asked.

"He's a stray; he showed up about eight o'clock. He's been here ever since." The big man picked up the dog and set him on the narrow counter, gently rubbing him behind the ears. "He has a collar but no tags. No one has come looking for him and my shift is almost over."

My rational side knew that rescuing this little wanderer was noble but totally impossible: I mean, what about Beaufort?

The token collector sensed a soft spot in me. "I've asked every person who has come through here if they wanted him. No one would take him."

"What about you?" I inquired.

He smiled and laughed softly, "Me? No honey, my wife would kill me."

I couldn't take my eyes off the dog. How in the world did he get here and why was no one looking for the poor little guy?

The collector made his final pitch: "You know, if you don't take him, I'll have to let him go when I leave."

I couldn't believe it! "What do you mean you'll let him go? We're downtown. He'll get killed. He'll starve! He's so... little."

He explained that there were only a couple more trains scheduled to come before he closed. He couldn't leave the dog in the booth, and he couldn't bring him home. No one else had taken him. I, in other words, was the dog's last hope.

I was wavering, and both man and dog sensed it. Oh, Lord, what was I going to do?

We stared at each other for what seemed a very long time.

"Is it a male or a female?" I sighed finally.

He grinned. "A female. I called her a 'him' just 'cause it's easier," he explained hastily.

I shook my head and added halfheartedly, "But I don't have a leash."

"That's okay, I've got it all worked out. Here's a piece of twine; it's stronger than it looks. What stop are you getting off at?"

"Andrew."

"Oh, great! That's only four stops. You'll be fine — the twine will last you until you get home."

His face flushed with excitement, the collector unlocked the heavy door, stepped out of the booth and without fanfare handed me my new pet. "Thank you so much," the guy said with relief, "I really didn't want to let him loose upstairs."

The dog and I looked at one another.

"Hey, you guys look good together!" the man crowed. With that he opened the gate and allowed me to pass without paying, a satisfied grin on his face.

The dog and I walked to the next set of stairs that would take us down one more level to the subway tracks. I spoke to my new friend in soothing tones. "It's okay, everything's going to be okay," I promised.

The minute the collector told me that the dog was female I had decided on a name: Phyllis, after Phyllis Diller, the comedienne with the wild, unkempt hair. It came to me immediately and was as right as rain. "Oh, Phyllis," I sighed, "Wait till Beaufort gets a look at you."

We descended the stairs, my new friend and I, stepping onto the dirty platform together. Park Street Station is one of the biggest and busiest train stations in Boston. It is so big that it has three platforms instead of the usual two. One side leaves Boston heading toward Dorchester and the other side goes farther into town and on to Cambridge and quirky Harvard Square. In the middle is an extra platform to accommodate the many riders who frequent the station.

As if on cue, my fellow travelers all turned to look at Phyllis and me. Even the young man who played guitar, collecting coins in his open guitar case, stopped.

All at once the whole crowd broke into applause. Looking around, I didn't recognize the place. Most nights, people kept to themselves—like me, burying their noses in books or newspapers and ignoring everyone around them—but not tonight. Tonight everyone was smiling and clapping, giving me a thumbs-up and a right-on! Phyllis began to bark, all bluster.

A young couple two tracks over on the far side to Cambridge pointed and waved. "Look!" the girl gushed, "She took the dog. She took the dog."

Joined by the length of twine the collector had given me, Phyllis and I stood together, basking in the attention of the cheering crowd. It didn't matter that we were big-city strangers in the middle of the night—for a brief moment we were all joined in the euphoria and camaraderie that only happy endings can bring.

~Elizabeth Lombard
Chicken Soup for the Dog Lover's Soul

The Night
Al Heel Broke Loose

In a certain northern city, in a certain regional hospital, a story is still whispered about the "Legend of Wanda May." It has grown some over the years, but as one of the few witnesses to the entire chain of events, I will try to stick to the facts.

Wanda, a rookie nurse, was a mighty mite of sorts. Standing four feet, eleven inches, she couldn't have weighed more than ninety pounds, yet every inch of her screamed spitfire! With her green eyes and shiny black hair, Wanda was a looker. Even her cap, which conjured visions of the flying nun, and her oversized scrub suit added to her allure.

Our fifteen-bed ICU ran like organized chaos. With whirring ventilators, beeping monitors, blaring code sirens, ringing phones, glaring lights and chatting nurses, sensory overload was a common problem for our patients. A unique phenomenon known as ICU psychosis afflicts about 10 percent of those treated in this environment. Without warning, a sweet and kindly grandmother could morph into a Linda Blair clone right before your eyes. With proper medication, the condition usually lasts only twenty-four hours. Still, the poor patients are often mortified by their reported behaviors.

On the night in question, the unit was unusually quiet. With only three patients, I stayed at the desk to read the cardiac monitors while Phyllis, a jolly seasoned nurse, looked after two patients. This left

Wanda to care for Alan Heel. Al looked much older than his twenty-seven years; he'd lived a hard life. Kidney disease and his penchant for alcohol proved a difficult combination. His heart strained to pump the extra fluids his body couldn't eliminate. Weekly dialysis is a hard lot in life. Long deserted by family, you could almost understand the root of Al's addiction. He was a frequent patient in our unit, and we all knew it would be a miracle if Al saw thirty. This huge grinning fellow with an unruly shock of black hair loved the attention he received in the unit. And he was never happier than when Wanda was his nurse. He swore she looked exactly like his favorite stripper, and we teased and regaled him with "Hey Big Spender" whenever Wanda was at his bedside. In spite of all of his shortcomings, Al was easy to like.

By midnight on this particular night, the patients were settled and the checks were done. Sitting at the desk, Wanda entertained us with the latest chapter of her ill-fated romantic life. Suddenly, multiple monitor alarms screamed. In the time it took to look up, there was Al, looming over us, huge and naked—except for the monitor leads flapping from his chest. We could have taken his pulse by watching the blood spurting from his thigh where he'd yanked the arterial line. If not for the blood, the absurdity of Al dragging his urine bag might have been comical—but there was nothing funny in his eyes.

Wanda and Phyllis tried to cajole him back to his room. Grabbing the phone, I paged security and then put in a call to his doctor. The next few moments unfolded like a scene from the Keystone Kops!

Al ran, followed by Wanda, Phyllis, two seventy-year-old security guards and several nurses from the step-down unit. He charged from room to room, fleeing a demon only he could see. Patients screamed, guards yelled, staff raced in all directions. The arrival of three police officers and his doctor only added to the chaos. Cornering him in the hallway, they nearly subdued him, but the power of his psychosis proved too great.

When he darted into the four-bed ward in the adjoining step-down unit, panic reigned. The screams of the four elderly female occupants almost drowned out the alarms from their collective heart monitors.

Jumping on top of the nearest bed, Al took a hostage. Now debate often ensues about the weapon Al used. I hear tell now that it was a butcher knife, but to the best of my recollection it was a letter opener he picked up from the patient's tray table. Flipping the poor woman so she was perched on top of his naked body, Al held the letter opener to her neck. The frantic look in his eyes gave us all cause to believe he would use it. Backing off as he demanded, we all tried to think of a way of getting a shot of Valium into him. In this truly desperate, life-threatening situation, the legend of Wanda May was born.

Holding us at arm's length, Wanda stepped forward. Slack-jawed, we watched as she flipped off her cap, undid her braid and fluffed her long, luxurious hair. In a sultry voice, she belted the song, "The minute you walked in the joint...." With her eyes focused on Al's, she pulled her scrub shirt over her head and sent it sailing across the room. His wild eyes softened as she shimmied closer. It was plain to see that the occupant with the "knife" to her throat didn't know which of these evils was greater. In two more seductive moves, Wanda was down to her skivvies. With a crooked finger, she beckoned Al to follow her. As if in a trance, he put down his weapon and rose from the bed. In utter silence, the assembled onlookers parted and Wanda, clad only in bra and panties, walked through the center, with a docile Al directly behind. She continued humming the strains of "Big Spender" all the way back to the unit. Patting Al's bed, she prompted him to lie down. Now I was frightened for Wanda's safety. But instead of venting aggression or male energy, Al began to cry. With his head nestling on her chest, Wanda held him and stroked his hair while the doctor and I started an IV and a flurry of drugs. In moments, an exhausted Al drifted off to sleep. Extricating herself from his grasp, Wanda casually asked, "Could someone get my clothes?"

She may have been small of stature, but Wanda May will forever remain a giant to those who continue to whisper her legend.

~Elizabeth Turner
Chicken Soup for the Nurse's Soul

Living on the Ledge

Take the first step in faith.
You don't have to see the whole staircase, just take the first step.
~Dr. Martin Luther King Jr.

Three months before my husband, Mel, was diagnosed with terminal lung cancer, we went on vacation to Glacier National Park in Montana, a place I had wanted to see since I was ten years old.

Within six months, my husband of thirty-five years was dead, and I was left with a shattered heart. Before he died, I made him promise that he would somehow let me know he was with God and that he was with me in spirit. I had his body cremated, knowing that someday I'd want to put his ashes down in Montana. I dreamed of one day having the courage to go back without him at my side. Mel had always believed I could do anything. He was always encouraging, always cheering me on to greater heights, but I never had his faith in me. How could I possibly do this alone now?

Two-and-one-half years passed before I could call the funeral home and arrange to pick up his ashes. Another six months went by before I could muster the courage to arrange a trip with Elderhostel to return to Glacier.

When we finally assembled at Big Creek for the first day of hiking, every one of the seventeen mountain hikers was experienced—except me. I was a flatlander who had walked only at sea level all her life. If I had known what hiking in the Rocky Mountains was like, I never would have signed up. I just knew I was going to die on those mountain ledges. Every step of the hike, I kept saying over and over, I can do all things through Christ who strengthens me. By lunchtime I was sitting on the top of a mountain peak, looking down at Two Medicine Lake on one side and a wide prairie on the other.

After lunch, we continued climbing with an elevation gain of 2,300 feet in just three miles—and a temperature of at least 95 degrees. One of the most empowering moments of my entire life was when I reached the summit and finished in the top ten. I felt energized with faith, and I knew that with God's help, and the memory of Mel's faith in me, I could face any challenge life had to offer.

Of course, then I had to hike back down—but that's another story.

I had previously arranged with the director of Elderhostel in Montana to put down my husband's ashes. After four days of classes and hiking, the time and the place were set, and eight of the eleven women on the hike wanted to be part of the ceremony.

On Thursday, July 12, the same date that Mel and I had visited Glacier, the group went for our final hike together. The trail was twelve miles long at 6,700 feet. The last four miles descended 2,400 feet to our pickup point. We literally traversed the Continental Divide and the scenery was spectacular. When we returned to camp, however, I wondered how any of us would have the strength to carry out the plans for that evening's ceremony. To make matters worse, for the first time that week it had started to rain. I checked with the instructor after dinner, and she agreed we should carry on as planned, but take our umbrellas.

We met on the banks of the creek that eventually flowed into Glacier National Park, where I wanted the ashes to end up. The banks were too steep, and I knew I would slip if I tried to go down to the water's edge. I suggested that we go farther down the road to a clearing I had been to the night before.

As we approached the clearing, a large deer stood looking at us. Mel had had a fascination with deer and he often took me to watch them. I knew then that Mel was there with me and that I had chosen the right place. The deer retreated back into the forest, and we all gathered into a circle just a few feet from the creek's rocky edge. As we joined hands and closed our eyes, the instructor told everyone how important this week had been for me, that Glacier was the last vacation spot for me and Mel, and that, after several difficult years, I was putting the past behind me. She remarked that although life was a challenge, I could do anything I set my mind to do—even hike twenty-six miles in the Rockies at 7,000 feet.

We opened our eyes and the instructor, who was standing across from me, told me to slowly turn around. I turned and looked straight into the eyes of the same deer standing about twenty feet away. After it saw me, it retreated into the woods. We were all flabbergasted. At the next moment, the woman on my left told me to look to my right. At that moment, the sun came out and everything turned golden. There below the mountains, between two trees and stretched across the creek, was the loveliest rainbow I have ever seen.

I finally collected myself enough to open the black box with the ashes, walk out into the creek and put them into the water. But it was nearly anticlimactic as I watched them flow down the stream to Glacier National Park.

~Denise Mizell
Chicken Soup for the Christian Woman's Soul

Woman to Woman

Motherhood

*I looked on child rearing not only as a work of love and duty
but as a profession that was fully as interesting and challenging
as any honorable profession in the world,
and one that demanded the best I could bring to it.*
~Rose Kennedy

34

The Day I Became a Mom

When you are a mother, you are never really alone in your thoughts. A mother always has to think twice, once for herself and once for her child.
~Sophia Loren, Women and Beauty

The day I became a mom was not the day my daughter was born, but seven years later. Up until that day, I had been too busy trying to survive my abusive marriage. I had spent all my energy trying to run a "perfect" home that would pass inspection each evening, and I didn't see that my baby girl had become a toddler. I'd tried endlessly to please someone who could never be pleased and suddenly realized that the years had slipped by and could never be recaptured.

Oh, I had done the normal "motherly" things, like making sure my daughter got to ballet and tap and gym lessons. I went to all of her recitals and school concerts, parent-teacher conferences and open houses—alone. I ran interference during my husband's rages when something was spilled at the dinner table, telling her, "It will be okay, Honey. Daddy's not really mad at you." I did all I could to protect her from hearing the awful shouting and accusations after he returned from a night of drinking. Finally I did the best thing I could do for my daughter and myself: I removed us from the home that wasn't really a home at all.

The day I became a mom was the day my daughter and I were sitting in our new home having a calm, quiet dinner just as I had always wanted for her. We were talking about what she had done in school and suddenly her little hand knocked over the full glass of chocolate milk by her plate. As I watched the white tablecloth and freshly painted white wall become dark brown, I looked at her small face. It was filled with fear, knowing what the outcome of the event would have meant only a week before in her father's presence. When I saw that look on her face and looked at the chocolate milk running down the wall, I simply started laughing. I am sure she thought I was crazy, but then she must have realized that I was thinking, "It's a good thing your father isn't here!" She started laughing with me, and we laughed until we cried. They were tears of joy and peace and were the first of many tears that we cried together. That was the day we knew that we were going to be okay.

Whenever either of us spills something, even now, seventeen years later, she says, "Remember the day I spilled the chocolate milk? I knew that day that you had done the right thing for us, and I will never forget it."

That was the day I really became a mom. I discovered that being a mom isn't only going to ballet, and tap and gym recitals, and attending every school concert and open house. It isn't keeping a spotless house and preparing perfect meals. It certainly isn't pretending things are normal when they are not. For me, being a mom started when I could laugh over spilled milk.

~Linda Jones
Chicken Soup for the Mother's Soul 2

35

Second Skin

The best conversations with mothers always take place in silence,
when only the heart speaks.
~Carrie Latet

My favorite pair of old jeans will never fit me again. I have finally accepted this immutable truth. After nurturing and giving birth to two babies, my body has undergone a metamorphosis. I may have returned to my pre-baby weight, but subtle shifts and expansions have taken place—my own version of continental drift. As a teenager, I never understood the difference between junior and misses sizing; misses clothing just looked old. Now it is all too clear that wasp waists and micro-fannies are but the fleeting trappings of youth. But that's okay, because while the jeans no longer button, the life I exchanged for them fits better than they ever did.

For me, this is a barefoot, shorts and t-shirt time of life. I have slipped so easily into young motherhood; it is the most comfortable role I have ever worn. No tough seams, no snagging zippers. Just a feeling that I have stepped out of the dressing room in something that finally feels right.

I love the feel of this baby on my hip, his soft head a perfect fit under my chin, his tiny hands splayed out like small pink starfish against my arms. I love the way my eight-year-old daughter walks alongside us as we cross the grocery store's sunny parking lot. On gorgeous spring days, the breeze lifts her wispy ponytail, and we laugh at how the sunshine makes the baby sniff and squint. I am constantly reaching out to touch them, the way a seamstress would two lengths of perfect silk, envisioning what might be made from them, yet hesitant to alter them, to lose the weight of their wholeness in my hands.

On those rare mornings when I wake up before they do, I go into their rooms and watch them sleeping, their faces creased and rosy. Finally, they squirm and stretch themselves awake, reaching out for a hug. I gather them up, bury my face in them and breathe deeply. They are like towels just pulled from the dryer, tumbled warm and cottony.

Sometimes, I follow the sound of girlish voices to my daughter's room, where she and her friends play dress-up, knee-deep in garage-sale chiffon, trying life on for size. Fussing and preening in front of the mirror, they drape themselves in cheap beads and adjust tiaras made of sequins and cardboard. I watch these little girls with their lank, shiny hair that no rubber bands or barrettes seem able to tame. They are constantly pushing errant strands behind their ears, and in that grown-up gesture, I see glimpses of the women they will become. I know that too soon these clouds of organdy and lace will settle permanently into their battered boxes, the ones that have served as treasure chests and princess thrones. They will become the hand-me-downs of my daughter's girlhood, handed back to me.

For now, though, my children curl around me on the sofa in the evening, often falling asleep, limbs limp and soft against me like the folds of a well-worn nightgown. For now, we still adorn each other, and they are content to be clothed in my embrace. I know there will be times that will wear like scratchy wool sweaters and four-inch heels. We will have to try on new looks together, tugging and scrunching, trying to keep the basic fabric intact. By then, we will have woven a complicated tapestry with its own peculiar pattern, its snags and pulls and tears.

But I will not forget this time, of drowsy heads against my shoulder, of footy pajamas and mother-daughter dresses, of small hands clasped in mine. This time fits me. I plan to wear it well.

~Caroline Castle Hicks
A Second Chicken Soup for the Woman's Soul

Rites of Passage

Our attitude toward life determines life's attitude towards us.
~Earl Nightingale

For some time, my fourteen-year-old son Tyler had been acting more responsibly: doing his chores without having to be told, keeping his room organized, keeping his word. I knew he was making his transition into manhood.

Memories of other turning points flooded my mind. I remembered breathing in Tyler's scent as a baby, and then one day noticing that scent had shifted, changed—my baby had become a little boy. Then I recalled the day the training wheels came off his bicycle. Another time, I'd watched wistfully as he had thrown out all of his toys, only saving a stuffed gorilla that my mother had given him when she was alive. Now another, bigger change was brewing. So, with tears welling up inside, I began to plan a rite-of-passage day for my son.

Tyler's special day began with breakfast at a restaurant. It was just Tyler, his father, stepmother, stepfather and me—no other children. He seemed so happy being with us all together for the first time by himself.

After breakfast, we all went to a heavily wooded park outside of town. I gave him a special journal created just for the day. In the weeks before the ceremony, I had written numerous questions in the journal for him to think about and answer. Questions like: Who was his hero and why? When did he feel the deepest connection to God? What gift in his life had been his favorite and why?

He had chosen several adults who were important in his life, and I had arranged for each of them to come and walk with him for about an hour over the course of the day. The adults were told that this was Tyler's time to "pick their brain," and they were asked to be as open and candid as they comfortably could.

His school principal, whom Tyler had invited to walk with him, shared his favorite prayer—the St. Francis prayer—with Tyler. This had special meaning for my son as it is the same prayer my mother read every morning of her life. She and Tyler were very close, and later he told me it almost felt as if she were there reading it to him.

As dusk began to settle, family and friends gathered for a ceremony on a dock by a lake. A brief rain had freshened the air, which held a fall chill. A tape of Indian flute music played as we sat around a dancing fire. During the ceremony, Tyler shared his intentions about his responsibility to the planet, guests publicly blessed him and we, his parents, made a verbal commitment that—from that moment on—we would hold him as a man in our hearts.

The guests had been instructed to bring nonmonetary gifts to share with Tyler. He received a box of "What I Love About Tyler" notes filled out by the guests, an acorn of a mighty oak tree, handmade pouches and more. One man read a poem aloud that he had written about his father.

During the ceremony and in the weeks following, numerous people came up to me and said, "I would be a different person today if my parents had given me the gift of a rite-of-passage ceremony." Never in my wildest dreams as a mother could I have anticipated the feelings and sacredness that my son and I experienced that day.

Things are different in our house now; there is a deeper, richer feeling of respect for each other. Frequently, before I speak to Tyler, I ask myself, "How would I say this to a man?" And Tyler seems less self-absorbed and more sensitive to how others feel.

This was clearly demonstrated several months later, when our family was planning a fun outing. It was a cold rainy day, and everyone wanted to go to play games at the arcade—except for me. I had made some feeble attempts to recommend something different, but their enthusiasm won out. I did not have the energy to stick up for myself that day.

We were walking out the door when Tyler, now a head taller than I was, came over and put his arm around my shoulders and said, "I can see that you don't really want to go to the arcade. Let's sit down and decide on something we ALL want to do. 'Cause I'm not going anywhere unless you're happy, too."

I was so surprised, I burst into tears, but they were tears of happiness. It felt wonderful to be cared for and to know that my son would be a loving husband and father to his own family someday. Yes, Tyler had become a man—a good man.

~Kathryn Kvols
Chicken Soup for the Mother's Soul 2

Boarder Baby

I was working as a pharmacist at the hospital in 1969 when Billy was born with Down syndrome. His unwed mother intended all along to put the baby up for adoption. When she was told that the child had been born with "problems," she didn't even want to see him. She left the hospital during the night, abandoning the baby.

The law stated that in such cases Children's Services must be contacted. If no immediate placement was available, the baby would be transferred to a municipal hospital to wait for foster care or adoption. Armed with this information, the nurses from the maternity floor and nursery went to the director of nursing.

"Why can't we keep Billy here until he can be placed?"

The director said, "You know he can't stay here. It's against the rules of the Board of Health. We're not certified to have a boarder baby. We simply can't keep him here; there is nothing I can do about it."

"You know he won't be placed easily," they persisted. "It's hard enough to place a baby with no problems, much less a baby like Billy. Please, don't call Children's Services yet. Speak to the administrator first, or better still, let him come up and see the baby. Tell him we will take care of Billy and all the expenses. Just let us keep him up in maternity."

By this time, every employee of the hospital had seen Billy and was aware of the situation. And everybody had fallen in love with him. The administrator, a very religious man, was sympathetic to the pleas of the nursing staff and soon acquiesced.

The problem now was where to keep Billy. He couldn't stay in the nursery because he might subject the other newborns to germs. He couldn't be housed in the pediatric ward because the sick children would expose Billy to their infections. It was decided he would stay on the maternity floor.

One of the three isolation nurseries was commandeered as Billy's private quarters. Through the viewing window Billy could see out, and visitors and nursing staff could see in. Initially he had only a crib, but the employees bought him clothes, a playpen, high chair, toys, a stroller and anything else he needed. The entire hospital staff became his family, constantly showering Billy with affection and attention during breaks, lunchtimes and days off. They took turns taking him outside for walks.

All the maternity and nursery staff mothered him, but no one more than Miss N, who, although she was an excellent nurse, had never shown any maternal instincts. In fact, she was the prototype of a tough army sergeant. Actually, she'd been a captain when she served as an army nurse. Billy's face lit up whenever she approached him. Her coworkers had never seen Miss N even smile before, so they were astounded to see her cooing and cuddling Billy. He truly melted her heart, and she cared for him zealously. She adored Billy and desperately wanted to adopt him. Unfortunately, during the sixties, unmarried women were not considered good candidates as adoptive mothers. Knowing it was hopeless, Miss N didn't even try. But Mrs. B, one of the newborn nurses who loved him specially, applied to adopt him.

Meanwhile, Billy was a happy, gurgling boy thriving as a boarder baby in this nurturing, albeit conspiratorial environment. Every member on the staff was in on the secret. No one even mentioned Billy's name outside the hospital corridors.

One day, the Board of Health came to do an impromptu routine inspection of the hospital. Word of the inspectors' arrival traveled quickly to the maternity ward. The administrator led the inspection team to the opposite end of the facility where each department head delayed the inspectors as much as possible. Billy was spirited away from the maternity ward and taken to the apartment of one of the nurses across the street. Nurses and other staff members emptied his room, moved the furniture to the basement, covered his window with examining-table paper and locked the door.

The inspector arrived on maternity and inquired about that room. The head nurse explained it was one of the isolation nurseries being remodeled. The hospital passed the inspection, the inspectors left, the room was refurbished, and Billy returned to his home.

When Billy was fifteen months old, Mrs. B's application for adoption was somehow expedited and approved. We were all overjoyed when Billy became a sibling of her loving brood. Miss N shared a greater joy when she became his godmother.

Staff members sent gifts and had parties for Billy on his birthdays and holidays. Mrs. B and Miss N kept us informed of Billy's progress with pictures and stories.

And brought him often to visit his family in his "first" home.

~Zaphra Reskakis
Chicken Soup for the Nurse's Soul

Confessions of a Stepmother

Shared joy is a double joy; shared sorrow is half a sorrow.
~Swedish Proverb

When I met Larry, my husband-to-be, he came complete with an eighteen-month-old daughter, McKenna, and a four-year-old son, Lorin—on weekends.

The day I met the children, we walked around a pond, Larry holding the diapered McKenna in his arms while Lorin ran around finding frogs to show me. I was stunned. These children were an enormous piece of the man I loved and yet had really nothing to do with me. How did this stepmother thing work?

I quickly fell in love with Lorin's impish grin and McKenna's pudgy baby body, warm against my chest as I held her. I was completely captivated by my new and charming "instant family," but the children's mother, Dia, was a different story. We had a wary relationship, the edge of hostility between us only thinly veiled. I did my best to ignore her and focused instead on the two adorable children she'd borne.

The children and I got along well, though Lorin was somewhat standoffish. Perhaps it was loyalty to his mother, or being a boy, or at four simply wanting more independence. McKenna, being so little, had no such qualms. She loved me and let me know it, unreservedly and with a sweetness and innocence that took my breath away. I couldn't resist her love and when I fell, I fell hard. Almost immediately, we formed our own mutual fan club—two hearts that beat as one.

In fact, it was McKenna who proposed to me first. We sat together in an airport waiting room, on our way to visit Larry's parents. She was almost three, and she sat facing me in my lap, playing with my necklace and every so often looking into my face with worshipful eyes. I smiled at her, feeling the fullness of love for her present in my own heart. Larry sat beside us and Lorin was motoring around the rows of plastic seats, making engine noises with his mouth. To the casual observer, a typical young family. But we weren't a family because Larry hadn't popped the question yet. And although I didn't want to be pushy, we both knew my patience was wearing thin. What, I wondered, was he waiting for?

Then McKenna pulled her pacifier out of her mouth and returning my smile, said brightly, "Will you marry me?" After a moment of shocked silence, we all laughed till our sides hurt. Me with delight, Larry with the release of tension and the children simply because the grown-ups were laughing. Happily, it didn't take Larry long to follow up with his own proposal.

As time went on, I got used to part-time parenting—and having the children's mother as an unavoidable part of my life. I really liked Dia, but our positions seemed to dictate a certain grumpiness with each other that I did my best to squelch. Sometimes I had the guilty wish that the children's mother would simply disappear. A quick and painless illness and on her deathbed, she would make me promise to raise her children for her. Then the children could stay with us—truly be mine—and we could be a "real" family.

Fortunately that never happened. I didn't really want her to die; I just was jealous that she'd had children with my husband. All right, so he was her husband at the time—it still rankled.

I watched the children grow, changing from toddlers to school-kids. And their mother and I continued our civilized and awkward interactions, arranging for the children to come and go and negotiating vacations and holiday schedules.

My friends all told me that Larry should deal with his ex-wife, and for a while we tried that. But as an active and willing caregiver, I was involved with decisions, so Dia and I went back to our previous arrangement. And as the years went by, I noticed that our phone calls changed. I actually enjoyed talking to Dia about the kids. And I think she realized that there were very few people in the world who were as interested in, charmed by or concerned about her children as I was. We began a slow but perceptible metamorphosis that was completed the year Dia sent me a Mother's Day card, thanking me for "co-mothering" her children.

That was the beginning of a new era for Dia and me. And while it hasn't always been perfect, I know now it's been extraordinary. I have a few thank yous of my own:

Thank you, Dia, for being big enough to share your children with me. If you hadn't, I would never have known what it was like to hold a sleeping infant and feel the complete trust displayed in the limp, silky-skinned limbs gathered carefully in my embrace. I wouldn't have had the opportunity to marvel at the twists and turns a little boy's mind makes as he tries to make sense of a large and complex universe.

I would never have known that children could cry so loudly when their stomachs hurt or that after they threw up, they could smile so radiantly at you, the tears still wet on their cheeks, their pain already forgotten.

I would never have watched a boy struggle to become his own person, or have been so closely involved with the painful and serious process of "growing a teenager." I would never have had the awe-inspiring privilege of watching that squirty twelve-year-old who could drive you wild with his questions turn into a heartbreakingly handsome hunk with the megawatt smile and charming personality. As he gets ready to leave for college, I know he will drive a new generation of women wild — for entirely different reasons.

I wouldn't have felt the thrill of seeing our beautiful daughter on stage, expressing herself with a grace and depth of emotion that seemed too old for someone so young. Or had the distinctly undeserved (and guilty) thrill of vanity and pride when someone who didn't know us commented that McKenna looked like me.

Thank you for making Christmas morning a communal occasion,

so the children never had to feel divided on the holiday they held so dear. I looked around one year as we all sat around the tree, while the children delivered the gifts. There we were, you and your husband, Larry and me, the kids... and surprisingly, I felt at home.

I understood then that you didn't have to disappear for us to be a real family.

~Carol Kline
Chicken Soup for the Mother's Soul 2

All Our Hearts Have to Offer

*N*o classroom course I ever took prepared me for one of the most difficult lessons I learned during my nursing career. Feeling fully confident and armed with cutting edge knowledge of critical care, I embarked into the incredibly exciting field of flight nursing. Life on the helicopter was full of ups and downs—literally. I was constantly placed in a pivotal position impacting the way families dealt with instantaneous life-changing events.

During my first pregnancy, I worked with a pediatric resident who predicted my outlook on my patients would change dramatically when I gave birth to my child. I'd always felt I had compassion for my patients and their families, but her words proved prophetic and have echoed in my mind and heart many times since that day in 1984.

I was called to a small emergency room to airlift a five-month-old who had stopped breathing. I was immediately confronted by a hysterical mother, distraught over the possibility that she had somehow caused this catastrophe. She desperately looked to me for reassurance that all would be well. Based on the lab values, X-rays and the child's condition, I could not promise that. In those days, our helicopters were much too small to accommodate a parent, and this child was so critically ill and in need of advanced care, that it became a "scoop and run" situation.

In my haste, I failed to allow a momentary interaction between mother and child. I cuddled the little girl in my arms, and we flew with all the speed the machine could muster to the awaiting pediatric critical-care facility. Her condition proved too critical, and resuscitation attempts were futile. As I realized this sweet mother would never again have the chance to hold her live, breathing, warm baby, a haunting feeling pervaded my soul. A feeling I would not soon forget.

Since that day, and following the arrival of my four beautiful, healthy children, I have been faced with countless opportunities to extend healing to family members. My outlook on my patients has, in fact, changed dramatically. While I still carry charts, calculations, medications, equipment and skill, I have learned there truly is no replacement for the human touch. Since most of the patients I transport are extremely critical, the window of opportunity for technology passes for many of them. Yet families still count on me and countless other flight programs around the world to deliver one last miracle. Thankfully, a God-given feeling of compassion encircles me when I realize the time has come to help heal the nurturers. Now I allow human contact to begin the healing process for family members.

I spent time with a distraught father several days after his daughter was killed in an accident. He came to pick up her purse, left in the back of the helicopter. He begged to know of her last words, to know if she suffered, to know if there was anything he could have done to change the tragic outcome. Tears flowed freely as I reassured him she had been in good hands and given every opportunity available to her. We parted having given each other a small measure of comfort.

I arrived to pick up a three-year-old who had been found submerged in the family pool. Fourteen family members cried out, "Thank God, they're here to save our baby!" A review of his condition soon revealed his little body and brain had been deprived of life-sustaining oxygen for too long a period. His six-year-old sister stepped forward with his stuffed animal; he needed it with him at all times. Kisses were given, touching encouraged, cautions for them to drive safely issued, and we flew to the receiving facility, teddy bear in tow. Gratefully, the little boy survived long enough for the family to arrive. Seeing it was hopeless, the father begged to hold him one last time "while he still feels alive and warm." We disconnected all technology and wrapped his son snugly in a blanket for his daddy to spend precious moments embracing him.

I broke all the rules when I brought family members past the yellow "Caution" tape so they could touch and whisper hasty good-byes before departing from highway accidents, certain they will never again see their loved ones alive. I violated the posted hospital visiting rules and carried small children to their mother's side to kiss, touch, cry and lie next to mommy on the way out to the helicopter.

I'm asked by patients, en route to trauma centers, the status of their husband, wife, friend or sibling. The looks in their eyes indicate their knowledge of the inevitable, and my heart aches as I try to soften the truth.

How grateful I am for all that medicine has to offer, for living in a time when technology changes as rapidly as the second hand ticks. But I am more grateful for those opportunities when soul touches soul, when communication is perfect despite the silence, and when the only thing I have to offer family members is one last memory with their loved ones.

Sixteen years have passed since I listened to words that would shape my care of patients. I have witnessed untold tragedies, but through it all my solace has been the gift of a last touch, a last kiss, a last word, and the hope that these moments would alleviate some of the suffering. I pray that other caregivers will learn this lesson sooner than I did and extend not only all that technology has to offer, but all that our hearts have to offer, as well.

~Janie K. Ford
Chicken Soup for the Nurse's Soul

40

Cards for Mom

God gave us memories that we might have roses in December.
~J.M. Barrie, Courage, 1922

'd lost my dad three years earlier, and my mom was visiting for what I suspected would be the last time. We still were hoping that there'd be a rally. We thought she might be able to beat brain cancer the way she'd beaten lung cancer, but we weren't nearly as confident.

My "white tornado" of a mother—so named because the cleaning product ad reminded us of her whirlwind energy—was suddenly weak. She was becoming accepting instead of being the defiant warrior we'd observed during her first battle with cancer. I recognized the signs of impending death because I'd too recently been through it with Dad.

Mom pulled a box from her suitcase just before she left and she handed it to me, asking me not to open it for a few months. I knew what that meant, and I braved out the next few hours with her, only cracking as she drove away. The tears seemed to flow from then until Christmas Eve. The call that she was gone came just as we were leaving to drive the seven hours to be by her side. I'd seen her many times since she'd left the box for me. We'd talked about everything but what was really happening.

The week of Christmas passed in a blur. My sisters and I all tried to salvage the holiday for our children even as we were coming to terms with the fact that we no longer would be able to lean on the strength of our parents.

I'd been home from the funeral for several weeks before I even remembered the box... a few more weeks before I could bring myself to open it. I steeled myself with a cup of tea (the panacea used by all Scottish girls) and sat cross-legged on the floor to open the battered blue file box that my mother had left to me.

To my surprise, the box was full of greeting cards. My mother, the same one who'd incurred my wrath as a teenager for indiscriminately throwing out my treasures, had saved every single card we'd ever sent to her. The card on top was a recent one, a get well card from her time in the hospice, received while she'd been fighting her first cancer. It was from my sister. Inside my mother had written her own note to us about how much it had meant to her that we'd been there for her and with her. Her spidery writing reached out to me from the card and made me cry.

I dug to the middle of the box and came up with an anniversary card from another sister who had been sixteen when it was sent. My heart skipped as I saw that there was another note written from Mom inside, in a bolder hand: "Hen, I'm looking at you and Terry and feeling so proud of what a beautiful woman you're becoming. Seeing you with your first boyfriend makes me look forward to the day when I'm sending you anniversary cards, too."

Mom's reserved Scottish upbringing kept her from lavishing praise out loud, yet every card, from the fanciest store-bought ones to the crudest childish drawings, was etched with my mom's hopes and dreams for us. More than that, these were the words she rarely expressed to us in life. She was proud of us. She loved us. She thought we were wonderful. We'd always known these things, but in her urgency to see us succeed and surpass her goals for us, more often she'd push and nag us.

I could see evidence of her own tears on the card that was signed by her first grandchild. I read of her joy as each of us married the men who would become the sons of her heart. I laughed as she shared her worries for us in a voice I could hear as clearly as if she were standing next to me.

I was suddenly hungry to see my own cards. I quickly found one. Reading it, I began to sob. I reached for another... and another. Over and over, my mom told me I was beautiful and smart and funny. She wrote about how much it meant to her that I chose cards that were so beautiful and then put my own lovely words on them. She told me she wished she could express herself as well as I could.

In the months that followed, I wished I could have told her that the way she had expressed herself on all those cards would help her four daughters through some of the hardest days of their lives. And that she'd left behind a more lasting legacy than anything else she could have done.

The blue box is much lighter now that I've given the appropriate cards to each of my sisters, but there's a new layer forming. After each holiday, every card that I receive is put into the box with my own heartfelt message—and the vow that I'll say those words out loud as often as I can.

Even so, I will leave my own stack of cards behind so they can buoy up my dear ones when I'm gone, and keep my love for them alive... the way my mother's cards have for me.

~Mary Ann Christie
Chicken Soup for the Mother's Soul 2

Woman to Woman

Through the Generations

*I am a reflection of my past generations
and the essence of those following after me.*
~Martha Kinney

41

Step on a Crack, Bring Your Mother Back

"Step on a crack, break your mother's back," my best friend Franny laughed. She stomped her detested new white bucks on every scar on the cement, giggling. From that call to attention, our walk to school became dangerous. I marveled at her risky rebelliousness as I tiptoed my Mary Janes around the sprung concrete of those New York City sidewalks. I come from a superstitious tribe. A broken Mom was a big threat, something I could never—would never wish on my mother.

These days my mother lives on the Pacific side of the continent in a small group home. Several of the other residents, like my mother, have Alzheimer's disease.

It was no surprise to me when my mother was diagnosed with Alzheimer's. Over a period of years her optimistic eyes began to dim and the mental agility of this eternal student began to disappear. The process was slow and subtle; at first she made jokes about her forgetfulness, but gradually the benign humor vanished, to be replaced by a more severe helplessness. At the memory disorder clinic of a nearby teaching hospital, they described the prognosis; they recommended to me the books I could read that would help. They were kind and caring. The rest of my mother's life, though, seemed a frightening pathway, cracked and distorted by the unpredictable course of a debilitating disease.

"Does she still know you?" This was the first question people asked when I mentioned my mother's disability. Not understanding the slow course of the disease, they always pictured the worst and were surprised and reassured when I told them that my mother did indeed still recognize me. In fact, I told them, her humor surfaced frequently, like when she coyly introduced me as her mother. Her vocabulary was often startlingly original and, with great effort, she still had pockets of usable memory.

A better question emerged: Did I still know her? Who was that woman who looked like my mother but whose eyes could not belie her bewilderment? She was a woman of independence who had lived alone for more than twenty years after my father's death. Unprepared for her sudden widowhood, she learned over the years to manage well on her own, physically, financially and socially. She was determined to survive the poverty of her first generation immigrant upbringing and, finally, in her later years, she came to enjoy a freedom she wasn't raised to expect.

Alzheimer's, a thief in slow motion, stole that freedom and left a woman who could no longer remember her personal history or how many years ago her husband had died. She couldn't recall where her money was or how much it amounted to. Her supposedly golden years were spent living in a house she never called home and enduring a sense of disorientation that she did not understand.

One morning, her arm threaded in mine, we strolled out of her group house for our walk around town. The sidewalk in front of the house was slowly giving way to a mighty cedar tree that dwarfed the Victorian structure.

Suddenly, my boot wedged in a deep crevice in the walkway, and I was pitched forward. My mother reacted instantly, making her arm rigid and yanking me upright. I regained my composure and smiled at her gratefully.

"Are you okay?" she asked with concern. I looked at her, and the thrill of recognition gave me goose bumps. My old Mom, the Mom that I had always known, was smiling at me, her eyes clear, bright with the light of purpose, not a trace of confusion evident.

For a brief moment, my mind flashed back to another time, many, many years ago, when I had seen my mother smile at me in just that way. It was a rainy winter's day in Queens, New York. The weather had been stormy all week and our '54 Plymouth didn't like the rain any more than we did. It stalled just after we picked up my father's shirts at the cleaners. As we sat together in the car, patiently awaiting the tow truck, my mother took my rain boots off and tickled my feet under her coat. We laughed and talked as a car pulled up and parked behind us on the downward incline of a slight hill. A woman in a red kerchief and dark coat sprinted to a shop across the street. Something in the rearview mirror caught my mother's attention. In a flash, she thrust open the car door and swooped me out into the street as the car behind us rolled from its parking spot and slammed our Plymouth into the car parked in front. But we were safe. I huddled against her in the rain, peering up with surprise. She hugged me closer and smiled with relief.

"Are you okay?"

She needn't have asked. Of course I was. I was in my mother's arms.

Those same arms now wrapped around me after my stumble on the sidewalk, and that same smile reassured me.

"I love you so much," she said as she kissed me. "I don't want anything to happen to you." I had heard her say this many times in my life but not recently. I felt overjoyed to have her back.

We continued on down the street where we had walked several times a week since I moved her closer to me. "I haven't been on this street in years," she announced. As she turned to me for confirmation, something she does often given the erratic universe of her mind, I saw that my real mother had slipped away again.

Nothing in my life could have prepared me for the complicated task of caring for a parent with Alzheimer's. Our tender relationship has become an act of balancing familiarity with strangeness. It is one thing to grieve for a parent gone; it is quite another to have to learn to love one you still have but no longer know.

Even though I see my mother often, I miss her very much. I

keep looking forward to the next time I might stumble across her endearing old self, feel her love wrap around me and, if only for a moment, keep me shielded from the pain of losing her.

~Sandra Rockman
Chicken Soup for the Mother's Soul 2

42

The Blessing of Old Age

Happiness is an attitude.
We either make ourselves miserable, or happy and strong.
The amount of work is the same.
~Francesca Reigler

My coworkers and I had lunch together every day. As with any group of women, our conversation ranged from our families and work to our female problems. One day, the conversation centered on our litany of complaints over getting older.

One coworker described her hot flashes in detail, how in the middle of the night she got out of bed, got naked and lay on the cool tile floor in her bathroom to calm her night sweats. Another described dressing and undressing constantly depending on her body temperature. One woman commented that between her mood swings and arthritis, her family compared her to Dr. Jekyll and Mr. Hyde, never knowing what personality was going to show up next. They all bemoaned the fact that their behinds had spread and that they seemed to work harder to try to maintain a decent weight. Then there was the existential question: "My life is half over and what have I done with it?"

Throughout this entire conversation, I remained silent, listening to their complaints. Finally, one woman turned to me. "You're going to be fifty this year. You must have some complaints."

I smiled and sipped my tea. "Well, I guess I look at age differently.

Sure, I wish I were twenty pounds lighter, and I have hot flashes and bursitis in my shoulder, but I can live with those things. But you know what? I can't wait to turn fifty. I'm finally starting my writing career and I feel great. I'm looking forward to getting my AARP card and never paying full price for anything anymore."

Everyone laughed, but I could tell by their curious looks that they thought I was just a little strange.

"My mother died of cancer when she was forty-eight years old. She never got to experience what I'm experiencing now," I said. My coworkers suddenly became quiet. "So I welcome old age with all its aches and pains. Old age is a blessing, and that's just how I'm going to treat it."

"You know, I never thought of it that way," one woman said. "I guess you're right."

Suddenly, the conversation changed from the aches and pains of old age to older persons they knew who were still active, and how they hoped to be like them. Old age, they agreed, might have its aches and pains, but it was indeed a blessing. A blessing to be embraced with an open heart and mind.

~Sharon M. Stanford
Chicken Soup to Inspire a Woman's Soul

43

The Tablecloth

It takes a long time to grow an old friend.
~John Leonard

Last year, my mother, Rose, lost her best friend of fifty years, Rosa, to cancer. Over a lifetime, Mom and Rosa forged a relationship that transcended the two of them, tightly intertwining their families as well. The two women knew and understood each other thoroughly and plainly, and deeply valued each other's company and wisdom.

Their friendship began when they were young brides, inviting each other to barbecues and cocktail parties where they tried out and polished their cooking skills. A few years later, each became pregnant, beginning parallel journeys of motherhood. As the years passed, together they experienced the normal ups and downs of raising a family, providing one another with daily comfort, encouragement and companionship.

When Rosa's cancer was diagnosed, my mother was her greatest cheerleader. Galvanized by fear and a loss of control, Mom organized meals, shuttled Rosa to doctor appointments, ministered to Rosa's husband and grown children, and when possible, translated medical lingo to a bewildered family. My mother, a quintessential helper, gave Rosa and her loved ones much-needed support, gratified to be the scaffolding on which her fragile friend leaned.

Rosa's prognosis was poor from the start, and within a year, she died. As arrangements for the funeral were made, Mom, herself grief-stricken, played a critical role stabilizing Rosa's family and assisting with important decisions. The fact that she was needed was, of course, good therapy as she struggled through her own emotions.

Shortly after Rosa passed away, her bereaved husband, Jean, called my mother on behalf of their daughter, Marsha, who lived out of town. "Rose," he said, "when Marsha was here for the funeral she turned the house upside down looking for a tablecloth she said Rosa had been working on, embroidery or something. I have no idea where it is, and Marsha is devastated about it. I think Rosa was working on it for her. Do you have any idea where she might have put it?"

The next day, my mother, her heart heavy with loss, pulled up in front of her friend's house. Walking into the dining room, fifty years of knowing Rosa's habits her guide, she opened the bottom drawer of the china cabinet, revealing the tablecloth and napkins Marsha was searching for. Unfolding the embroidered cloth, she said to Jean, "I remember Rosa telling me about this cloth before she became sick. She was working on it for Marsha, but it looks like she finished only half of it before she had to give it up. Do you mind if I finish it?"

My mother carried the cloth home and lovingly studied her friend's handiwork. With tears in her eyes but with a sense of renewal, she threaded the embroidery needle tucked into the fabric and began to sew. For days, she embroidered, each stitch fortifying and healing her.

The tablecloth finished and ironed, Mom draped it over her lap, examining the commingling of her stitches with Rosa's, contemplating the weight of their joint effort and thinking how true it is that the whole is much more than the sum of its parts. With great care, she swaddled the cloth in tissue, placed it in a box and mailed it to the daughter of her best friend.

~Bohne G. Silber
Chicken Soup for the Girlfriend's Soul

Gran

When I was a young mother, my grandmother, who was lonely after my grandfather's death, visited me every month for a few days. We'd cook together and talk, and she'd always babysit, so I could have time to myself.

By the time she was ninety-five, practically deaf and very frail, I was working part-time, and two of my three children were in school. Gran would come to our home on days when I wasn't working. Once when she was visiting, my older children were in school, my eighteen-month-old was sleeping, and Gran and I were having coffee. I always felt protected and relaxed when we were together. Then I got a telephone call that there was a crisis in my office—would I please come in for an hour or two. Gran assured me that she and Jeff, the eighteen-month-old, would be fine, and I left.

As I drove to work, I panicked. I'd left my deaf, elderly grandmother with an eighteen-month-old she was not strong enough to pick up and could not hear if he cried. But Gran inspired so much confidence that I felt it would be all right. And perhaps, if I was lucky, my son would sleep the whole time I was gone.

I returned two hours later and heard happy sounds coming from Jeff's room. He'd awakened, she'd dragged a chair next to his crib, and she was reading him a story. He sat there, enchanted by her voice, unperturbed by the bars of the crib that separated them. And our German shepherd lay at her feet, also completely content.

The drama of that day did affect Gran, who later admitted that communicating with an eighteen-month-old presented some problems. Unlike adults, if he'd needed something and wanted her to know about it, of course he couldn't write it down. The next week she enrolled in a lip-reading course at a local college. The teacher was a young intern, and Gran was her only student. After the first session, the teacher made the trip to Gran's apartment each week, so Gran wouldn't have to travel to the college, changing buses twice. By the end of the semester, Gran's ability to lip-read had greatly improved, and she felt infinitely more comfortable with Jeff and with the rest of the world.

Gran continued to communicate with Jeff in this way until she died, a few days before her hundredth birthday — leaving an unbearable void in my life.

~Mary Ann Horenstein
Chicken Soup for Every Mom's Soul

Disaster on the Mountain

Faith makes things possible, not easy.
~Author Unknown

When Ruth Hagan was seventy-eight years old, she visited her daughter Judy and teenage granddaughter Marcy in California. They headed for their cabin, zigzagging forty miles up and down the mountains in their Bronco, from pavement to gravel to a narrow one-lane road of brittle shale and powdery dirt that wound terrifyingly close to cliffs.

After dinner, Marcy announced the water tank was low and that she would take the Bronco down to the pump and get water. Ruth was nervous about her young granddaughter driving down the narrow dirt road by herself, but Judy reminded her that Marcy had been driving vehicles up there on the ranch roads since she was twelve.

"Just be careful, Marcy," her mother warned. "They've had a dry spell up here and the cliff side is pretty shaky. Be sure to hug the mountain side."

Ruth said a quick prayer as she and Judy watched Marcy from the big window where they could see the road winding down the mountainside. Fifteen minutes later Judy was still watching when suddenly she screamed, "Oh no! God help us! She went over the cliff, Momma! The Bronco and Marcy—they went over! We have to help her! Come on!"

The cabin door slammed and Judy took off running. Ruth ran

behind her, but Judy was quickly out of sight after the first turn in the road. Ruth raced down the steep hill, breathing hard. She ran on and on, down the hill, up the next, trying to catch up with her daughter. It was getting harder and harder to see anything at dusk. Ruth stopped cold and looked around.

She screamed into the darkness "Judy, where are you?" Off to her immediate right and down the cliff she heard, "Down here, Mother! Don't come near the edge! I slipped on loose rocks and fell over. I'm down about twenty feet."

"Oh dear God, Judy, what can I do?"

"Just stay back, Momma! The road is giving out all over! I think I can crawl back up. I saw the white roof of the Bronco when I was falling, Momma, and I heard Marcy calling for help. She's alive! But she's way down there in the ravine. You have to go back to the cabin and phone for help. Tell them to send a helicopter. We have to get Marcy out!"

Ruth resisted looking over the edge to make sure Judy was really okay. She turned around and started running back up the hill she'd just stumbled down. Up one hill, down the next. She had one hill left to climb when she stumbled on loose dirt and rocks and fell on her face. Chest pains took her breath away. She started to sob. "Dear God," she prayed, "please help me get back to the cabin so I can call for help!"

At that moment something went through Ruth. It was like a powerful energy and she knew for certain that somebody was there to help her. She heard the words, "I am here." She stood up, completely relaxed and rested. A surge of pain-free energy propelled her forward.

Ruth ran on confidently, faster than she had before, and up that last big hill. She turned into the cabin driveway, pushed through the front door and dialed 911. She sputtered out details of the disaster but unfortunately, she had no idea where she was. The dispatcher was totally confused. Ruth had to get Judy up to the phone so she could give directions. Ruth stepped out of the cabin into total darkness. She grabbed a three-foot-long walking stick propped against the cabin door and started running back down the switchback road.

She continued to run with energy and determination through the darkness. Up the hill, down the hill, up the second hill. Suddenly she stopped, not knowing where she was. "Marcy! Judy!" she shouted.

A faint voice cried from directly below. "I'm here, Grandma."

Another voice. "Momma!" It was Judy.

Ruth dropped to her knees, then lay flat on her belly as she scooted herself closer and closer to the edge of the cliff. She held the walking stick over the edge and asked Judy if she could see it.

"I see it, Momma, I'm almost there."

Ruth heard gravel rolling around where Judy was climbing. Within minutes, Judy grabbed the other end of the stick and Ruth pulled her 140-pound daughter up and over that cliff. Judy crawled into her mother's lap, shaking and sweating and immediately passed out.

Ruth held her close and stroked her wet forehead. "Judy, Judy, wake up. We have to get help for Marcy!" Ruth kept talking and rubbing her daughter's head. Finally, Judy came to. Ruth pulled her to her feet, and the two women started walking. Dazed and bleeding, Judy fell three times as they worked their way back to the cabin in the darkness.

When they reached the cabin they heard the phone ringing. It was the volunteer emergency crew on the other end. Judy sputtered out directions to where Marcy was. As soon as she hung up, she and her mother started down the mountain again to meet and guide the rescuers. They trudged up the hill, down the hill. Still full of energy, calm and confident, Ruth held on to Judy, for Judy's sake, not hers.

An hour later, the fire trucks, ambulance, paramedics and, finally, the Flight for Life helicopter arrived. It took three-and-a-half hours to cut Marcy free from the wreckage at the bottom of the cliff. At last the sheriff pulled her out of the back end of the Bronco and carried her to the waiting ambulance. She was rushed to the hospital for treatment of a crushed ankle and severely broken leg, foot and finger.

The next day, when the sheriff came to visit Marcy in the hospital, he shook his head and said, "That mountain didn't beat you."

Ruth Hagan knew the mountain didn't beat them because God was there that night, protecting her, guiding her, breathing strength into her frail body. Ruth, Judy and Marcy all have their lives to prove it.

~Patricia Lorenz
Chicken Soup for the Christian Woman's Soul

46

The Mirror Has Three Faces

And thou shalt in thy daughter see,
This picture, once, resembled thee.
~Ambrose Philips

I am fifty-one years old. My mother was fifty-one when she died. I remember that last day of her life only too clearly. It was a rainy Monday, and my mother could not breathe.

"It's fluid," the doctor said. "We'll tap her lungs." They sat my mother up in the hospital bed and plunged the long needle through her back into her lungs. Again and again they tried, but no fluid came. And no relief.

"It's not fluid," the doctor said. "It's all tumor. We can't help her breathe."

I remember my mother's desperate words. "I can't... breathe. Turn up the oxygen... please." But turning up the oxygen didn't help. Her lungs, bursting with cancer, fought to make room for the air. My mother whispered her final words to me, "I want the quickest way."

My mother should have grown old. Her dark hair, peppered with gray, should have become snowy white. The fine lines, etched in her face from her smiles, should have become soft wrinkles. Her quick step should have given way to a slower, more seasoned gait.

My mother should have watched her five grandchildren grow

up. She should have had the chance to enfold them in her very special brand of love and to impart to them her considerable wisdom. She should have been arm in arm with my father—she was the only girl he ever loved—sojourning into their shared golden years. She didn't. She wasn't. She never had the chance. She was fifty-one, and she died.

I was twenty-seven when my mother died. Over the years, not a day went by when I didn't think of something I wanted to tell her, to ask her or to show her. I railed bitterly against the injustice of it. It wasn't fair that my mother died at fifty-one.

Now I am fifty-one. I look into the mirror and it strikes me: I have slowly but surely been transformed. There she is with that gray peppered hair, those dark intense eyes, that expression on my face. When I hear my voice, it is her voice. I have become my mother.

I am entering a new and strange stage of my life. I have always looked ahead to see my mother. Ever so briefly, I stood next to her. Now I'm beginning to be older than my mother. The direction in which I gaze to see her will change. Soon I will look back at my mother.

Gradually my mother will become young in comparison with me. I will grow old instead of her—acquire the white hair she should have had but never did. I will develop that seasoned gait she never experienced, see those soft facial wrinkles she never had, and so it will continue on and on until one day when I'm seventy-five, as she would have been today. On that day, the reversal of our roles complete, I will turn around to look at her, but see instead my own daughter, at fifty-one—my mother.

~Kristina Cliff-Evans
Chicken Soup for the Golden Soul

47

Emma's Bouquets

It was a hot June day when my mother and I crossed the Texas border and made our way to Minden, west of Shreveport, Louisiana. Although it wasn't far to the old George family farm, where my great-grandparents had homesteaded 100 years earlier, I had never been there before.

As we drew closer to the family homestead, through softly rolling hills of longleaf pine, sweet gum and red oak, I thought about what connects us with earlier generations of our family. Is it just a matter of eye color, height or blood type? Or are there other ties that bind us? If my great-grandmother Emma could find her way into the present, would she discover something familiar in my generation?

When my mom and I turned into the George property, we saw before us a real Southern farmhouse—mostly porch with a house attached. Although it was just a simple farmhouse, its front windows were graced with ornately carved dental moldings, and the steps from the porch—flanked by large brick pillars with granite plinths—were a palatial ten feet wide. The house bore a startling resemblance to the houses my brother and sister and I owned, even though none of us had ever seen this place. When I'd bought my old farmhouse in North Carolina, for example, the first thing I'd done was to add a replica of this porch. Similarly, my brother's and sister's Louisiana homes, although newly designed by architects, bore an uncanny resemblance to the old George homestead.

As my mother and I strolled through the garden, where roses, day lilies, irises, vitex and phlox still bloomed, my mother remarked, "Your great-grandmother Emma loved flowers." Wanting to keep a part of this, my heritage, I knelt down and dug out one of the iris pips.

Because I also wanted to preserve something from the inside of the house, before it crumbled and was lost to time, we gingerly explored the interior, noting the twenty-inch-wide virgin pine boards, the hand-hewn beams and the handmade clay bricks, each marked with a G. Then, in the bedroom, I discovered Emma's 1890s wallpaper—a floral motif, naturally, with a repeating pattern of large bouquets of ivory and pink roses. It was peeling off the pine boards, but still lovely after all this time, just like my great-grandmother's garden. I knew this was the memento I wanted to take with me. With the tiny penknife on my key ring, I carved off two square-foot pieces, one for me and one for my younger sister, Cindy.

Before we headed for home, Mom and I stood on that familiar front porch for a moment of silent leave-taking.

At that instant, I felt very connected to my ancestors, as though there were invisible wires running between us, anchoring each successive generation to the earlier ones. However, on the drive home, I began to wonder if I weren't making too much of this family ties thing. Perhaps a penchant for wide porches was just a coincidence.

The next day, eager to share the story of this trip with Cindy, I dropped by her house. I found her in the kitchen, happily perusing the materials she had bought on a recent trip to England in order to redecorate her home. We sat at the table together, and I told her about our great-grandparents' farmhouse with its verandah, floor-to-ceiling windows and high ceilings that had somehow found their way into the design of the homes of the Georges' great-grandchildren. We laughed about my muddying my dress in order to dig out a flower pip, and then I produced the little square of wallpaper I'd brought for her as a keepsake.

She appeared stunned, sitting stone-still and dead-quiet. I thought I had, in my big-sister way, offended her with my story. Then she reached into the box of her renovation materials and pulled out the rolls of newly purchased wallpaper from England. The design was exactly the same—the ivory-pink sprays and bouquets of roses were Emma's.

Emma's bouquets had found their way into the present.

~Pamela George
A Second Chicken Soup for the Woman's Soul

48

Lessons from Aunt Grace

The day we moved away I hit bottom. Saying goodbye to my friends and to the house I had loved made me feel as though my moorings had been ripped loose. Now, in what my husband kept calling "our new home" (it wasn't new, and it wasn't home), I was so awash in self-pity that I almost ignored the white leather book I found while unpacking an old trunk. But something prompted me to examine it.

The gold Victorian script on the cover spelled My Diary. Opening the book, I recognized the spidery handwriting of my great-aunt Grace, who had lived with us when I was a little girl. Aunt Grace belonged to a species now extinct—the unmarried, unemployed gentlewoman forced to live with relatives. All the cards had seemed to be stacked against her. She was plain-looking; she was poor; she was frail.

Yet the thing I remember about her was her unfailing cheerfulness. Not only did she never complain, but she never seemed to lose her gentle smile. "Grace always looks on the bright side," people said.

I sank down on the rolled carpet to read her diary. The first entry was dated 1901; the last was the year of her death, 1930. I read casually at first, and then with riveted attention.

Three years have passed since my dear Ted was killed at San Juan Hill and yet every day is still filled with pain. Will I ever be happy again?

Ted? I thought of Aunt Grace as the complete old maid. She once had a sweetheart! I read on:

> *My unhappiness is a bottomless cup. I know I must be cheerful, living in this large family upon whom I am dependent, yet gloom haunts me.... Something has to change or I shall be sick. Clearly my situation is not going to change; therefore, I shall have to change. But how?*
>
> *I have given much thought to my predicament and I have devised a simple set of rules by which I plan to live. I intend this to be a daily exercise. I pray that the plan will somehow deliver me from my dismal swamp of despair. It has to.*

The simplicity of Aunt Grace's rules-to-live-by took my breath away. She resolved every day to:

1. *Do something for someone else.*
2. *Do something for myself.*
3. *Do something I don't want to do that needs doing.*
4. *Do a physical exercise.*
5. *Do a mental exercise.*
6. *Do an original prayer that always includes counting my blessings.*

Aunt Grace wrote that she limited herself to six rules because she felt that number to be "manageable." Here are some of the things she did and recorded in her diary:

Something for someone else. She bought three calves' feet, simmered them for four hours in water, with spices, to make calf's-foot jelly for a sick friend.

Something for myself. She trimmed an old blue hat with artificial flowers and a veil, receiving so many compliments that she thought the thirty-five cents well spent.

Something I don't want to do. She "turned out" the linen closet — washed three dozen sheets by hand, sun-bleached them, and folded them away with lavender sachet.

Physical exercise. She played croquet and walked to the village instead of going by horse and buggy.

Mental exercise. She read a chapter a day of Dickens's Bleak House, "which everyone is talking about."

To my surprise, Aunt Grace had trouble with number six. Prayer did not come easily. *"I can't concentrate in church,"* she wrote. *"I find myself appraising the hats."* Eventually she discovered a solution: *"When I sit in solitude on the rock overlooking our pasture brook, I can pray. I ask the Lord to help me bloom where I am planted, and then I count my blessings, always beginning with my family, without whom I would be alone and lost."*

When I put down Aunt Grace's diary — aware now that "cheery Aunt Grace" fought the battle against darkness that we all fight — tears filled my eyes. But at first I ignored her message. I was a modern woman who needed no self-help crutches from a bygone era.

Yet settling into our new life proved increasingly difficult. One day, feeling totally depressed, I lay in bed and stared at the ceiling. Should I try Aunt Grace's formula? Could those six points help me now?

I decided I could continue to be a lump of misery, or I could test Aunt Grace's recipe by doing something for someone else. I could, for instance, phone my eighty-five-year-old neighbor who was ill and lived by herself. One of Aunt Grace's sentences echoed in my head: *"I alone can take the initiative to escape from 'the sarcophagus of self.'"*

The sarcophagus of self. That did it. I would not be buried by my own ego. I got up and dialed Miss Phillips. She invited me for tea.

It was a start. Miss Phillips was delighted to have someone to talk with—and in her musty parlor I listened to details of her illness. Then I heard her say something that snapped me to attention.

"Sometimes," said Miss Phillips, "the thing you dread doing is the very thing you should do, just so you can stop thinking about it."

I walked home, turning over that insight in my mind. Miss Phillips had cast a new light on Aunt Grace's third rule. Do something I don't want to do that needs doing.

Ever since we moved, I had avoided organizing my desk. Now I made up my mind to get the blasted pile of papers in order. I found a file and folders, and every paper on my desk went into one of them or into the trash.

Two hours later I put down a new green blotter and a small philodendron plant. I beamed. I had done something I did not want to do, and it made me feel good.

At first, "doing a physical exercise" wasn't quite so successful. I signed up for a jazz-exercise class and hated it. I tried jogging, until it dawned on me that I hated it, too.

"What's wrong with walking?" my husband asked. He offered to join me each morning before breakfast. We found walking to be wonderfully conducive to communication. We enjoyed it so much that evening walks eventually replaced our evening cocktail. We felt healthier than we had in years.

At "doing something for yourself" I excelled. I began with Aunt Grace's idea of bath therapy. "A bath should be the ultimate place of relaxation," she wrote. "Gather fresh lemon balm, sweet marjoram, mint, lemon verbena, lavender and rose geranium. Steep the dried leaves in boiling water for fifteen minutes and strain into the tub. Lie in the bath with your eyes closed, and do not think while soaking."

Miss Phillips happily supplied me with herbs from her garden. I put the herbal mix in the tub, turned on the water and stretched out to let the tensions of the day melt away. It was sensational.

Soon I started an herb garden of my own and made herbal sachets for Christmas gifts. Doing something for myself had turned into doing something for someone else.

The "mental exercise" was more of a challenge. I couldn't decide what to do until I read about a poetry course at the local community college. The teacher was a retired college professor who made poetry come alive. When we reached Emily Dickinson, I went into orbit. I read all 1,775 of her poems and was enthralled. "I dwell in Possibility," wrote Emily. Marvelous.

Our professor was big on memorizing, which turned out to be the best mental exercise of all. I began with "I'm Nobody! Who are you?" and progressed to more difficult poems like "I felt a Funeral, in my Brain." How I've enjoyed recalling these poems while waiting in supermarket lines or at doctors' offices!

Aunt Grace's prayer assignment was the most helpful of all. I try now to make up a short prayer every day, and I always include some thanksgiving in it. Writing a prayer isn't easy, but it's a valuable spiritual discipline. I don't have Aunt Grace's meditation rock, but I do have a peaceful village church where I can attend to that inner voice.

I don't worry how well I fulfill Aunt Grace's six rules, so long as I do them daily. I will give myself credit for just one letter written, or one drawer cleaned out, and it's surprising how good feelings about a small accomplishment often enable me to go on and do more.

Can life be lived by a formula? All I know is that since I started to live by those six precepts, I've become more involved with others and, hence, less "buried" in myself. Instead of wallowing in self-pity, I have adopted Aunt Grace's motto: "Bloom where you are planted."

~Nardi Reeder Campion
Chicken Soup for the Single's Soul

49

A Legacy in a Soup Pot

The time to take the time is when you don't have time for it.
~Attributed to both Jim Goodwin and Sydney J. Harris

Have you ever noticed the busier your life seems to be, the more empty it appears to become? I remember staring at my date book early one Monday morning—scores of meetings, deadlines and projects leered back at me, assailing my senses and demanding my attention. I remember thinking for the umpteenth time, "What does all this really matter?"

And lately, with all this introspection, I had been remembering my beloved grandmother. Gram had a sixth grade education, an abundance of kitchen table wisdom and a wonderful sense of humor. Everyone who met her thought it was so appropriate that she had been born on April 1—the day of practical jokes, good laughs and hearty humor—and she certainly spent her lifetime buoying up everyone's spirits.

Cerebral she was not, but to a child, she was Disney World personified. Every activity with Gram became an event, an occasion to celebrate, a reason to laugh. Looking back, I realize it was a different time, a different sphere. Family, fun and food played an important role.

Meals were Gram's mainstay—occasions to be planned, savored and enjoyed. Hot, sit-down breakfasts were mandatory. The preparation of lunch began at 10:30 every morning, with homemade soup simmering, and dinner plans started at 3:30 P.M., with a telephone call to the local butcher to make a delivery. Gram spent a lifetime meeting the most basic needs of her family.

Stopping to pick up yet another take-out meal for dinner, my mind traveled back to her kitchen. The old, oak kitchen table, with the single pedestal... the endless pots of soups, stews and gravies perpetually simmering on the stove top... the homey tablecloths stained with love from a meal past. My gosh, I thought with a start.

I'm over forty, and I have yet to make a pot of soup or stew from scratch!

Suddenly the cardboard take-out containers next to me looked almost obscene. I felt as if I had been blessed with a wonderful legacy, and for one reason or another, I had never quite gotten to the point of passing it on.

The following day, I rummaged through the attic searching for a cardboard box that had been stowed away. Twenty-five years ago, that box had been given to me when Gram decided to move from the old homestead. I vaguely remember going through my "inheritance" as a teen. Every granddaughter had received a pocketbook. Mine was a jeweled evening bag, circa 1920. I remembered I carried it at my college graduation. However, being a headstrong teen at the time of my "inheritance," I never really bothered with the rest of the contents. They remained sealed in that same box, buried somewhere in the attic.

It wasn't that difficult to locate the box, and it was even easier to open it. The tape was old and gave way easily. Lifting the top, I saw Gram had wrapped some items in old linen napkins—a butter dish, vase and at the bottom, one of her old soup pots. The lid was taped to the pot itself. I peeled back the tape and removed the lid.

At the bottom of the pot was a letter, penned in Gram's own hand:

My darling Barbara,

I know you will find this one day many years from now. While you are reading this, please remember how much I loved you, for I'll be with the angels then, and I won't be able to tell you myself.

You were always so headstrong, so quick, so much in a hurry to grow up. I often had wished that I could have kept you a baby forever. When you stop running, when it's time for you to slow down, I want you to take out your Gram's old soup pot and make your house a home. I have enclosed the recipe for your favorite soup, the one I used to make for you when you were my baby.

Remember I love you, and love is forever.

Your Gram

I sat reading that note over and over that morning, sobbing that I had not appreciated her enough when I had her. You were such a treasure, I moaned inwardly. Why didn't I even bother to look inside this pot while you were still alive!

So that night, my briefcase remained locked, the answering machine continued to blink and the disasters of the outside world were put on hold. I had a pot of soup to make.

~Barbara Davey
A Second Chicken Soup for the Woman's Soul

50

Old People

Age is an issue of mind over matter. If you don't mind, it doesn't matter.
~Mark Twain

At age ninety-two, Grandma Fritz still lived in her old two-story farmhouse, made homemade noodles, and did her laundry in her wringer-washer in the basement. She maintained her vegetable garden, big enough to feed all of Benton County, with just a hoe and spade. Her seventy-year-old children lovingly protested when she insisted on mowing her huge lawn with her ancient push mower.

"I only work outside in the cool, early mornings and in the evenings," Grandma exclaimed, "And I always wear my sunbonnet."

Still, her children were understandably relieved when they heard she was attending the noon lunches at the local senior citizens' center.

Yes, Grandma admitted, as her daughter nodded approvingly, "I cook for them. Those old people appreciate it so much!"

~LeAnn Thieman
A Second Chicken Soup for the Woman's Soul

Woman to Woman

Inner Strength and Courage

*Wisdom is meaningless until
our own experience has given it meaning.*
~Bergen Evans

51

Starting Over

Courage is the power to let go of the familiar.
~Raymond Lindquist

My husband of twenty-five years had died only three weeks before, and I was alone—running a business and worried about keeping house and home together. Everyone remarked how well I was doing. I looked composed on the surface and was comforted by the convincing role I was playing. But frightening questions arose when I didn't expect them. Could the business support my daughter Lexi and me without Paul helping us run it? Where would we move if I had to sell our house? Most frightening of all, I was terrified that if I surrendered to my grief, let myself really feel it, I would be sucked downward into a dark, bottomless spiral from which I would never return to sanity. I knew I had to do something.

Several years earlier, Paul and I had been very impressed by a man named Tim Piering. He helped people work through their deepest fears by leading them through the very things they were most afraid of. I decided to make an appointment with him.

The following Saturday, I drove to Tim's office in Sierra Madre, located in the foothills of the San Gabriel Mountains in Southern California. Tim, a tall ex-Marine with a big heart, asked me questions and listened to me for a while, then asked if Paul would want me to grieve for him. I thought about it.

"No, I can't imagine that he would. In fact, I think he'd strongly object."

"I'm sure he'd object, and I really think I can help, Diana. I think we can process some of the grief you're feeling, and lessen it. Would you like to try?"

"Y-yes," I managed to say. It was as if I wanted to hold onto my hidden grief out of loyalty to Paul, although I knew he'd want me to do everything I could to move ahead.

"Notice the thoughts going on in your head," Tim said. "All your fears, your considerations, sound like radio voices, don't they? Of all these thoughts, fear is the most debilitating. Not only does it sap your energy, but it also will cost you many great opportunities. Just think of how many times you have held back from doing something because of fear. If you are willing, Diana, I'm going to give you a quick course in stretching your ability to do anything you want to do. Basically, what will happen is you will have a completely new image of yourself, and you will see how you can take any action—any action you want—regardless of what your mind is saying. Your mind can be yakking away, even screaming, and you can go ahead and do things in spite of the racket going on in your mind."

Tim drove me in his truck high into the nearby mountains. He pulled onto a shoulder and parked. Carrying ropes and other equipment from the back of his sports utility vehicle, he led me out onto a bridge that spanned a dry wash several hundred feet below. I watched as Tim attached a pulley to the bridge railing and to his body and threaded the pulleys with ropes. Suddenly, he climbed over the railing and lowered himself slowly to the bottom of the canyon. Climbing back up the hill, he called, "Want to try it yourself?"

"Not on your life!"

Tim went over the side once again, showing me how he could maneuver up and down with the pulley, and how a safety rope was in place just in case. It did seem very safe, and I began to feel I could do it, and said I might try it someday.

With that small crack showing in my armor of fear, Tim wasted no time strapping the gear on me and attaching the rope to my rappelling ring. He showed me how to gradually roll the pulley and come to a complete stop during the descent. He attached the safety rope to himself.

"Okay, now just step over the railing."

"Ha! Easy for you to say!"

"It's a metaphor, Diana, for how willing you are to really 'go for the gold' in your life."

I've never, ever felt more terrified. Since childhood I've been afraid of heights and had recurring nightmares of teetering on a cliff or window ledge. I trembled at the mere thought of standing on the outside of the railing. Very, very slowly I eased one leg over the railing, saying, "Oh, my God, I am so scared!"

Tim held both of my hands firmly on the railing as I lifted the other leg over, leaning as far toward him as I could for protection. My heart was pounding and I began to whimper.

"Let's just forget the whole thing!"

"It's your decision, Diana. You don't have to do it."

No one was making me do this, I realized. I'd come to Tim for help. I had a hunch that if I could only do this, it would make all the difference. Again, I resolved to try.

"Okay, I'm going to do it. I'm committed."

"Let go with one hand and hold the rope tightly so you won't start moving until you're ready."

I was bleating like a terrified sheep, I was so frightened. But I did what Tim said—I let go of the railing with one hand. Then came the crucial moment. I released the other hand—and there I was, swinging in small arcs over the canyon.

So far, so good.

"Now—very slowly—inch your way down a foot or two."

I did. At that moment, my fear was transformed to excitement. It was easy for me to operate the pulley. I took a long time lowering myself to the bottom, relishing the view and my victory over the terrified voice in my head. Tim ran down to meet me.

"Look what you did, Diana! You did it!"

And so I had. Li'l old me, exactly like a U.S. Marine! Wow! If I could do that, I could do anything! I thought to myself. I felt elated and more powerful than I ever had before.

Then Tim took me to a firing range and had me fire an automatic revolver repeatedly, another thing I would never have dreamed of doing. I realize now that Tim wanted me to feel a different kind of fear than what a woman—suddenly alone—would normally feel. Survival in a physical sense—not an emotional one. I could feel my life beginning again.

"Diana, you've stretched your reality of what you thought you could do. This is a benchmark that will allow you to rise to new levels of action in spite of fear. Whenever you feel confronted by an action you need to take, you can think back to this experience, and whatever challenges you face will seem easy in comparison. This one short event—committing to the action of going off the bridge—will propel you years ahead in how you operate in scary situations. And it will stretch your limits for all the things that frighten you. Regardless of your thoughts, you can do almost anything just because you commit to doing it. You've opened the door to the possibility of achieving all your dreams, Diana.

"In the beginning, you may spend most of your time fighting the negative comments of the radio voices that try to justify all the reasons why you shouldn't do something. But, as you remember what you accomplished here today, Diana, keep this thought in mind: The world owes you nothing. You've landed on the playing field of life. The only question is: will you play?"

~Diana von Welanetz Wentworth
Chicken Soup to Inspire the Body and Soul

52

Leadership Material

*I*was new to the church the first time I went to a women's fellowship meeting. Had I known it was their night to reorganize their committees, I would have stayed home. Since then I read my church bulletin very carefully.

After explaining what the various guilds did, they asked everyone to choose which one they would be part of. I chose the Parish Guild. That committee sent out cards to new parents, the sick and the bereaved. They also provided food for the funeral suppers. I could do the cards. The food, if I had to cook it, would be a problem. I wondered how they felt about store-bought desserts.

I was about to raise that question when Lori asked if I wouldn't mind being chair. I stared at her like she had spoken Swahili. Then I told her I really was not leadership material. She smiled. It was a "pat-on-the-head- and-don't-worry-about-a-thing-dear" smile. Lori said, "Everyone will help. You only have to make the calls."

"Okay," I relented.

"It'll be fine," she reassured me.

And the first months were. I selected cards and sent them out. It was easy. It was a joy. Then someone died.

Helen, my pastor's wife, called me and told me. She said I was to call the family and ask if they wanted the guild to provide food for the gathering after the service. I practically dropped the phone.

Nobody had told me I had to call the family. Nobody had told me that was part of my job.

I called. I was awful at it. I hemmed and hawed my way through the whole conversation, although I wanted to be so sensitive.

The day of the memorial service I stopped by church to check on the food. The guild women, as promised, had come through—three entrees, three salads, three desserts so far. I hoped that other people would bring food to the house. I left with my small daughter to do errands.

On my way home, I stopped by church to make sure that all the food had been picked up and taken to the house. The organ was playing as I passed the sanctuary. I looked at my watch. This sure is a long service, I thought as I rounded a corner. I nearly knocked Helen over. She was wearing her best black dress and practically running, her hands loaded with a huge silver platter.

I recognized the meatloaf entree on it. "They think the meal is here at the church," she whispered. "Pastor is stalling for time while we set up." The sound of a metal tray crashing to the floor echoed from the parish hall. Helen flinched.

Then she straightened. "I've started the coffee," she continued bravely. "The oven in the kitchen is on the fritz. I'm taking the meat home to warm it. I'll be back as soon as I can."

I nodded like a person caught in a whirlwind—which I was.

"Nancy, did you tell them the meal was to be at their home?"

"I, I just assumed that...."

"Never mind," said that saintly woman, "it'll be all right." She dashed toward the parking lot.

I sighed and watched her departing figure. Holding my daughter's hand, I trudged across the patio to the kitchen. On the island counter were the three salads, the three desserts and the two entrees minus the meatloaf. I glanced over my shoulder, out the door. The church parking lot was nearly full.

God, what are we going to do? There must be over 100 people at the service. This is going to be a fiasco. I closed my eyes as if to shut out the future. The giant coffeepot perked away merrily. How dare it?

I set out the napkins and brought up plates from the cupboards. I removed the plastic wrap from the food containers and put serving spoons in them. The organ stopped playing. My stomach fluttered as footsteps and voices approached the kitchen.

People began streaming in. In their hands they carried green salads and macaroni salads and Jell-O salads, casseroles and sandwiches, bread and cold cuts, pies and cakes, plates of cookies and brownies. For a moment it was happy chaos as we found places for all the food. Then people lined up. Smiling graciously I stepped behind the counter and handed out coffee. I hoped that the tall people wouldn't notice that I was wearing blue jeans.

Later, as one of the daughters of the deceased was gathering up the remains of the leftover food she smiled. "It was great having this at the church," she said. "Mother was worrying and making herself sick over how she would ever get the house ready."

Her words filled me with awe. God, I thought, You sure do move in mysterious ways.

I managed the next funeral okay. Helen said pointedly, "Tell them, Nancy, that the meal is to be at their house." I did.

However, the funeral after that one found me dog-paddling in disaster again. While loading the food into my car, I broke a salad bowl and chipped a crockpot lid.

At the end of my one-year tenure as Parish Guild chair, I heaved a sigh of relief. I hadn't gotten through unscathed, but it had all worked out. God had made it work out. I congratulated myself that I had done my bit as a leader and now could retreat into being a committee member.

Then the women's fellowship elected me president.

~Nancy Ellen Hird
Chicken Soup for the Christian Woman's Soul

53

Dancing for Fireflies

Other things may change us, but we start and end with the family.
~Anthony Brandt

On a Saturday morning a few years back, I made a difficult and irreversible decision. My daughter was at the piano, galloping through *Unchained Melody*. My son was polishing the hallway mirrors, eager to earn a few extra dollars for a new CD. I couldn't decide if it was the warm mug of coffee cupped in my hands—brewed just right for a change—or the sense of harmony that seemed out of character in a house that had become a war zone as of late, but I realized how crucial it is that a home be a peaceful place away from the turmoil of work and school. And, in those moments, a startling thought welled up in me. I suddenly realized that little by little, I was jeopardizing the greatest source of safety my children can possess: the home that my husband and I have provided for them.

A safe home has little to do with physical elements, even though we judge other people's homes by the craftsmanship of the woodwork or the quality of the drapes. I'm referring to the "atmosphere" of a home—or maybe "soul" is the definitive word. I recall one weekend years ago, visiting a college friend's elaborate home. I was so impressed that each bedroom had its own bathroom with the thickest, most luxurious towels. Yet that detail seemed marred by the chilling silence that existed between her parents—a silence so loud that I still recall it vividly. I also remember a rather ramshackle house on the outskirts of my hometown. The lady who lived there was a seamstress, a kind woman who listened with eyes that smiled through peculiar blue-rimmed glasses. Whenever my mother took me for a fitting, I was never quite ready to leave. One evening when I went to pick up a dress, she and her husband, Eddie, with the oil-field grime scrubbed from his skin, sat at the table with their kids. They were eating peach cobbler, laughing loudly and playing Yahtzee, and on that evening, their home, with its worn furniture and framed paint-by-number artwork, was clearly one of the finest.

Uncontrollable hardships may plague a home's well-being: the loss of a job, a serious illness or even death. But it's the circumstances many of us encounter on a day-to-day basis that often wear us down and more often contribute to the breakup of a home. I know many couples just like my husband and myself. Once upon a time each other's company charmed us. Our infatuation with each other seemed to cast a rosy glow over the fact that we could barely make ends meet as we struggled to balance part-time jobs with our college classes. Our furniture was the cast-offs our relatives were glad to unload, we guarded the thermostat with a frugal eye, and tomato soup was a common meal staple. Yet the two of us created a mansion with our passion. We graduated, found our niche in the working world, bought our first house, and when our children came along, we were even more enchanted with the cozy feeling their wide-eyed wonder contributed to our home. Long walks with the stroller, Dr. Seuss, dancing for fireflies in the warm twilight—we were happy.

But somehow twenty years passed and neither my husband nor I could account for the past five. Our jobs demanded more of our time, and our passion for each other slipped away so gradually I scarcely noticed. Our children grew older and fought more so we bought a house twice as big where we were soon spending our time in four remote corners: my husband with his work or evening TV, I with my nose in a pile of bills, my daughter's ear glued to the telephone, and my son, depending on his moods, lost in the world of alternative music or ESPN. When my husband and I did talk, it was to argue about how to discipline adolescent angst, or whose turn it was to take out the garbage. What happened to the long walks, "Sam I Am" and the fireflies?

On that Saturday morning months ago, I faced a reality I had been denying. Something I never imagined could happen to me, had happened. I grew dependent on the attention of another man. Despite his graying hair, he's uncannily like the strong-willed but sensitive guy who charmed me almost two decades ago. Our friendship sparkled because we'd never raised headstrong children, never lived together during hay-fever season, and never woken up to each other's foul breath or puffy eyes. We had never experienced any of the tribulations, minor or major, which test and shape a relationship. In the months that followed, visits with him had grown more intense and drew me farther away from my husband, the other anchor in our children's home. In fact, I had actually begun to imagine life without the man I had promised to love until my last breath.

And so, in one of the saddest and most awkward moments of my life, I told my friend that I could no longer see him. I ended a friendship with a person who had begun to matter very much to me. As I struggled to abandon my feelings for him and embrace the logic of closing the door, the days which followed were filled with a frightening revelation: somehow, unthinkingly, when half of marriages end in divorce, I had threatened our home with the most common reason: a lack of commitment. I had pursued a selfish desire to the point that I could no longer distinguish between right and wrong. I had been entrusted with a loyal husband and two remarkable children, yet I risked their well-being with every moment I spent in this other person's company.

After my decision, there was a wave of emptiness that continually washed through me as I moved through each day. I felt it when I lay awake next to my husband who snored peacefully at three in the morning. It came again at work when my mind drifted away from the pile of paperwork in front of me or the discussion at a meeting. It welled up once more as I sat on the front porch with the evening paper, and my two kids fought over the basketball in the driveway.

Gradually, though, that feeling has been replaced with a sense of relief that, despite my temporary insanity, my family is safe. But a thousand "I'm sorries" will never take away the sting of remorse I feel nearly every time I look in my husband's eyes and they smile back at me. While the passion we first had doesn't always seem as strong, passion is meaningless compared with the qualities he possesses. I hadn't a clue how much I would come to value his integrity, his work ethic or his devotion to our children. It wasn't until I was confronted with the fear of losing the world that he and I had created together, that I recognized the pricelessness of his friendship.

So tonight, on an unusually warm evening for this time of year, my husband has agreed to join me for a walk. As I study the sky from the window by my desk, I see that there must be a thousand stars tonight, all sparkling like fireflies.

~Sarah Benson
Chicken Soup for Every Mom's Soul

Low-Fat and Happy

When you're a kid, it's tough being different. By the time I was ten, I was taller than most kids and overweight. It was then that I began to hide my eating. I felt bad enough about my size, but when the others laughed at me, it only made me feel worse, and I turned to food for comfort.

For a time I tried slumping, so that I'd be closer to my friends' sizes, but my mother wouldn't allow it. Mom always said to me, "Be proud of your height. You've never seen a short model, have you?" That got my attention. To me, the word "model" stood for beauty, which certainly wasn't included in the vocabulary I would have used to describe myself.

One day, I was crying about how some of my friends got attention from boys that I didn't. Mom sat me down again. I remember the soft, comforting look in her beautiful baby-blue eyes as she told me the story of The Ugly Duckling—how the little bird's beauty was revealed when its time arrived. Mom told me that we all have our time on earth to shine. "This is their time," she said. "Your time will come when you become a woman." I listened to Mama's story over and over throughout my growing-up years, but my time never really seemed to come.

Grown and married, I started to have my babies. After the birth of each of my three sons, I always hung on to twenty pounds. When I got pregnant with my last son, I went into the pregnancy weighing

209. After that, for a period of eight years, I gave up on ever being a normal weight again. I was the first to crack jokes about my size, laughing with the others on the outside but crying intensely on the inside. I hid my eating binges from my family, hating myself for what I was doing, but unable to control myself.

At the age of thirty-four, I weighed 300 pounds. I was in pain twenty-four hours a day, with degenerative disc problems. My body felt stretched and crushed all at the same time. Stepping on the scales at 300 pounds was a turning point in my life. The scale registered that enormous number, but I felt like a zero. And I realized with startling clarity that if I didn't gain control of my life, I wouldn't be around much longer. I thought of my precious sons—I wouldn't be there to watch them grow up. I'd miss their first crushes, first heartaches, proms, driver's licenses, graduations, weddings—I'd never hold my grandbabies. At that moment, I knew I had two choices: live or die. Something inside me broke free and I heard myself screaming, "I'm going to live! I deserve to live, live, live!"

I screamed loud enough to awaken a new me. How I wanted to live that day! I had a drive inside I'd never felt before. I knew then that I was going to do everything in my power to win this battle. I wasn't going to give up on me ever again.

This powerful force inside me for life was a force of love as well. I felt a spark of love for myself—as I was—that had been gone for a long time. I decided, for the first time ever, that I was going to lose weight the healthy way. In the past, I had abused diets as much as I'd abused food. I had starved the weight off to the point of losing my hair and developing blurred vision.

This time, I would set small goals, so that when I reached them it would give me the confidence to continue. I learned to prepare and enjoy low-fat, healthy foods. I also developed a new way to talk to myself about food. When food "called out to me," instead of saying, Go ahead, girl, eat. Who's going to know?... the new Teresa was firm. No! I will not eat in private and guilty silence anymore. I will eat when I choose, not when food dictates. How wonderful it felt when I made it through another day without cheating.

Toughest of all, I had to concentrate on the positives in my life. I had always been so good at encouraging others; now I realized the person who needed me most was me. I made myself wear make-up because it made me feel prouder of myself. Some days that was just the little push I needed to get me through. As the weight came off and I got smaller, my confidence in myself grew and grew.

I remember the first time I went to the regular, not plus size, section of the local department store. I cried as I looked around at all the racks of clothes I knew I could wear. I grabbed twenty outfits and went to the dressing room. The attendant raised her eyebrows in surprise, saying, "All of these?"

I smiled broadly. "All of these," I answered proudly.

Zipping up a pair of jeans, I felt a wonderful sense of freedom. I'm going to make it, I thought.

In nine months, I lost 108 pounds, but then I hit a plateau. For years I had blamed my weight on a slow metabolism, and had always fought exercise like I fought losing weight. Now I knew I couldn't go any further without getting my body moving. I remember telling myself, Girl, you weren't blessed with a great metabolism, but you were blessed with two legs, so get out there and do something about that slow metabolism. So I did.

Parking my car near a wheat field by my home, I walked along the fence till I reached the end of the one-mile long field. If I wanted to get home, I had to get back to my car, so I had no choice but to walk the return mile. It was hard at first, but it got easier and easier as the weeks and months went by.

Within another eight months, I was at my target weight of 170 pounds. I had lost 130 pounds! At five feet, eleven inches, I am a size twelve. Best of all, I am alive not only in body but in spirit as well.

Now, my husband flirts with me, and our kids think we act weird because we're so happy together. Plus, I'm able to be the active mom with my sons the way I'd always dreamed. We fish, play ball or just hang out together, and amazingly, I have the energy to keep up.

Today, at age thirty-six, I'm blessed with a new career. Writing and publishing my low-fat cookbook has been one of the most exciting adventures I have ever been on. Because of the book and the motivational speaking I do to promote it, I've been given the opportunity to reach out to others who, like I once had, have all but given up hope of losing weight and gaining control of their lives.

For me, losing weight was about choosing life over and over and over again. I remember a day on one of my walks by the wheat field, when I reached over the fence and grabbed a stem of wheat to hold in my hand as I walked. I remembered from school that, to the ancient Greeks, wheat represented life. Whenever I felt like giving up that day, I looked at the wheat in my hand and it spurred me on to finish my two-mile hike.

I still have that piece of wheat. When I have a tough day, I look at it and it reminds me of a girl, and later a woman, who for years thought there was no hope, but through faith, courage and love, found her hope—and her life—again. It is, finally, my time to shine.

~Teresa Collins
A Second Chicken Soup for the Woman's Soul

55

Wild Waters Run Deep

If we wait for our hands to stop shaking, we will never open the door.
~Naomi Newman

No doubt about it, a fortieth birthday requires a spectacular celebration. So I did what I thought a self-respecting, bold woman who has learned that she is responsible for her happiness might do—I decided to make my own party and take it with me! That my celebration took place in a foreign country, where I was alone, surrounded by a group of strangers and involved a near-death experience that coincided with my birthday was grist for the mill.

I decided to go white-water rafting because it was something new and wild and adventurous that would push the fear envelope. As Eleanor Roosevelt said, "You must do the thing you think you cannot do." White-water rafting through class IV and class V rapids down the Rio Pacuare in the Costa Rican rain forest seemed like just the ticket! So, I packed my Spanish tape, water bottle, bathing suit, sandals and sunscreen, and set off for my "Fortieth Birthday White-Water Rafting Adventure of a Lifetime." Little did I know, wild waters run deep.

I should have taken it as a premonition when our bus made a pit stop along the road to the river where a vendor was selling "I survived Rio Pacuare" T-shirts. I bought one and put it on; people on the bus with me all laughed! Maybe I should have thought better of getting in a raft with a group of total strangers, most who had never rafted before, and going down a river with such potential danger. And, it probably is not the best thing to be with guides who speak limited English and give only cursory lessons in rafting, which mostly included telling us to hold on, a lot. And, maybe there is something to the proliferative liability laws that we have in the United States, at least as far as the safety protection they may offer toward the assumption of risk.

Well, you probably guessed it. Not too long into the experience, I was knocked out of the raft, went over a small waterfall into a whirlpool (they call it a "hydraulic"; I call it "hell") and got sucked to the bottom of the river in a swirling confusion of water. And that was just the beginning of the ride. Fortunately, I did have on a helmet and life jacket. I can't imagine what I would have done without them. Nevertheless, I did get quite an exfoliation from the numerous rocks I hit, not to mention all the water I swallowed.

While I was busy getting more than I bargained for, I had an epiphany about life. While being tossed about by those wonderful, wild waters and flopping in and out of submersion like a rag doll, my mind took me to another place. Somehow, I got my feet pointed downstream as you're supposed to. And, I did my best to keep my head above water as much as possible, which, actually, was nearly impossible. It was horrible trying to breathe and not being able to get enough air. But, I became incredibly calm, despite the sheer terror of the situation and the possibility that I might die.

I thought, Oh wow. I fell into the river in the middle of a rapid. Boy, this really hurts my lungs to try to breathe. Hmmm. Wow. Hey, I might die! I actually felt pretty neutral about the whole thing, living or dying, that is, and I had a strange sort of peacefulness and the ability to watch myself almost from the outside. Maybe all those Buddhist meditation exercises and books about "mindfulness" had paid off!

They tell me that the primary reason I survived that day is precisely because I did not fight the river, because I did not try to swim against the almighty power of rushing water, because I did, in a sense, surrender to the experience. I let the river take me where it would. I actually went through three whirlpools, and each time it got easier.

The drama that day was high magnitude. All the other rafters pulled over to the shore. People were crying and praying and most just looked on with terror at what was unfolding. There were several ropes across the river and three experienced kayakers went in for my rescue. It was quite a scene.

Later, the guides talked about how amazingly polite I was during my rescue. I don't remember that at all. Inside, I am pretty sure I felt like grabbing some guy by the shirt and growling, "Get me out of here, now!" But, in reality, they say that when a kayak came toward me, I simply held out my hand and arm and meekly said, "Could you please help me?" Please? I said that? I learned that often a rescuer is nearly drowned by someone who desperately wants out of the river.

I was dragged to shore and given medical attention and lots of people cheered and some pretty cute Costa Rican guys were all giving me high-fives. I enjoyed the moment and the attention I was getting, until they told me I had to get back in the raft and continue down the river. I really did not want to do that at all, but I found out I had no choice. Also, I could tell everyone's morale seemed to be hanging on my getting back in that raft and going on.

Not feeling very brave, I did go on. I got through the whole course of the river and lived to tell about it. I do have to admit to hunkering down in the middle of the raft a few times when I was supposed to be paddling, but I was scared, and that was the best I could do.

One thing I learned that day is that your best is all you can do and that is exactly what you should do—and your best is very often good enough. Sometimes you fall out of the raft and have to get back in and continue on down the river. And sometimes the best way to get through a difficulty is to just let it be! Don't fight it. Let it be difficult. Know that that is what is happening and that your reaction to it, is what it is. Surrender doesn't mean doing nothing, being passive. Or being perfect. On the contrary, it is a very active thing to let yourself have the experience and not try to control it.

Certainly, I will always remember how I survived that day and how I handled the challenge—who could forget? Even more important, I will carry with me always and be grateful for the lessons I learned from those "wild waters" about how to live my life.

~Benita Tobin
Chicken Soup to Inspire a Woman's Soul

56

Mercy's Time

S he was almost my mother-in-law. I was nineteen, and she was in her late fifties.

She welcomed my presence into her son's life and treated me like a daughter. Our mutual love for her son was our commonality and created a strong bond between us. Invited into their world, I shared meals and trips to the family cabin. A year and a depleted box of Kleenex later, we left her son at boot camp.

To fend off long winter nights, I visited her after work. We had warm talks of possibilities. She, a patient right-hander, taught me, a left-hander with dreams of marriage, to crochet a bedspread. I helped her pick out a puppy at the Humane Society; Doris named her Precious.

When the engagement was announced, she started my hope chest with gifts of a silverware chest and milk-glass butter dish. Though she often said she was a terrible cook, my first recipe of Mexican stew, which I still make, came from her.

Sadly, when I broke the engagement, I broke my friendship with Doris. Awkward and young, I didn't know how to say goodbye. So I didn't.

On occasion, in the twenty years since, she came to mind. As hard as I tried, I could not put her out of my head. I knew I would never forgive myself if something happened to her before I said I was sorry for my rude behavior.

On a Florida vacation as I read a novel filled with estrangements and reconciliations, she visited my thoughts again. Whether Doris chose to forgive me or not, it was time to apologize for the abrupt severing of our friendship. I had no idea where she lived, but I knew that her sister, Elsie, lived in town. Through the phone directory, I found Elsie's telephone number. It took me two weeks to muster the courage to call.

Elsie informed me that the years had been harsh to Doris. She had gone through a divorce, suffered through several seizures and then brain surgery, and was now in the final stages of emphysema. Elsie gave me Doris's address and said it would be fine if I wrote to her.

Now that I had permission, I was terrified. I had broken her son's heart and shattered a seemingly perfect dream of togetherness. Surely she must hate me. Certainly no good could come from a simple, handwritten apology.

A sleepless week went by. It was no use—until I put pen to paper, there would be no peace in my heart. Lord, give me the words to convey how sorry I am, was my quiet plea.

"Dear Doris," I wrote. "I know it's been many years since you and I last had contact." It took until page three to get to my reason for writing. "I know when I broke your son's heart, I broke part of yours," I continued. "Knowing you like I once did, you probably forgave me years ago, but what good is an apology that no one hears? I'm sorry for the pain and the way I ended it all," I wrote. I asked for forgiveness; if she found it in her heart to do so, I wanted to hear it.

Two weeks went by before her familiar curly handwriting appeared in my mailbox. The envelope was heavy. My fears resurfaced. I prepared for a severe lecture.

"You can't know what your letter has done for me," she wrote. "Came at the right time, too." Her letter was delightful. She gladly accepted my apology and forgave me, recalled some happy times and even asked for a recipe.

Her words lightened a burden I had carried for too long.

As I put the letter back in the envelope, a picture of Precious slipped out. On the back she had written, "Remember when you went with me to pick her out? She died last year. I miss her so." That dog, like the Mexican stew, was a part of our togetherness that had carried into Doris's life, too.

God's merciful timing taught me it's never too late to say you're sorry. Two months later her sister called to tell me Doris passed away. I'm grateful God knew I needed to say goodbye.

~Julie Saffrin
Chicken Soup for the Christian Woman's Soul

You Can Do Anything!

> *The only disability in life is a bad attitude.*
> ~Scott Hamilton

I was a twenty-year-old nursing student in 1968, preparing for a rotation through the pediatric unit. Compared to cardiac units or the operating room, how hard would this be? After all, I'd always cared for and played with children. This rotation would be a snap. I'd breeze right through it and be one step closer to graduation.

Chris was an eight-year-old bundle of energy who excelled in every sport he played. Disobeying his parents' instructions, he explored a neighbor's construction site, climbed a ladder and fell. His broken arm was casted too tightly, leading to infection, sepsis and gangrene. Sadly, his condition required amputation.

I was assigned as his postoperative nurse.

The first few days passed quickly. I provided Chris's physical care with forced cheerfulness. His parents stayed with him around the clock.

As his need for medication decreased, his level of awareness increased, as did his moodiness. When I saw how alert he seemed as he watched me bring in supplies for a sponge bath, I offered him the washcloth and suggested he take over. He washed his face and neck, then quit. I finished.

The next day, I announced he'd be in charge of his whole bath.

He balked. I insisted. He was more than halfway through when he slumped down and said, "I'm too tired."

"You won't be in the hospital much longer," I urged gently. "You need to learn to take care of yourself."

"Well, I can't," he scowled. "How can I do anything with just one hand?"

Putting on my brightest face, I groped for a silver lining. Finally I said, "Sure you can do it, Chris. At least you have your right hand."

He turned his face away and muttered, "I'm left-handed. At least I used to be." He glared at me. "Now what?"

Suddenly, I didn't feel so snappy. I felt phony and insincere, and not very helpful. How could I have taken right-handedness for granted? It seemed he and I both had a lot to learn.

The next morning, I greeted Chris with a big smile and a rubber band. He looked at me suspiciously. Wrapping the rubber band loosely around my wrist, I said, "You're left-handed and I'm right-handed. I am going to put my right hand behind my back and keep it there by winding the rubber band around my uniform buttons. Every time I ask you to do something with your right hand, I will do it first, with my left hand. And I promise not to practice before I see you. What should we try first?"

"I just woke up," he grumbled. "I need to brush my teeth."

I managed to screw the top off the toothpaste, then placed his toothbrush on the overbed table. Awkwardly, I tried to squirt toothpaste onto the wobbly toothbrush. The harder I struggled, the more interested he became. After almost ten minutes, and a lot of wasted toothpaste, I succeeded.

"I can do it faster than that!" Chris declared. And when he did, his triumphant grin was just as real as mine.

The next two weeks passed quickly. We tackled his daily activities with enthusiasm and a competitive spirit. We buttoned his shirts, buttered his bread and never really mastered tying his shoes. Despite our age difference, we were playing a game as equal competitors.

By the time my rotation ended, he was almost ready for discharge, and ready to face the world with more confidence. We hugged each other goodbye with sincere friendship and tears.

More than thirty years have passed since our time together. I've encountered some ups and downs in my life, but I've never let a physical challenge pass without thinking of Chris and wondering how he would cope. Sometimes I put a hand behind my back, hook my thumb in my belt and give it a try.

And anytime I feel sorry for myself, for some petty grievance or another, I take myself into the bathroom and try once again to brush my teeth with my left hand.

~Susan M. Goldberg
Chicken Soup for the Nurse's Soul

Beauty Contest

Beauty is not in the face; beauty is a light in the heart.
~Kahlil Gibran

A successful beauty product company asked the people in a large city to send brief letters about the most beautiful women they knew, along with the women's pictures. Within a few weeks, thousands of letters were delivered to the company.

One letter in particular caught the attention of the employees, and soon it was handed to the company president. The letter was written by a young boy, who wrote he was from a broken home, living in a run-down neighborhood. With spelling corrections, an excerpt from his letter read:

> *A beautiful woman lives down the street from me. I visit her every day. She makes me feel like the most important kid in the world. We play checkers and she listens to my problems. She understands me and when I leave, she always yells out the door that she's proud of me.*

The boy ended his letter by saying, *"This picture shows you that she is the most beautiful woman. I hope I have a wife as pretty as her."*

Intrigued by the letter, the president asked to see this woman's picture. His secretary handed him a photograph of a smiling, toothless woman, well-advanced in years, sitting in a wheelchair. Sparse gray hair was pulled back in a bun and wrinkles that formed deep furrows on her face were somehow diminished by the twinkle in her eyes.

"We can't use this woman," explained the president, smiling. "She would show the world that our products aren't necessary to be beautiful."

~Carla Muir
A Second Chicken Soup for the Woman's Soul

Woman to Woman

The Power of Support

The hearts that never lean, must fall.
~Emily Dickinson

59

The Miracle of My Sister's Laughing

Mirth is God's medicine. Everybody ought to bathe in it.
~Henry Ward Beecher

Some of the lowest days of my life came shortly after my husband's death. While still grieving, I came face to face with the reality of raising our four children alone. The funeral was over, friends and family gone. It was the kids and I, each of us grieving as our ages and personalities allowed. One son angry, the other quiet; one daughter demanding, the other mothering. And somehow I was supposed to deal with it all. I was supposed to give the sole direction, the lone understanding and single wise responses.

While at the bottom of this inadequacy well, my sister arrived. She'd planned it that way, saving her visit until everyone else had left. Within hours, the closeness we had shared in the past came flooding back. She let me talk and cry but also helped me begin doing things. We got my kids returned to school, and then started tackling projects. We started with my closet since its half emptiness constantly reminded me of my now-gone husband. We decided to install a closet organizer, so I could add my sweaters and other clothes to fill it up.

Things didn't go well. While she held one end, I'd try to install and hammer the other. Nothing fit. As we improvised, things got worse. Then in the midst of our frustration, I noticed the picture on the organizer's box. A two-dimensional woman smiled back from it while she single-handedly installed what my sister and I were failing to do. While still holding up my end, I said, "Hey Jeanne, look at that picture. I wish!"

She took one look at the woman and said, "Yeah, right. She's even wearing a dress." That's when it happened. Somehow the whole situation turned into a joke.

Every fumble we made, every board that slipped, every screw that refused to twist brought us back to the perfect lady on the box and made us laugh. We laughed until the tears came. We laughed until we had to drop the organizer and run for the bathroom.

It was the first time I'd laughed in weeks.

That laughter happened fifteen years ago, yet I remember it as if it happened yesterday. It changed nothing, yet it changed everything. My kids were still grieving. I was still hurting, overwhelmed and inadequate. But when I hugged my sister goodbye, I knew God had used her to give me a miracle. For in the hard months following her departure, on my worst days, I inevitably opened my closet and spotted my slightly tilting organizer. No matter how I felt, I just couldn't help smiling.

~Deborah Hedstrom-Page
Chicken Soup for the Sister's Soul

And When I Was in Prison, You Visited Me

I tried not to stare as several dozen female inmates entered the gym one by one, some in white, some in maroon jail suits. A gray-haired woman walked with a cane in small, steady steps. A blond with six inches of brown roots patted her very pregnant belly. Another smiled effusively, revealing only three or four teeth. One seemed so young—barely twenty. Her scrubbed-clean face and simple ponytail didn't hide her natural, model-like beauty.

They sat silently, despondently, in the last of four rows of semi-circled folding chairs. "Come on up," Tom coaxed as he walked down the aisle shaking hands with everyone. An Asian girl stared at the wall. A Hispanic woman rhythmically kicked the chair in front of her with her toe. "Here's a front row seat!" Tom beckoned. I watched his approach with them intently. I'd never visited a prison before—never dreamed I would. So why had I chosen ministering to women in prison as the charity for *Chicken Soup for the Christian Woman's Soul?*

I had a feeling I was about to find out.

"How many of you have read *Chicken Soup for the Prisoner's Soul?*" Tom beamed, and waved a copy of the book he had coauthored. A dozen women raised their hands. "What was your favorite story?" He pointed to the inmate with a three-inch tattoo on her wrist. *"Ivy's Cookies,"* she said with what seemed to be a rare smile.

I couldn't believe it. There were 101 stories in the book. How could she have chosen that one?

"It's one of my favorites, too," Tom said, nearly dancing with delight. "Why is it your favorite?"

"Because this teenage girl took cookies to prisoners like us and they wouldn't talk to her. They treated her all mean and ignored her, but she just kept bringing cookies every week. Then at the end of the story when Ivy is older, one of the prisoners' daughters brought cookies to her at her home. That was so cool." The young woman blushed.

"Well, we have a special surprise for you here today," Tom said. "The author of that very story, *Ivy's Cookies*, is here with us, and she's going to read that story to you!"

Some inmates smiled brightly at the news while two African Americans sat stoically.

It was Candy Abbott's first prison visit too, yet she stood in front of them and began reading her story with all her heart. She emphasized how Ivy Jones had questioned herself about why she kept coming to the prison week after week when the inmates clearly didn't appreciate or care about her. Then an evangelist came to the prison and ordered the inmates to make a circle and thank God for one thing. Candy went on to read about the lopsided, silent circle and how one prisoner finally said, "I want to thank Ivy for the cookies. Thank you, God, for Miss Ivy bringin' us cookies every week." Then one by one, the prisoners each thanked Ivy for her weekly visits.

Candy concluded the story and closed the book. "We have another surprise visitor for you today," she said proudly. "Ivy is here!"

Many inmates gasped and most clapped as Ivy walked from the second row to the front of the room. "We've never done this together before," Candy explained.

Ivy reminded me of the evangelist in the story as she addressed them. "I didn't know what I was doing when I was that teenager visiting the prison. I was scared, but I prayed to God to show me what to do and He did. And He'll show you what to do too. Just ask Him!"

she proclaimed. "If you need strength, ask Him for strength. If you need hope, ask Him for hope. He'll give you what you need just like He did me."

"Amen!" someone shouted.

"God disciplines those He loves." Ivy looked into each of their eyes and added softy, "And He must love you very much."

The model look-alike's face reddened. She fanned her hand in front of her face as if to wave the tears away.

Ivy completed her brief sermon to the applause of the inmates, and then Tom came forward again. "There is a new Chicken Soup book called *Chicken Soup for the Christian Woman's Soul*, and part of the money from the sales of that book will go into a special fund to buy copies of it and *Chicken Soup for the Prisoner's Soul* to give to incarcerated women. We plan to send some to you after the first of the year." A few inmates clapped; many whispered with excitement; some sat motionless, expressionless. "We have a final surprise for you today—the coauthor of *Chicken Soup for the Woman's Soul*, LeAnn Thieman." Most of the women clapped with enthusiasm, but a few sat scowling with their arms folded across their chests.

Until that moment, I hadn't a clue what I was going to say. I'd trusted God would answer my prayer and give me the words. "It seems we have a theme here today," I began. "Apparently God uses baked goods to help do His work on Earth." Some chuckled. Most smiled, except for those with the folded arms. "Twenty-five years ago I bought a dozen cupcakes at a bake sale to help support the orphans in Vietnam. That's all I ever intended to do for them, but God had a bigger plan. He just used those cupcakes to trick me into helping Him!" In one long deep breath I rattled off my story of how I joined the organization to help support the orphans, how my basement became the state chapter headquarters, how we had decided to adopt a son from Vietnam, how I agreed to go bring six babies back to their adoptive homes, and how, when I got there, I helped bring out three hundred as a part of Operation Babylift. The room broke into applause. When I told them the part about a baby boy crawling into my arms and heart and family, a collective sigh filled the gym. "I was not and still am not anybody special," I explained. "I was raised a poor Iowa farm girl with seven brothers and sisters and I wore hand-me-down clothes. I'm living proof that God uses ordinary women to do extraordinary things."

Tom stood behind the group and stared me right in the eyes. "Why did you pick a women's prison ministry for the charity of this book?"

I looked at the old woman with the cane, at the pregnant woman rubbing her belly, at the tattooed woman and at the one with few teeth. I breathed past the lump in my throat. "Because a lot of good is in this room." A tear escaped the model's eyes. The black women unfolded their arms. The Asian woman looked me in the face. I continued. "I know something very bad happened to put you here, but I know you have a lot of good in you."

"Amen," the voice came again.

Tom hugged me long and hard as I headed for my seat. Then he introduced his wife, Laura, a frequent companion on his prison visits and coauthor of the *Chicken Soup for the Volunteer's Soul* book. "Everybody has a story to tell," she said warmly. "And yours isn't over yet—you can still choose the ending." Many heads nodded in unison.

Tom lightened the mood. "Just like in *Ivy's Cookies*, let's all circle up," he cheered. To my amazement, the women followed him to the side of the gym and formed a circle, holding hands. "Now let's say one thing we are thankful for," Tom urged. "I'll start. I want to thank God for letting me be here with you today."

A woman with long graying hair spoke first. "I'm thankful for the people keeping my children strong while I'm in here."

"I want to thank Ivy for coming today—and next time, will you bring us cookies?"

"I want to thank Tom and Laura and Candy for coming here today when I'm sure they got better things to do."

"I want to thank LeAnn for donating money from that book so we can get a copy someday. Those stories give me hope."

The model spoke. "I want to thank God for sending me to prison. If He didn't love me enough to send me here, I'd be dead."

"Amen."

"Everyone take one step forward," Tom instructed and we inched ahead. "Now another step forward," he said with a giggle. "And another." We jammed in closer together. "Now that's a big Texas hug!"

There I stood with my arms wrapped around forty women prisoners, all smiling, all hugging. Indeed, a lot of good is in this room.

~LeAnn Thieman
Chicken Soup for the Christian Soul 2

61

It Takes One to Help One

You just give folks a key, and they can open their own locks.
~Robert R. McCammon

I've been a single mother for nearly seven years and have a terrific twelve-year-old son, Connor. Divorce forced me back into the working world, a world I had left far behind with the birth of my first and only child. I had always intended to go back to work at some point, but had also thought the choice would be mine as to when that point would be. Angry, disappointed and unable to return to my former high-paying graphics position because of the technology jump during my "hiatus," I realized I would have to start over at the age of thirty-six. I had attended college off and on over the years, but never finished my degree, now much to my dismay. I had never thought I'd need a college degree to raise happy, beautiful children, or to cook sumptuous meals for my husband and friends, or to attend every "Mommy & Me" class I could find, in search of other lucky mothers like myself to befriend.

Well, all that came to a screeching halt as my son entered elementary school and my rocky marriage gave way to an avalanche of accusations and arguments, finally ending in divorce. I knew it was for the best, but it still hurt. We would remain friends and raise our son together, both of which have miraculously happened with much more ease than trying to stay together "for the sake of the child." I often wondered if getting a divorce made me a "quitter," but have since decided it definitely did not. I can honestly say I tried my very best to make that marriage work—it just didn't.

When I put on work clothes for the first time in years, I also realized I would have to put on a façade, too—a façade that I was a capable, hardworking, enthusiastic woman who just couldn't wait to come to work every day, leaving my little boy to ride that big bus to school every morning for forty-five minutes, then be cared for by others until I could pick him up after a long workday. Gone would be the lazy afternoons of playing Candy Land, watching cartoons or building Lego airplanes, while he munched carefully carved apple slices and homemade cookies.

Through a friend, I heard about a secretarial position in the hospital where she worked. It was entry-level and the pay was less than half the salary I was making when I left the workforce. My shock gave way to dismay when I was told there were many applicants for the position, mostly from within the hospital itself. Still, I faxed over my freshly redone résumé (briefly dreading the six-year lapse in employment) and was scheduled for an interview with Robin, who would be my boss if I could somehow manage to make her see that this soon-to-retire "domestic goddess" was just what she needed! Not an easy task for a woman who hadn't spoken in complete sentences for years.

Since my wardrobe at that time consisted mainly of jeans and more jeans, I borrowed a suit from my sister and nervously drove to the interview. Taking a deep breath, I walked into the office, an office of women, two to be exact, both well dressed and obviously younger than me. My hopes sank as I faced a consummate career woman who surely wouldn't understand why I hadn't worked in many years, not to mention the fact that as her assistant I would be several years her senior.

However, I liked her immediately—she was warm and obviously very intelligent. She asked me all the right questions, taking note of my lack of certain computer skills, yet kindly saying, should I be hired, there were in-house courses offered that would bring me up to speed quickly. Then she dropped the bomb. She asked if I had any children. At the time, I did not know that this question is a big "no-no" on an employer's part. (Even so, I would have answered honestly, anyway.) But I thought that surely this would end my chances of getting this position—I had seen her type before (heck, I'd been one), and I figured she'd have no interest in hiring a soon-to-be-divorced mom when she could have her pick of qualified candidates already working for the hospital. My heart sank, but I told her proudly about my wonderful son and the fact that I was returning to work a "little earlier than planned," so that I could take care of him on my own.

I sat across from Robin, in front of her big mahogany desk, while she studied me briefly, certain she was trying to find a nice way to say, "Thanks, but no thanks." Instead, she reached for a large framed photo on her desk and turned it around for me to see. There, smiling from the picture were a brother and sister, both younger than my son, who looked exactly like their mother. My eyes quickly looked to her left hand—it was ringless. I looked around the desk for other photos of the family—there were none. Robin smiled at me and said, "When can you start?"

That was the beginning of my life as a working single parent, and I will always be grateful to the other working single parent who gave me a chance when she clearly might have had a better choice, at least based on what she read on a résumé. I will never forget her, and when she left to pursue other career opportunities, I cried and thanked her again. Sometimes, it takes one to help one.

~Laurie Hartman
Chicken Soup for the Single Parent's Soul

62

The Friend Who Listened

If you're alone, I'll be your shadow.
If you want to cry, I'll be your shoulder.
If you want a hug, I'll be your pillow.
If you need to be happy, I'll be your smile.
But anytime you need a friend, I'll just be me.
~Author Unknown

I placed the peony on June's grave. Looking at her name on the stone brought back memories of the special lilt in her voice.

"Joan, this is June. How about meeting me for lunch today?" I hadn't been interested in leaving the house for some time and started to give her my list of rehearsed excuses. But I liked June, even though I didn't know her well, and I was touched that she'd called with the invitation. We made arrangements to meet.

As I put down the receiver, I felt panic. What had I done? Small talk held no appeal, and I certainly didn't feel like eating. Then I remembered what my ten-year-old son said the evening before, "Mom, you don't smile anymore."

"That's silly," I told him, "of course I do." I gave him a large toothy grin. Then I went into the bathroom and looked in the mirror. I smiled at that face, but my mouth felt stretched and strange. I locked the door and sat on the edge of the bathtub and let the tears have their way.

Bill, our oldest son, had been killed in an accident six months before, and I thought I had been presenting a healed person to my family. I was a fake.

I brought armloads of books home from the library, looking for a word or sentence that might help explain or comfort. The faith that had been a part of me no longer held answers. I realized my beliefs seemed childlike. Although our minister, family, neighbors and friends had been there for my husband and me, the emptiness and longing for an end to the pain continued. I realized that perhaps June's telephone call would herald a new beginning. It was probably what I needed — to get away and just visit for a while.

But while June and I sat at the table in the restaurant waiting for our order, it was obvious that chatting was not what she had in mind. "I've been wanting to talk to you," she started, "to see if you are all right and to let you know I'm hurting right along with you. You see, years ago my son died." I asked her questions about his death, wanting to hear her feelings and reactions, how she coped. Talking about that time in her life, reliving it, she cried — and I cried with her. She placed her hand on mine, "It was a long time ago, but I can feel it as though it were yesterday."

I don't remember if I ate my lunch that day but I do remember sitting there, finally pouring out my despair; and she listened. It was the first time anyone had allowed me to do this. I had wanted so much to talk about Bill, but whenever those with me heard me say his name or saw tears in my eyes, they were uncomfortable. It seemed a signal to leave or to immediately change the subject to some lighthearted topic. Now, at last, I could get rid of some of the feelings and questions I'd not been able to come to terms with. I told her how I missed my son, his presence in my life, his smile, his voice. I told her I wondered if I would ever have any enthusiasm for the things I needed to do, and about my constant concern for the safety of my two other sons. I told her how differently my husband and I were dealing with his death and about my struggle with God and the thought that, perhaps, I had somehow failed and not been a good mother. She confided she had worked through some of the same questions. We talked and talked and hugged, and I went home.

I realized I felt a sense of relief I could not explain, a relief I had been searching for. Perhaps, I thought, God speaks to us through our friends.

Our friendship deepened and we planned outings that included our husbands. We had pleasant times in each others' homes, eating out or sharing activities. June had a lively sense of fun and a wonderful laugh, but that was only one part of her. The woman I knew and loved was the questioning June, pondering on something she'd read or giving the details of a concern—even if tears and hurt were involved.

We enjoyed this comfortable relationship for many years and always, when I answered the phone and heard, "Joan, this is June," I felt pleasure. During one Christmas season, I told her I had read that the greatest gifts were not ones we buy. We discussed the gift we would give each other, that of complete acceptance.

One fall day she asked if I could drop over. When I got there she seemed upset. "Something just isn't right," she explained, "I don't feel like myself lately." We talked about getting older, about our needs. But when I got up to leave, I could see her face reflected a worry we had not been able to touch upon or identify. She gained no peace of mind from our conversation. I left feeling inadequate, as though I'd somehow failed her.

Before the end of the year, she was diagnosed as having a brain tumor. On New Year's Eve after her surgery, my husband and I visited June in the hospital. Seeing her that night, with memories of the New Year's Eve we spent together the year before, was an agony. The surgery was not successful. She went through treatment and therapy but made little progress. Her condition worsened, and she was confined to a wheelchair, unable to return home. I visited almost daily, stopping in for a few minutes. I watched her month after month, praying for her recovery and, if that wasn't to be, praying for the peace of mind she sought.

I'd promised to accept her that Christmas, just as she was, and I found it very difficult to keep my promise. I had to face the realization that I would never be able to give her the wonderful relief, the help, she had given me when I needed it.

June died that August. I realize now, many years later as I stand looking at her grave, that I still grieve. My wonderful friend, June. She taught me what a friend really is: one who listens.

~Joan Downey
Chicken Soup to Inspire a Woman's Soul

63

A Gift of Grace

As the nurse had instructed, I walked up and down the halls of Mercy Hospital over and over again. I was seventeen—and pregnant. This was the last place I ever imagined myself. I had planned to become an interior designer and move to New York. Not anymore, I thought glumly. As I walked past room after room filled with husbands and wives, giggles and encouragement, I was only reminded of how alone I was.

I couldn't help but notice the bright bouquets in so many of the rooms. One woman had at least fifty pink roses on her nightstand. The florist deliveryman seemed to live on this floor of the hospital. Every time he arrived, I said a little prayer, hoping he'd walk into my room in the back corner, but he never did.

I got pregnant the summer before I was to leave for college. My boyfriend, three years my senior, was leaving for medical school at the same time. He left on schedule in the fall, and I never heard from him again. My parents were almost as unsupportive. They begged me to "consider all the options." But even in my pain, I knew that having my baby was the right decision. They were infuriated and gave me money to have the baby in another state, "so you won't be embarrassed."

I moved in with my grandparents. They were well up in age and weren't able to go to the hospital with me. So, on that rainy day when the contractions began, I drove there by myself.

I had never felt so lonely. I wanted desperately to have my hand held by someone who wasn't trying to prick my finger or take my temperature. As I continued to walk, I passed a room so filled with people, it looked like they were having a party, not a baby. I stuck my head in to see what all the commotion was about and heard a pleasant voice come from the bed.

"Hi! It looks like you're getting ready to have one of these!" The new mother was holding a beautiful baby in a white gown and a pink cap.

"Let's hope so," I said, trying to sound cheerful. I was mesmerized by the tiny baby she held with such confidence and pride.

"My name is Laura. Would you like to hold her?"

I was so touched by the woman's kindness, all I could do was nod yes. Getting to her was the hard part. Laura had more balloons and flowers in her room than I had seen all day. She had beautiful orchids and lilies, too. The whole room was so inviting partly because of the flowers' gentle scent.

As I held the precious infant in my arms, she cooed and strained to open her eyes.

"Are you having a boy or a girl?" Laura asked.

"I don't know yet. I'm crossing my fingers I'll find out tonight." I delicately handed her back her gorgeous child, praying mine would be as healthy and alert.

"Well, good luck. You're going to be a great mom."

In my nine months of pregnancy, no one had ever said that. It was the nicest thing I had ever heard.

Hours later, I lay in my own hospital bed, alone, waiting to deliver a child whom I could offer only love. I was beyond scared. As tears fell down my face, I heard a knock at my door. A nurse came in and sat down next to my bed.

"I have a surprise for you, Amanda."

For a passing second, I thought my parents would stroll in, but instead, another nurse walked in with a bouquet of flowers. It was the most beautiful arrangement I had ever seen. It was filled with daisies and lilies and baby's breath and even roses! I was so excited

I could hardly keep from jumping out of bed. When I thought it couldn't get any better, another nurse came in, her arms full of more flowers and balloons. Nurse after nurse came in until the room was completely filled with every flower imaginable. I felt like I was in a florist shop!

I was in shock. Who would have gone to so much trouble to send me such thoughtful gifts? I hurriedly looked at the cards and found that they all said the same thing, written in the same handwriting: "You are loved and created with a special purpose. For love."

I had no idea who they were from, but suddenly I did feel loved—and ready to bear and love a baby of my own. That night I gave birth to a beautiful baby girl. I named her Grace. A few days later, I walked around the hospital, as proud as only a new mother can be. I stopped by Laura's room to visit and saw that all her flowers were gone.

"What happened to all your flowers?" I asked.

She smiled and said, "You are loved and created with a special purpose. For love."

I fought back the tears, as I realized who had sent my flowers. Only God could have put me in the hospital at the same time as such an angel. Laura told me she had given birth alone years earlier. She said she could sense I was hurting when I passed by her room, so she gave me her flowers to lift my spirits. Little did she know how much her gift had meant: It had given me the strength to deliver my beautiful Grace.

Laura has been my best friend for almost ten years now. To celebrate our friendship, every year on our daughters' birthdays, we send each other flowers. And every year I thank God again, for his grace—and for mine.

~Amanda Dodson
Chicken Soup for the Gardener's Soul

64

A Friend, Indeed

A true friend reaches for your hand and touches your heart.
~Author Unknown

It was three in the morning. Rolling over in bed, I reached for the ringing telephone. Instinctively, I knew who it was — who else would be calling at this hour? I had been expecting this call but why did it have to come when I was alone? My husband had just left for the East Coast on business eight hours earlier. How would I get in touch with him? I picked up the telephone and heard my mother's voice gently come through the receiver: "Honey, Dad's gone." As if she could read my mind, she quickly assured me that he had not been alone and he had died peacefully.

I assured my mother I would leave for home first thing in the morning but I had to go to work first and reschedule my patients. I hung up the telephone and pulled the covers up. I would let my daughters sleep while I started gathering our things together for the twelve-hour trip home.

I had not turned on the bedside lamp. The house was quiet and dark. I lay in bed thinking about my father's seven-year battle with cancer and what he had taught me. He had said, "When the treatment becomes worse than the disease, it is time to rethink your plan of action." Only one week earlier, I had been at his bedside. I found myself wanting to ensure that those caring for him understood that he was not an old man, but one about to celebrate his fifty-eighth birthday. As a birthday gift, I placed a picture of my father, taken a year earlier, in a frame that had the poem "Footprints" on it. I remember thinking, This picture looks like a fifty-seven-year-old man. I looked at the poem. How could I trust God to carry my father if I would not release him to God's care?

The telephone call had been no surprise. I had been holding on to my father and was finally able to entrust him to God, the true healer. Lying in my bed, I silently prayed for any sign to let me know Dad was okay. Seeking reassurance, I drifted off. I was back in my childhood house. My bedroom window was open, allowing the night breeze to blow across my room. I snuggled up under my quilts. I felt warm and safe. I could see my father standing at the foot of my bed. He was checking to see if I was all right before going to bed himself.

As I awoke, I felt a peace flow over me and knew my father was all right. I realized he would always be looking over me. I turned on the lamp and started gathering my things. Dawn came, and I sat down with my daughters. I shared the news of their grandfather's death, trying to ensure that they felt my strength and love enveloping them. I called my friend Carolyne, a fellow visiting nurse, trying to give her a heads-up that I was preparing to go out of town and would be at work to make the appropriate arrangements. Carolyne and I had become good friends as a result of all we did together: working, attending college classes and going to church. Few words were needed for me to inform her of my plan to drive home.

When I reached the office, I realized my coworkers were all aware of my situation and my patients were already reassigned to other nurses. Carolyne proceeded to tell me she had a bag packed and would be driving with me to Washington. Her mother had arranged a return flight for the following day and our supervisor had given her the time off. I was overwhelmed by this generous offer, but I could not ask her to do this. In addition, I knew I would be going straight to my parents' house, which would be filled with family. Where would Carolyne stay? Carolyne told me to call my mother. I made the call so I could graciously say "no thank you" to Carolyne's kind offer. As

I spoke to my mother, she breathed a sigh of relief, knowing I would not be alone on the icy roads.

My daughters, Carolyne and I drove straight through to my parents' house. My friend listened as my daughters and I told stories celebrating my father's life. The twelve-hour trip over the mountains went safely and quickly. The healing had begun.

Upon our arrival, my mother's gratitude for our safe arrival was evident. Carolyne was welcomed and thanked profusely. The house was filling up, and Carolyne and I wound up sharing my parents' bed. As we ended our day in prayer and closed our eyes, Carolyne sensed I needed my husband and reassured me that he would be joining me shortly. I smiled to myself knowing this special friend had been sent to carry me when I most needed support.

In the morning, I drove my friend to the airport. She refused my multiple offers to reimburse the cost of her airfare. Instead, she asked me to accept this gift of friendship.

As I drove back to my parents' house, I felt overwhelmed by the goodness of this woman. She had given me a gift that my family and I would never forget.

It has been ten years since my father passed away, and he continues to look over me. Carolyne has become my best friend. We continue to share our love of God, family and nursing. She knows me as few people do, and a special connection and trust exists between us. People often ask if we are sisters. Maybe we are, because there is no doubt in my mind that she is family and my sister in Christ.

~Vivia M. Peterson
Chicken Soup for the Girlfriend's Soul

65

A Pocketful of Love

Dogs are miracles with paws.
~Attributed to Susan Ariel Rainbow Kennedy

DebbieLynn never set out to be a fashion model, it just kind of happened. Although she had other interests she wanted to pursue, it was hard to walk away from the success she'd achieved modeling. The exciting lifestyle meant Deb traveled constantly, which left little time for other interests. She'd thought about taking the gamble, quitting and trying something new, but told herself she'd model just one more year. For more years than she could count, it had been, "Just one more year."

Everything changed the day Deb returned from an overseas modeling job and caught a taxi at the airport. Instead of delivering her home, the drunken cabbie stole her career and health in a horrible car accident that Deb barely survived. Suddenly, the "one more year" of modeling wasn't an option. Deb was left with a kaleidoscope of disabling health problems, some caused by side effects of the drugs meant to keep her alive. She had no choice—this time, Deb had to start over, from scratch.

Although she'd had dogs as a child and had wanted a dog for a long time, her travel schedule kept her from adopting a pet for many years. Finding the perfect canine companion was now the first thing on Deb's wish list. Not just any dog would do, though. The scleroderma racking her body left her skin so fragile, a tiny bump could tear it and cause bleeding. On top of that, secondary hemophilia kept cuts from coagulating, and Deb could die if the bleeding wasn't stopped in time. Doctors who feared a large dog could accidentally hurt her warned Deb that two and a half pounds was the top weight limit she could tolerate. With her lung capacity so severely diminished, shedding was also a problem.

Nevertheless, Deb was determined to have her dream dog. It took her eighteen months to find the perfect two-pound Yorkshire terrier, whom she named Cosette. Her puppy had special needs of her own—because of her tiny size, Cosette couldn't digest commercial dog foods and required a special vegetarian diet. Deb was happy to do whatever it took to keep her new companion healthy and happy.

They'd been together only a few weeks, and Cosette was only five months old when the pocket-size puppy began "acting weird." Cosette ran up to Deb, gently pawed her leg in an odd way, and squeaked a peculiar sound Deb had never heard before. The dog wouldn't stop—she repeated the behavior time and again. What was wrong? Deb worried the pup had gone nuts. Didn't Deb already have enough to deal with—what if the pup she'd fallen in love with had emotional problems? Deb knew she could manage the homemade diet, but could she handle something worse?

It never occurred to Deb that Cosette was trying to tell her something, until the doctor saw them together. During a house call, Deb's doctor witnessed one of Cosette's strange episodes. Other patients of his had dogs who alerted them to health conditions, so he immediately recognized that the puppy somehow "knew" in advance Deb would suffer a health crisis. Sure enough, seven minutes later one of Deb's dangerous migraines began.

Deb was amazed! She had heard about this ability and knew dogs couldn't be trained to have it; they either "know" or they don't, and it's the bond between the pet and person that makes it happen. She'd never considered having a service animal, but Cosette had taken matters into her own paws. The pup's ability offered a freedom Deb never expected, and allowed her to take medicine and prevent the headaches that not only were painful, but also could cause bleeding and kill her.

The doctor told Deb that her puppy should get additional training and certification so Cosette could go with her everywhere. The Delta Society, a national group that certifies therapy dogs, recommended a trainer. It took only four months for the little dog, with her inborn service-dog instincts, to be certified.

Deb had also suffered hearing loss from the accident, making it difficult for her to hear buzzer-type sounds like the doorbell, the telephone, and the washer and dryer, so Cosette learned to alert her to any of these. She also was taught to tell Deb when something or someone approached from her peripheral blind spots.

But Cosette figured out ways to help Deb that not even the trainer anticipated. Cosette's acute sense of smell allows her to alert Deb to tiny cuts that Deb doesn't even know have happened. First, she pushes and pushes against Deb's ankles to make her get down to the dog's level. Then Cosette puts her tongue against the cut, finds a position that gives her good traction, then applies pressure. Deb says that the tiny dog can make herself feel like a lead weight. A treatment lasts for twenty to forty minutes—or until the bleeding stops, and somehow, Cosette knows when it has been long enough. Without Cosette's skillful attentions, Deb would need to spend all day at the emergency room.

Another serious health problem Deb faces are her heart irregularities. She's often not aware that her breathing has become shallower until she blacks out. Now when Deb's heart skips a beat, Cosette warns her so she can take medicine in time to ward off the problem. When Deb sleeps, sometimes her heart stops altogether, until Cosette leaps into action—literally, by jumping on Deb's chest. That almost always gets the heart going again, but if it doesn't start right away, Cosette even knows to dial 911!

Cosette was trained to dial 911 on any push-button telephone by tapping out the individual three numbers, so she can call for help anywhere, anytime, even from a cell phone when they're away from home. Deb leaves phones in their home always within paw-reach.

Cosette has called 911 and saved Deb's life more than thirty times during their years together.

The little dog who saves her life also helps Deb make a living. Cosette inspired Deb to create three Web sites that cater to pet lovers. Cosette's Private Collection is a line of all-natural, botanical grooming products for dogs. Cosette's Choice includes organic biscuits, nutritional supplements for dogs with special nutritional needs (like Cosette herself), and includes a Biscuit-of-the-Month Club. The third, Cosette's Closet, leverages Deb's experience and taste from the world of fashion modeling to provide a specialty line of canine clothing, including doggy bridesmaid gowns, sundresses and tuxedos. Cosette, of course, has her own closetful of designer doggy togs.

Cosette wears her special outfits when she accompanies Deb to restaurants. On her last birthday, Cosette enjoyed eating rice and beans at her favorite Mexican dining spot and greeting the restaurant manager, a member of her "fan club," who insisted on singing "Happy Birthday" to the special dog.

Her biggest fan, though, is DebbieLynn. The former model—now successful entrepreneur—never knew she could become so attached to a dog, yet her tiny companion and service dog has become everything to her. And Deb knows the feeling is mutual; she is amazed at the depth of Cosette's love for her. Today they live for each other.

~Amy D. Shojai
Chicken Soup for the Dog Lover's Soul

66

The Purpose of My Soul

The view of tree-lined, snowcapped mountains, with Mt. Lassen towering above all, was majestic. Our campground, filled with tiny four-person cabins nestled near a mountain stream, added to the tranquil autumn atmosphere. Forty-seven women and eight men had assembled at this church youth camp for a five-day workshop called Empowering the Authentic Self.

The attendees, from affiliate churches throughout California and Nevada, seemed relaxed and friendly. Everyone was eager to begin their search for "the purpose of their soul," for their true mission in life and for the tools to carry out that mission. Our spiritual leader, Reverend David, and his wife, Carolyn, traveled from Oklahoma City to guide our journey.

We began each day with an early morning meditation in a warm, fire-lit room adjacent to our meeting hall. This special sanctuary was reserved for quiet time and reflection. The fire, tended by our camp hosts, would remain lit during our entire visit, signifying an eternal flame of peace and spiritual healing. It wasn't unusual to find an individual sitting by the fire at two or three in the morning, meditating in search of God's plan for them. The workshop was a time to explore unanswered questions and new possibilities in a place of worship and peacefulness.

At the beginning of every workshop session, we spent time sharing dreams, expectations, disappointments and lessons learned from the previous day's activities. For some, standing in front of total strangers and divulging personal stories was painfully difficult and often tearful. In fact, many participants weren't able to do this, and they were never made to feel that they had to share an experience with the group. Their presence alone helped create a safe haven where sharing was welcome and accepted without judgment.

We often, in groups of three or four, shared intimate details of our lives. For twelve to fourteen hours a day, we dug into our pasts and struggled to find a connection between our adult selves and our inner child. Every night we were asked to describe in our daily journals what we had experienced in the day's workshop.

The second evening of the workshop, during a group session focusing on traumatic events that had affected our lives, Jan spoke for the first time. She was quite shy and had trouble beginning her story, but with Reverend David's compassionate encouragement she began. Emotionally distraught and tearful, Jan told us about how she had recently attended a class reunion. Many years had passed since her graduation and this was her first reunion. Coincidentally, she was now a teacher and loved her work with children, though she often wondered if she was truly inspiring them.

Jan was approaching middle age and her body had changed. As her weight increased, her self-esteem decreased. Nevertheless, before the reunion, she decided to do her best to lose some weight, have her hair styled and her nails manicured, and buy a new dress. When the big day arrived, Jan was excited. She had transformed herself and felt beautiful. Her enthusiasm carried her right into the reunion where she mixed with the crowd.

As the night progressed, the band started playing wonderful music. The songs brought back many glorious memories of Jan's childhood, and she remembered how she loved to dance. She found a seat near the dance floor to be available when another single partner asked her to dance. Too shy to ask anyone herself, she sat alone, silently listening to the music. Her soul danced every dance, but as the night wore on and no one asked her to dance, sadness overwhelmed her. Devastated and feeling rejected, Jan went home, her spirit broken. She wasn't pretty enough, petite enough or charming enough to be asked to dance.

The room was silent as Jan finished her story. Our hearts were wounded, too. We wept with her, gave her comfort and held her hands.

The next morning, as we assembled for our early session, the room was unusually dark. As we took our seats, Reverend David's first request was that we hold hands and pray together. He prayed that our lessons would bring God's word to us abundantly and open our hearts to his offerings. We sat in prayerful silence, then we heard the song—"I Hope You Dance," by Lee Ann Womack—softly begin to echo through the room. Reginald, a male singer from the group, stood up and walked across the room toward Jan. As he approached her, he gently held his outstretched hand for hers. "May I have this dance?" he asked.

They danced gracefully around the room, holding each other closely as Jan cried. I stood, made my way to the dance floor and asked Reginald for Jan's hand. As we began dancing, all the males in the room gathered and waited in line to dance with Jan, too. Reverend David was the last to dance with her. When the music stopped, the men all gathered around Jan. We hugged her and escorted her back to her seat.

Reverend David, fighting back emotion, said he hadn't planned on bringing that CD to the workshop. While driving to the camp, however, he had stopped at a music store, saw the CD and sensed he was supposed to buy it. He didn't know why. When Jan told her story the day before, he knew why. It had been God's plan that he purchase the music and be a "messenger."

Jan changed that day. She talked a few more times before we completed our five-day workshop, and on the last day she told us how the dance had healed her heart and made her feel accepted. Before she left for home she said, "Now I will inspire students—and teach them not to be judgmental or form opinions based on appearance."

Jan had found the purpose of her soul.

~Duane Shaw
Chicken Soup for the Christian Woman's Soul

67

Angel to the Bone

You give but little when you give of your possessions.
It is when you give of yourself that you truly give.
~*Kahlil Gibran*, The Prophet

When I met Cindy, she seemed like any one of us women dropping our children off at school: thirty-something, a wife and a mother of two with a minivan, a dog, a house in the suburbs—a middle class woman living a middle class life. But things aren't always the way they seem.

Shortly after I met Cindy I found out she had leukemia. Her appearance gave no hint, nor did her attitude reflect it. If it weren't for the fact that she was listed with the National Bone Marrow Registry, I wouldn't have believed it.

While days for the rest of us passed with relative normalcy—kids with stuffy noses, trips to the vet, grocery and dry cleaners—Cindy continued with business as usual too—except that her young life was slipping away as each day passed without word of a donor match. She went to the market, drove carpool, baked cookies for her younger daughter's preschool and cheered as she watched her seven-year-old daughter perform gymnastics. She even went on daily, one-hour power walks with her friends, met us gals for the occasional lunch and managed to laugh during our many silly get-togethers. When I think back on it now, I marvel at her strength. Cindy set an example for all of us.

The only time I can remember her broaching the subject of her illness is when one of her young daughters asked Cindy if she was really dying, or whether it was just a bad dream.

Those were the hardest days, when she thought about her children. She was a mother and wife first, and a cancer patient a distant second.

Overcoming the odds was Cindy's specialty: one match out of 20,000 possible donors was located in a few months. The donor had passed the initial screening and follow-up tests; all systems were go. Cindy's husband could breathe again, her children had fewer nightmares and her family and friends rejoiced.

But this was real life, not a medical television drama.

After seven months of indecision, the donor backed out. It was as simple and as devastating as that. (The names of all donors are confidential until a year after the transplant.)

The agonizing awareness of the odds in finding another matching donor was almost too much to bear. As much as Cindy tried to hide it, the strain was beginning to show in her beautiful eyes. Her laugh, when it came, was no longer as easy or as deep. Days now seemed like weeks, and we all knew that time was the enemy, and the enemy was closing in.

Lightning rarely strikes twice in the same spot, but in Woodland Hills, California, one winter afternoon, a second miracle appeared in the form of a telephone call. Another donor had been found. And because of what had happened the first time, the registry had waited to make sure this donor was committed.

Most angels are easily identifiable, given away by their gossamer wings and opaque halos. But sometimes they live here on Earth—even disguised as a twenty-eight-year-old married mother of a two-year-old daughter from New Hampshire. Although Cindy didn't know anything about her donor—her angel—she received a note as she waited in her hospital room for the gift of bone marrow from this perfect stranger.

It said simply:

"I know this marrow will help you. My mother will be watching over you, Patty."

Patty was released the next day after the bone marrow aspiration. Cindy had a six-week hospital stay. After a fever and an additional week in the hospital to remedy that, as well as some drug modifications, the first year of Cindy's recovery went well. The doctors explained that the biggest hurdle was the first hundred days; after that, if the disease stayed in remission for one year, the prognosis would improve significantly.

At first, her friends handled Cindy like fragile crystal. We networked on the telephone, confirming with each other that she seemed to be getting stronger, looking better, acting like herself again. But before long, as we were swept into the business of our own daily lives, Cindy's illness faded into history.

Then, exactly one year to the day after Cindy's transplant, that harbinger of life-altering news — the telephone — rang again. Cindy's husband answered the call and handed her the phone.

"It's your sister," he said.

When Cindy put the receiver to her ear, the voice on the other end was not familiar to her. "This isn't my sister," Cindy mouthed to Hal.

"Oh yes it is," insisted her husband, his voice trembling.

Then she realized it was Patty.

Tears ran down Cindy's cheeks; on the other end, Patty was crying, too. They spent an hour on the phone, swapping information through the telephone lines back and forth between New Hampshire and California. Cindy learned that Patty had lost her mother to cancer, and although she couldn't help her mother, she was determined to help someone else. She had originally registered as a donor with the City of Hope to help a little boy. She called every two weeks to inquire about the status of her compatibility with him. Ultimately, she discovered she was not a match for the boy, but she was for a woman in California: a wife and mother named Cindy.

Patty had recently given birth to another daughter — but she had waited to get pregnant until she was able to donate her marrow to someone in need. Cindy described her battles with the life-threatening disease and how she eventually emerged victorious due to Patty's generous and loving act. They made plans to meet the following month.

Cindy and her family flew to Boston, then drove to Portsmouth, New Hampshire. Patty arrived at their hotel with her tiny daughter. When the door opened the two women fell into each other's arms like the long-lost sisters they had now become. Between tears and laughter, these two women, once strangers, who now shared identical bone marrow, forged a permanent friendship and bond.

Five months later, Patty and her family made the trip to California to meet Cindy's family and friends, who all wanted a chance to personally thank the woman who saved Cindy's life. They met at a local restaurant—a modest setting for the thirty people who gathered to celebrate the kindness of strangers and to renew their trust in the goodness of people.

When Patty was introduced, some guests raised glasses and some broke out in applause; others wept openly as they beheld the face of an earthbound angel and everyday saint.

Every year, on October 14—the anniversary of Cindy's transplant—Cindy places a call to Patty and says the same heartfelt words: "Thanks for another year, angel." Eight priceless years of memories and cherished time have come and gone since the paths of these two remarkable women crossed: a story of love, character and courage. A gift of healing and hope.

~Lori Shaw-Cohen
Chicken Soup to Inspire the Body and Soul

Woman to Woman

It's All a Matter of Perspective

Nobody trips over mountains.
It is the small pebble that causes you to stumble.
Pass all the pebbles in your path and you will find
you have crossed the mountain.
~Source Unknown

Body Work

If you don't like something change it;
if you can't change it, change the way you think about it.
~Mary Engelbreit

I remember the moment when it first happened, the first time I found myself dissatisfied with my body. I was fourteen, lying on my back. I noticed with displeasure that my stomach did not curve inward the way my friend Lisa's did.

Since then I have been on a roller coaster ride. I have been alternately pleased by and disgusted with my body. I have received some positive comments — but also many negative ones — about my physique. One time while out jogging, I heard a man yell out to me, "Keep it up! You need to do a lot of running!" Even my family has gotten into the act, telling me when I am "plump" or advising me when my face has gotten "full."

I have had ambivalent feelings about my body most of my life. Pretty women — reed thin women — reap the rewards in our society, whether it's men, attention or jobs. If a woman is not attractive — and slender — she is ignored. So, like most women, I have wanted to be slim. But I have never gone on a strict diet or embarked on a rigorous exercise program. Clearly, part of me desires to have the perfect body while another part wishes it weren't so important.

A couple of years ago, I started volunteering for the Meals on Wheels chapter in my community. The people I brought meals to certainly weren't obsessing over their appearance and their weight. They had more important things to think about, such as long-term illnesses and perilous financial situations. I realized then that striving for the perfect body is a superficial pursuit, to say the least.

I realized something further. There is only so much I can do to alter my shape. I can exercise regularly and eat healthfully, but I will never measure up to the impossible ideal our society has set. Sure, there's starvation and plastic surgery, but I prefer not to resort to such extreme and potentially dangerous methods.

On the other hand, there is a lot I can do about my feelings of compassion for those less fortunate, my understanding of cultures different from my own and my actions on behalf of people not as healthy and fit as I am. I have decided to focus on these pursuits rather than the futile quest for a better body.

After all, I would rather be admired for the breadth of my kindness than the length of my legs, the size of my heart than the fullness of my breasts, and the shape of my thoughts rather than the proportions of my body. It's taken me twenty-seven years, but I've learned to love my body—after all, it's where I live.

~Carol Ayer
Chicken Soup to Inspire a Woman's Soul

Gifts

The greatest discovery of my generation is that
a human being can alter his life by altering his attitudes.
~William James

I worked closely with Mother Teresa for over thirty years. One day, after my conversation had been filled with a litany of problems, some seemingly insoluble, Mother Teresa remarked, "Everything is a problem. Isn't there another word?"

I confessed that I knew no other word that carried the same weight.

"Why not use the word 'gift'?" she suggested.

With that I began a shift in vocabulary.

One of the first times that this new vocabulary came into use was on our return to New York City from a conference in Vancouver. She had tried without success to be excused from the conference and was extremely anxious to have time with the sisters in New York.

I was dismayed to learn that the trip had to be broken en route with a long delay. I was about to explain the "problem" when I caught myself and said, "Mother, I have to tell you about a gift. We have to wait four hours here, and you won't arrive at the convent until very late."

Mother Teresa agreed that it was indeed a great "gift." She settled down in the airport to read and ponder a favorite book of meditations.

From that time on, items that presented disappointments or difficulties would be introduced with, "We have a small gift here," or "Today we have an especially big gift." Now there were smiles at situations that earlier had been described by the dour word "problem."

~Eileen Egan
Chicken Soup for the Traveler's Soul

Happy Birthday

’ve really been good the past four days: low-fat cottage cheese, tuna salad with lemon, broiled chicken with broccoli (no butter), grapefruit for breakfast.... Oh boy, I can hardly wait to step on the scale today. Slide out of bed slowly, stretch, savor the anticipated report from the scale. Slip off my robe, step lightly on the scale, look down with fragile confidence. I wonder how many pounds I’ve lost. Two, three, four maybe? Relishing the anticipated news, I let my eyes slip down to the mechanical device beneath my feet.... Disbelief! Confidence destroyed! Not only did I not lose four pounds, I gained one! I’ve been tricked, fooled, betrayed. The scale says I’ve been bad; the scale says I’m fat. Four minutes ago I didn’t think so, but now I do. I’m fat. I’m bad. Devastated by the condemnation from the scale, I skulk back to bed wearing my robe like a shroud.

I am accustomed to stepping on the scale in the morning and to having the weight report determine what kind of a mood I will be in for that day. But today I am thirty-four, and I’ve been dieting in preparation for my birthday. I wanted to feel good today, not old and... But the scale has passed judgment on me: I’m fat. I’m bad. Sullenly I trudge back to bed where I feel, not think, the memories.

I remember.

I am four. My cousins romp circles around me, their loud obnoxious shrieks assaulting my ears. I suppose my quiet granddaddy loves them, too (though I don't know why), but I also know he loves me best. I don't know how I know this, but I do. Though he can hear them—they all scream so loud—and he can hardly hear me at all. My family doesn't talk loudly. We talk quietly in my house, and I talk quietest of all. But Grandpa and I don't talk much; we don't need to. Grandpa, I want to pick pink rhubarb I think, looking up at him. "Shall we go pick some rhubarb, Wee Ann?" he says quietly, taking my small, pudgy hand in his coarse, big one. Grandpa calls me his special version of my given name, Willanne—unlike my cousins, who call me "Pudgy." I am pudgy, as pictures thirty years later attest. But today I am four and I don't care if I'm "Pudgy," because Grandpa loves me best. I don't know how I know this, I just know, that's all.

I remember.

I am eleven. We are visiting Grandma's house and my detestable cousins have a friend over. My cousins are running around under the umbrella tree in the front yard and shrieking brainlessly. But their friend—a boy—is not running and shrieking. My cousins are gleefully teasing him, daring him to kiss me. I hate my cousins. My horrible cousins still call me "Pudgy," though I've outgrown the appropriateness of the name. I'm so embarrassed.

I remember.

I am sixteen. I pass the driving test easily, both the written and the driving portion. But the hard question comes after "Sex," "Color of eyes" and "Height." The question is: "Weight." How much should I say, I wonder. What happens if I lie? Will I have to step on a scale? If I lie will an alarm go off? Will the clerk repeat my weight out loud so everyone will know? Will she question me? Will she exclaim disbelievingly, "You weigh how much?" Filled with trepidation, I decide to lie. I wonder how much I can get away with. I take off ten pounds. I get away with it. No alarm sounds. The clerk doesn't even raise an eyebrow. She acts like she doesn't even care, though I'm sure she must.

I get away with my first ten-pound lie: Ten pounds becomes my permanent cheat number. No matter how much I weigh, from then on, I always take off ten pounds before committing my weight to paper. And I always know—no matter how much I weigh—that if I just lose ten pounds, I'll be just right. No matter how much I weigh, "just right" is always ten pounds less.

In the suburban morning quiet, I remember.

Six years ago, I was pregnant and looking like the Goodyear blimp. But today I am thirty-four, and I'm not pregnant. I'm also not fat. I'm not even pudgy. But the scale has just pronounced judgment and destroyed my mood by telling me I gained a pound.

I contemplate this: Maybe how much I weigh is not the problem; perhaps the problem is how I feel about how much I weigh.

Unhurried, I rise from the bed to which the bathroom scale has so recently sent me. I put on my robe, and go to the bathroom. I pick up the scale and carry it deliberately down the hall, past the dining room, through the kitchen, to the side yard where six empty trash cans await next week's trash. I raise the scale to the level of my shoulders, pause for just a moment and then drop the mechanical dictator into the waiting rubbish receptacle. And in so doing, I reclaim control over my own morale.

Never again will my mood be determined by the bathroom scale. A happy birthday belongs to me.

~Willanne Ackerman
Chicken Soup for the Unsinkable Soul

A Real Home

Attitude is a little thing that makes a big difference.
~Winston Churchill

Her world had shattered with the divorce.

Bills, house payments, health insurance. Her part-time job provided little income and fewer benefits. With no financial support, she had finally lost the house.

At wit's end, Karen managed to rent a cramped camper at the local RV park for herself and five-year-old Joshua. It was only a little better than living in their car, and she wished with all her heart that she could provide more for her child.

After their evening ritual of giggling over a table game and reading stories, Karen sent her son outside to play until bedtime while she agonized over the checkbook. She glanced out the window when she heard voices.

"Say, Josh, don't you wish you had a real home?" asked the campground manager.

Karen tensed and held her breath as she leaned nearer the open window. Then a smile spread across her face when she heard Joshua's response.

"We already have a real home," he said. "It's just that we don't have a house to put it in."

~Carol McAdoo Rehme
Chicken Soup for the Mother's Soul 2

Action Hero

Experience is not what happens to a man.
It is what a man does with what happens to him.
~Aldous Leonard Huxley

A few years ago, I stopped at a neighborhood market for some late-night ice cream. As I got out of my car, a young man hailed me from across the street. He was college-aged and dressed to the nines: expensive pullover, dress shirt and slacks so sharply creased they could have cut frozen fish. I thought he wanted directions; he had that urgent late-for-a-party look. When he reached me, he pulled up his sweater and smoothly drew a pistol from inside his waistband. "Get in the car," he ordered.

My brain went into hyperspeed. I remembered watching a personal-security expert on a talk show advise victims not to stare at an assailant's face. His reasoning was that if a robber thinks you cannot identify him, he's less likely to kill you. No one asked how much less likely. Given its importance to my future, I focused instead on his weapon—a .38 Smith & Wesson revolver, blued steel, short barrel. I'd fired others like it at pistol ranges. This was no mouse gun. Nervously, I directed my gaze lower. His shoes were highly polished. Strange as it sounds, I admired his sense of style.

The click of the revolver's hammer being cocked snapped my head up eye to eye with his. So much for not looking at his face. Contrary to the belief that when death appears imminent a person's entire life passes before him, I was completely focused on the moment. Instinct told me that a car trip with this guy would turn out to be a one-way journey for me. I held out my keys. "Take my car," I said in a tone I prayed would inspire calmness and reason. "I'm not getting in."

He hesitated, then ignoring my proffered keys, thrust out a hand and yanked off my shoulder bag. In it were my wallet and a couple of rented videos. He took a step back, his gun still aimed at me. Neither of us spoke.

Laughter broke the silence, making us both turn. Several couples were leaving a Chinese restaurant on the opposite corner. The gunman gave them a fast scan, then lowered his revolver. Holding it against his thigh to conceal it, he began to stride quickly across the almost trafficless street, my bag clutched under his arm.

Incredibly, I took off after him. "Hey," I shouted to the people in front of the restaurant. "This guy just robbed me." I was halfway across the street when I realized my would-be posse was not mounting up. The gunman, now aware of my proximity, pivoted in my direction. As I watched him raise his gun, everything went into slow motion. A tongue of flame flashed from the snub-nosed barrel, followed by a loud crack.

I lost my balance. I felt no pain, but when I looked down, I saw my left leg flopped out sideways at my shin. A half-dollar-size spot of blood stained my jeans. When I looked up, my assailant was sprinting down a dark side street.

Later that night at a nearby hospital, I was told that the bullet had fractured my tibia and fibula, the two bones connecting the knee and ankle. Doctors inserted a steel rod secured by four screws into my leg. They also gave me a "prosthesis alert" card to show security personnel if the rod set off a metal detector.

Almost immediately a remarkable thing began to happen—my popularity soared. When friends introduced me as "the guy who got shot," women who a moment before had no interest in me came after me like groupies. Men wanted to buy me drinks. They considered me "brave" for running after the gunman. I'm reminded of war movies in which the green infantrymen behave reverentially around the grizzled vets who have "seen action."

I found it difficult to forgive myself for what I considered an act of colossal folly. Sometimes I thought I had chased the kid out of anger at being victimized; other times I attributed my actions to an adrenaline rush that needed a physical outlet. Whatever the reason, I knew it had nothing to do with bravery.

Clearly, I was being given credit for something I didn't deserve, yet I was reluctant to give up my newly acquired status. After all, it wasn't as if I were taking an active part in any deception; I was merely allowing people to come to whatever conclusions they wished. I finally rationalized my decision to maintain the status quo: I considered any misperception to be my compensation for having gone through a horrible situation.

Things went well until the day I was approached by a panhandler. On a whim, I told him I had no money because I'd been unable to work since being shot in a robbery. His eyes grew large, and it was obvious that the information impressed him. "That's heavy," he said, then leaned closer, conspiratorially. "Did you get caught?"

~Rulon Openshaw
A 5th Portion of Chicken Soup for the Soul

73

All God's Children

There is no surprise more magical than the surprise of being loved.
It is God's finger on man's shoulder.
~Charles Morgan

The night receptionist handed me a slip of paper. "The volunteer chaplain would like to meet with you. This is her extension number."

Her? The hospital chaplain was a woman? I was tired, exhausted really, after a full ten hours supervising my son's third day of intensive therapy at Craig Rehabilitation Hospital. I was certainly not in the mood to explain—for what seemed like the thousandth time—the accident that brought us here.

"Maybe tomorrow," I muttered, ducking into the crisp night air. Street lamps lit my path across the pedestrian walkway, but cast deep shadows as thick as those weighing down my heart. At the guest apartment door, I fumbled with unfamiliar locks and tumbled into bed without even washing my face or brushing my teeth.

The next morning a different receptionist handed me another slip of paper. "The hospital chaplain wants to...."

"I know," I sighed, "I know. Is she in now?" She opened her mouth to answer but nodded and pointed instead. Peering over my shoulder, I was startled by the middle-aged woman lumbering toward me. Her walk was lopsided, like a gate swinging on one hinge, her eyes were skewed and even her arms seemed twisted, out of her control. She looked like she could be one of the patients. But her smile radiated warmth as she greeted me.

"Are you Kyle's mother? What a wonderful, charming son you have! I could hardly wait to meet the person who brought him into the world." Although her stumbling words slurred, I understood the message, and it melted the icy knot that had been lodged in my stomach for weeks. Here was someone who only knew my son after his head injury—and liked what she saw.

"Let's sit," she invited. We sat. And talked. And talked.

So began my brief relationship with Patty Cooper, lay chaplain, confidante, teacher and friend. Her regular visits to Kyle cheered him. Her regular visits to me gave me hope—a hope she spread as generously as her encouragement in a facility that treated only the worst of spinal cord and brain injuries.

Like many others at Craig Hospital, as I dealt with my son's infirmities and my own doubts, I came to rely on her unique mixture of relentless optimism and calm acceptance. I needed both in my grief over the losses and my adjustment to the changes.

Patty complimented Kyle's attitude and each small success as he worked hard to rebuild his body and to walk again. She encouraged my involvement and soothed my mother-fears. And she shared her personal story when I asked her how she found herself volunteering here, in this place, where heartache reigned supreme.

"I wanted to have a baby," she said simply.

Twenty-five years earlier during a straightforward, exploratory surgery of her fallopian tubes, a lethal dose of nitrous oxide gas was administered. It started Patty's life down an unexpected path. Her resulting complications and permanent disabilities read like an index of medical terms: cardiac arrest, anoxia, hypoxic brain surgery, forty-day coma, paralysis, peripheral blindness, impaired speech, cognitive lapses.

Patty awoke from the initial surgery months later to discover herself a patient at this very facility. Over a long period of months, she relearned the basics—how to walk and talk, how to feed and dress herself, how to brush her hair and teeth, and even how to tend to her most personal needs. Meanwhile, Patty's husband chose a different path—and a different woman—for himself.

"But you don't seem bitter," I pointed out. "And you've ended up here. By choice." After a month, I still struggled with the heart-wrench of each patient's pain and each family's problems, which I witnessed on a daily basis. How could she do it, night and day, year after year?

The crooked smile I had come to love lifted a corner of her mouth and crinkled her tender eyes. "I'm here because once I entered a hospital to conceive one perfect child of my own to love. But God taught me that love doesn't seek perfection." She paused to brush at a single tear.

"And now—now I voluntarily walk through these doors each day for a more important reason." Patty nodded toward the row of wheelchairs, walkers and weights lining the corridor. "To share my love with all of His children."

~Carol McAdoo Rehme
Chicken Soup for the Christian Woman's Soul

74

A Matter of Weight

Ever since grade school, when being the biggest girl in class landed me more than a fair share of snickers, I've had a difficult relationship with my weight. Kids called me all sorts of names—Pork Ball, Porcupine Rind, Jam Pudding and worse. I pretended to laugh along with them, but went home and drowned my anger in food.

It wasn't until I turned eighteen and fell in love with a tall, soft-spoken boy from Massachusetts that the weight slipped off. And when I married him six years later, I was a svelte 103 pounds. For someone who enjoyed food as much as I did, this was no small feat. Those were the Twiggy days, when being knitting-needle thin had become a cultural obsession; the fashion industry was relentlessly unforgiving towards natural bulges and buxom shapes.

But "skinny" didn't last long. Within two years, I gained over ten pounds, and with the birth of our first child three years later, I added another forty. The old grade school angst returned, and I decided to wage my own holy war against the bulge. I took up running, beginning with a brisk walk around the block, and then doubled my efforts until I was able to run comfortably for two miles without stopping. By the end of the year, I had shed thirty pounds and was permanently hooked on running. It made me feel brisk and clean, like a colt; it allowed me to eat what I wanted and it kept the weight manageable.

As long as I pounded the pavement for fifty minutes, five times a week, I was able to keep my weight within an acceptable range.

Still, I fretted over every bite. My husband, much more relaxed about body shape, said, "I wish you could just enjoy being what you are. You carry so much guilt about what you do and what you look like that you aren't enjoying life at all!"

"But I feel so fat!" I countered.

"I have a suggestion. Get rid of your scale."

I did—and miraculously discovered that my body had its own way of finding balance. I moved from "how much I weigh" to "how I feel." For several years, I ate when I was hungry and ran not because I had to, but simply because I loved the sense of exhilaration it gave me. I didn't choose one activity to cancel out the other, but did both because they fed my soul. And although I didn't know exactly how much I weighed, I was content because my clothes remained a comfortable fit.

Then everything changed the year I turned fifty. My husband passed away after an eleven-month battle with cancer. Food became a different kind of issue during his illness, when his body refused to eat because the radiation had scorched his throat and he couldn't swallow without pain. Day by day, I watched him shrink to a shadow.

After his death, I was plagued by a terrible loneliness. In the silence of an empty home, I ate, wept and ate again. I noticed my body becoming dumpy and thick. Despite a daily run, pockets of flesh flapped under my arms and my belly jiggled like Jell-O. A year later, my obsession with weight returned.

I bought a new scale, joined the local fitness club, placed myself on a high-protein diet and squelched my natural enjoyment of food. I ate only what was permitted: egg whites, cheese, onions, tofu, seeds, nuts and lentils, and drank designer whey drinks. I ran six days a week and did an hour of resistance training three times a week. I worked out this way for four weeks, like a soldier, then I stepped on the scale. You could have heard my scream ten miles down the road: I had gained three pounds. How was that possible?

An older friend had once said, "You just wait—the day will come when your body will stop performing for you. It will bloat, swell and gurgle; it will rise and spread and do all the nasty things you exercise freaks are trying to keep under control. Just wait and see." Her eyes gleamed with venom.

I would have believed her and turned the rest of my life into a lament had it not been for a vivid dream, which came like a message from my body:

I was on a dark, stuffy train. Several people were with me, and we were on a mission of some kind. They had wrapped me up in long sheets and placed me in the aisle. When the train stopped, the sheets peeled off, and I followed the crowd out the gates and down winding stairs towards some kind of underground cavern. The journey was long and tedious, but we finally emerged from the last flight of stairs into the depths of a cave. There, in the center, was my husband, lying on a hospital bed. He was bone-thin, cheeks sunken, eyes hollow. I walked up to him, placed my hand over my hip and complained to him, "I can't stand it. All this work coming down here and I haven't lost a pound."

Then I woke up, and it hit me: that dream showed the absurd irony of my situation. My husband could barely eat at all, and all I could think about was losing weight.

The next morning I threw away the scale.

Life, I decided, was too short for weights and measures. I would run and I would eat. I would take pleasure in both. I would neither deny my body nor starve my soul. I was going to love my body in whatever shape and form it took. My body was here to serve a higher purpose, my soul's purpose, and my soul was not here to be shaped or stuffed into a standard mold.

~Mary Desaulniers
Chicken Soup to Inspire the Body and Soul

Woman to Woman

Overcoming Obstacles

*You cannot discover new oceans
unless you have the courage to lose sight of the shore.
~Author Unknown*

75

A Day at The Tradition

Laughter is the shortest distance between two people.
~Victor Borge

everal years ago, I was diagnosed with cancer. It was the most difficult time I have ever faced. I think it was my sense of humor that allowed me to hold onto my sanity. Like many people who have gone through chemotherapy, I lost all of my hair and I was as bald as a cue ball. I always had enjoyed wearing hats, so when my hair deserted me, I ordered several special hats with the hair already attached. It was easy and I never had to worry about how my hair looked.

I have always been a big golf fan. In fact, I have been to twenty-three straight U.S. Opens. At one point during my cancer treatments, my husband John and I decided to get away from the cold Minnesota winter and took a trip to Scottsdale, Arizona. There was a Senior PGA Tour event called The Tradition being played, and that seemed like just the ticket to lift my spirits.

The first day of the tournament brought out a huge gallery. It was a beautiful day, and I was in heaven. I was standing just off the third tee, behind the fairway ropes, watching my three favorite golfers in the world approach the tee box: Jack Nicklaus, Raymond Floyd and Tom Weiskopf.

Just as they arrived at the tee, the unimaginable happened. A huge gust of wind came up from nowhere and blew my hat and hair right off my head and into the middle of the fairway! The thousands of spectators lining the fairway fell into an awkward silence, all eyes on me. Even my golf idols were watching me, as my hair was in their flight path. I was mortified! Embarrassed as I was, I knew I couldn't just stand there. Someone had to do something to get things moving again.

So I took a deep breath, went under the ropes and out into the middle of the fairway. I grabbed my hat and hair, nestled them back on my head as best I could. Then I turned to the golfers and loudly announced, "Gentlemen, the wind is blowing from left to right."

They say the laughter could be heard all the way to the nineteenth hole.

~Christine Clifford
Chicken Soup for the Golfer's Soul

76

Cultivating My Garden

The greatest gift of the garden is the restoration of the five senses.
~Hanna Rion

It was a summer's evening when my husband Tim's minivan spun out of control on a rain-slicked road, leaving me a young widow with a little daughter to raise.

On a fall day three months later, as I struggled to work through the grief, the pain and even the anger, I stood on the back steps of my house, surveying the large vegetable garden that Tim had put so much of himself into. From the yard, my eyes wandered over to the wooded slope beyond it and to the cemetery where Tim was buried, and then back to the garden.

The garden was a mess. I couldn't possibly keep up with it all. I didn't even know where to begin. The bright, green-bean wall Tim had constructed was covered with rotting beans, and every other green growing thing had been choked out by the ornamental gourds we had mistakenly planted last spring. What was I to do with it all? I certainly didn't want to turn it back into the sort of manicured greenery that both Tim and I had always loathed.

After much pondering, I decided to make an herb garden out of it. Something that I could lose myself in.

The bean wall came down and was hauled to the town dump. I closed my heart to the memory of the warm late-spring morning when Tim had been up early, painting it gaudy green, and threw myself into ripping down the ragged sunflowers and sadly faded cosmos he had planted all along the edges.

Then came the herbs. Lamb's ears, rosemary, angelica and costmary. Lavender, speedwell, lemon balm and valerian. Spearmint, apple mint and—would you believe?—chocolate mint.

In the strawberry bed that Tim had made for me the second Mother's Day after our daughter Marissa was born, I planted a white birch. Well, it was gray just then, but Eric, one of my garden wizards, told me that it would turn white some day. It became the Tim Tree.

In the spring, with the help of my friend Cel, I put down wood chips. Another friend, Jan, went on an herb shopping trip and came over with plants I'd never seen or even heard of, with names like woad, soapwort, felicity, amaranth and woundwort.

The garden was taking shape all right. But I still felt lost and unhappy in my own skin. I toyed with the idea of selling the house and moving with Marissa into my grandmother's old farmhouse. There would be no memories of Tim to gnaw at me there.

But I still kept puttering with that garden. I moved the white marble birdbath that Tim had given me on our last anniversary into the center. I bought a stone angel, her eyes downcast and her face filled with Renaissance piety, and placed her next to the birdbath.

Still, it seemed that something was missing. Then it occurred to me that my garden had no central theme. I had always been fascinated by "theme gardens"—Shakespearean gardens, moonlight gardens, witches' gardens and the like. But mine was simply a hodgepodge of herbs, flowers, trees and shrubs.

Late that summer, Marissa and I traveled to New York State. We stopped at an herb farm, and I came across some new herbs with bewitching names, such as boneset and all-heal. Boneset leaves, I learned, were originally used in setting broken bones and in tonics. All-heal, or self-heal, was a remedy for a variety of internal and external wounds. It was then that I decided that my garden would be a healing garden. Not only in the literal sense, but perhaps in the spiritual sense as well.

One afternoon not long afterwards, I stumbled right smack

into my epiphany. I had fallen in love with my garden. My bane had turned out to be my blessing. I gazed around me, just as I had the previous fall, but with such different eyes. The garden had made me remember what I had tried so hard to forget: that I loved this place where Tim and I had started our journey as husband and wife and as parents of a vivacious daughter. That part of the journey was over, but the journey continued. Marissa and I still had miles to go and promises to keep—to each other, to Tim and to the garden. We'd make good where we were.

Over a year later, I'm still working at my garden. I've moved the trees out and put a tiny iris garden in one corner. And I've been putting down flat bricks, fieldstone, and anything else I can lay my hands on, to make little wayward paths that branch out, then circle back on themselves. Sometimes I just sit on the marble bench that I put in, and at other times I hunt around for the four- and five-leaved clovers that often crop up, good luck signs that assure me nature is working for me.

I don't go down to the cemetery much now. If I want to find Tim, I feel him in this garden he gave me. The pain has gone from my memories now, leaving them full of laughter and warmth. The healing garden has lived up to its name.

~T. J. Banks
Chicken Soup for the Single's Soul

A Lesson from Luke

One bright, sunny afternoon in September our golden retriever, Luke, rose from a nap to go for our usual walk to the park. I should say he attempted to rise, because as he stood, he wobbled, tried to get his balance, then collapsed. My heart did somersaults as my husband and I carried him to the car and sped to the vet's office. After hours of blood tests, exams and an ultrasound, we learned the grim news: Luke had hemangiosarcoma, an inoperable cancer of the blood vessels.

"How long does he have?" I asked through my tears, my arms wrapped around Luke, hugging him to my heart.

"I can't say for sure," the vet told us. "Weeks. Maybe only days."

I barely made it to the car before I broke down in uncontrollable sobs. My husband didn't handle the news any better. We held on to each other and bawled. How could Luke have gotten so sick without our realizing it? Sure, he was ten years old, but you'd never know it. He ate every meal with the gusto of a starving piglet, and just that morning he'd chased his tennis ball as if it were filled with his favorite doggy biscuits. He couldn't have cancer, not our Luker Boy, not our baby.

For the next several days we hovered over him, studying him diligently. We took slow walks around the neighborhood, and instead of throwing the ball, we tossed it right to his mouth and let him catch it. One day while dusting the furniture, I picked up his blue pet-therapist vest — Luke had been a volunteer with the Helen Woodward Animal Center pet therapy department, and had visited centers for abused and neglected children. I held the vest to my cheek and started to cry. Why Luke? He was such a sweet dog; he deserved to live.

As I started to put the vest away in a drawer, Luke trotted over, wagging his tail. He looked at me expectantly, his ears perked up and his tongue hanging out.

"You want to put on your vest and go to work, don't you?" I knelt and scratched behind his ears. I could swear he grinned at me.

Although there could be no running or jumping, the following day Luke joined the other pet-therapy dogs on a visit to the children's center. I'm often envious of Luke's ability to light up kids' faces just by being himself. They giggle and clap their hands when he gives them a high ten or catches a cookie off his nose. But the best reaction by far comes when the children ask him, "Do you love me?" and he answers with an emphatic, "Woof!" The kids whoop and holler, continuing to shout, "Do you love me?" He always answers them.

On this particular day, I wanted to make sure that Luke enjoyed himself, so I wasn't paying as much attention to the children as I usually did. A girl about nine or ten years old inched over to us. Her narrow shoulders slumped and her head hung down; she reminded me of a drooping sunflower. Luke wagged his tail as she neared us and licked her cheek when she bent to pet him. She sat next to us on the lawn and smiled at Luke, but her large brown eyes still looked sad.

"I wish people would die at ten years old the way dogs do," she said.

Stunned, I could only stare at her. None of the kids knew that Luke had cancer. Luke rolled over on his back and the girl rubbed his belly.

Finally, I asked her, "Why do you say that?"

"Because I'm ten, and I wish I would die."

Her sorrow curled around my heart and squeezed it so tightly, my breath caught. "Are things so bad?"

"The worst. I hate it here."

What could I say to her? I couldn't tell her that she shouldn't feel that way, or that she had a wonderful life ahead of her. What good would that do? It wasn't what she needed to hear. I put my hand gently on her back and asked her name.

"Carly."

"Carly, you want to know something? Luke here has cancer. He's dying. And he wishes more than anything that he could go on living. You're perfectly healthy, yet you want to die. It just isn't fair, is it?"

Carly snapped her head up and looked at me. "Luke's dying?"

I nodded, swallowing back tears. "He doesn't have much time—a week, maybe two... or just a few days... we don't know for sure."

"Shouldn't he be at home or in the hospital?" she asked.

"He wanted to visit with you kids, to bring you some happiness. Just like you, things aren't good for him either. He probably hurts a lot inside." I paused, wondering if she was old enough to understand. "But by coming here, it's as if he's trying to make every minute of his life count for something."

Carly sat silently, looking at Luke while she softly rubbed his belly. "Poor Luke," she said, almost in a whisper. When she raised her head and met my gaze, her eyes looked wary, almost accusing. "You think I should be glad I'm alive and not wanting to die, don't you? Even if I'm stuck here."

I took a few seconds to try to gather my thoughts. "Maybe you could make it sort of like a game. Every day try to think of at least one good thing about being alive."

The counselors began calling the children back to their class-rooms. I looked straight into Carly's eyes, trying to reach her. "If nothing else, there's always hope things will get better."

"Come on, Carly," a counselor called out.

Carly stood. "Will you come back and see me?"

"Yes, I will. I promise. And you'll tell me lots of reasons to live, right?"

"Right." She gave me a big nod, and then ran off to join her classmates.

The next week, though Luke's walk was slower and more labored, we visited the children's center again. Carly didn't show up. Alarmed, I asked one of the counselors where she was. They told me that she'd gone to live with a foster family. My heart settled back into place. Good for you, Carly.

Twelve days later, Luke lost his battle with cancer.

When I think of him now, I try to focus on what I told Carly: that Luke made every minute of his life count for something. Perhaps he inspired Carly to do that, too. I hope that she, and all the other children we visited, benefited from being with Luke. I know I did.

~Christine Watkins
Chicken Soup for the Dog Lover's Soul

Angel in Black

All God's angels come to us disguised.
~James Russell Lowell

I had landed a dream job—a summer on Cape Cod as a mother's helper. Days were spent on the beach or the cabin cruiser; nights I was usually free to hang out at the teen center. One night, though, the mother I worked for asked me to stay on duty. Her husband was away on a business trip, and she planned to spend the night at a friend's. I readily agreed; they had been very kind to me. I was especially close to the woman, having worked for her several times a week all year. We often sat in the kitchen chatting after she came home from work. She treated me like a younger sister. Although her husband traveled and rarely saw me, he was always pleasant when he was home.

I tucked the kids in, listened to music until after midnight, then checked the sleeping children and turned in for the night. I don't know how long I slept, but later a presence beside me jolted me into full consciousness, sending a shock down my spine and paralyzing me with fear. The children's father was sitting on my bed, touching me, whispering to me. He smelled of alcohol. I couldn't believe this was the same man who had let me steer the boat a few days ago, asking me about my friends, my interests, my ambitions. Now I wondered if he had been planning this evening for days. The thought sickened me. With uncharacteristic courage, I sat up in bed and told him to get out of my room. To my amazement, he did. I lay frozen while he finished in the bathroom and went to bed. The sound of his snoring did not relieve my panic; the rest of the night stretched endlessly before me, and, in my mind, the rest of the summer after that. How could I pretend it didn't happen? What if he approached me again?

A crucifix hung on the wall opposite me. I had never been a praying person. Though I found God everywhere—in sunsets, on the rocky cliffs I loved to climb, in the cold sea spray—I saw no need to call on Him. But I called on Him now as I gazed at the cross. I prayed my first prayer that was not a "God bless everybody I know" formula. I don't remember my exact words, but I remember His answer distinctly. It was audible, but without vocal tone. And it was compelling: "Get out of the house."

Now this is something I would not ordinarily do. My Puritan work ethic went back many generations and was firmly ingrained. I had this job, I was responsible for the children and I never asked anyone for help. Yet seconds after I heard the command, I leaped out of bed, threw on some clothes and bolted barefoot for the front door. I walked on the beach until dawn. I was scared, hungry, penniless and lost, driven with murderous thoughts. The first person I saw was a fisherman. He nodded and smiled kindly. I narrowed my eyes to mean little slits, thrust both hands in my pockets and took off at a fast clip. "If you're gonna send someone to help me, God, it can't be a man," I muttered. "Not now."

Ten minutes later I came upon an unlikely sight—a nun in full habit, humming to herself, enjoying the morning. I had never spoken to a nun, and the stories I had heard from my friends in parochial school did not encourage me. But there was no one else in sight, and I was really at a loss. I needed some advice. What does one call a nun? I felt awkward with "Sister," since I wasn't Catholic, so I skipped the formalities altogether. "Um, what town am I in?" I figured that was as good a conversation starter as any. She must have assumed I was a runaway. In a sense, I was. My story unfolded as we walked together, and to my surprise I found myself trusting her. "So what do I do now?" I finished.

"You must call your mother."

"I don't want to worry her."

"Your mother is your God-given guide. She will tell you what to do."

I thought of several excuses why this was impossible. There was no phone nearby; I didn't have any money. The nun offered me a ride in her car, gave me some change and waited for me outside the phone booth during the tense conversation. I returned and slumped in the front seat. "Okay, I told my mother. She's really nervous. My father's out of town and she's getting my aunt to drive here with her. She says I have to come home."

"That is good advice. Now there is something else you must do."

"Yeah, sneak into the house and get my stuff while they're at the beach."

"No. You must face them and tell them why you are leaving. The woman is your friend, you said. Friends don't leave without a word. The truth is hard, always, but it must be told."

"I have to tell her what her husband did to me? And break her heart? Some friend!"

"Her heart is broken already. Go and talk to her. Would you like me to drive you?"

I declined. I was in no hurry to face my friend. "Thanks for your help and the change," I said. "Maybe I'll write. What's your name?"

"Sister Fitzgerald," she answered, "just like President Kennedy's middle name. I live at the convent here," she continued. "It's the only one."

We said our goodbyes and I dragged my feet during the long walk back down the beach to the house. My friend was waiting for me at the front door—angry, worried, thinking I had taken off and left her children. "Could we go upstairs alone?" I said to her. "We have to talk."

She was incredulous and could not believe me. It must have been some huge mistake. He'd been drinking. He thought I was one of the children. I was compassionate but firm. "No, he didn't think

I was someone else, because he called me by name. I'm going home today. My mother is coming."

Saying goodbye to her was the hardest thing I have ever done. She knew the truth; I could sense it. She couldn't accept it. We never saw each other again. I did, however, learn from a friend at home that it had not been the only time her husband had behaved this way.

Several months later my family was vacationing on Cape Cod. While driving through the area where I'd stayed, we stopped at the convent to visit Sister Fitzgerald and thank her for helping me. We inquired for her at the front door.

"Sister Fitzgerald? There's no one by that name here."

"I met her in July. Has she moved to another convent?"

"I've lived here for years. We've never had a sister by that name."

Thirty years later the story still stirs my heart, a reminder of God's love and very real presence for all who call on Him.

~Nancy Massand
Chicken Soup for the Christian Woman's Soul

Chicken Soup for the Soul

A Little White Lie

> *Friends are relatives you make for yourself.*
> ~Eustache Deschamps

When my friend, Sadie, was taken to the emergency room at a local hospital, I rushed over to be with her as soon as I received the news.

Sadie was both surprised and pleased to see me. "How did you get them to let you in?" she asked, knowing visitors were not usually allowed in the emergency room.

I, too, had been concerned about that on the drive over. However, I knew Sadie needed a friend to comfort her. In desperation, I had decided if worse came to worst, I would be forced to tell a lie and say I was Sadie's sister. I hoped I wouldn't have to resort to that.

After I explained all this to Sadie, she threw back her head in hearty laughter. While I was trying to figure out why Sadie was laughing, I glanced down at our clasped hands—my very white one held gently between her two black ones.

~June Cerza Kolf
Chicken Soup for the Sister's Soul

Wigged Out!

"So," my oncologist's nurse continued, handing me a list of names and addresses, "you may want to check one of these out."

Glancing at the sheet, I caught my breath: "Stores Specializing in Wigs for Chemo Patients."

Chemo. I still could hardly bring myself to accept the word. Numbly, I headed for one of the wig stores on the list. Inwardly I seethed. Not fair, God. You know I hate wigs. Last time I wore one was in the seventies. Loathed it. I looked like something in a B-movie. No, make that a D-one. Surely You don't want me to look like that!

Stepping into the little shop, I felt even worse. Almost every inch was filled with row upon row of artificial heads with artificial smiles topped with artificial hair.

The shop owner's smile, though, was warm and real. An older Asian woman, she tried to put me at ease. She picked out a few of her treasures that seemed closest in style, length and color to mine, then tried them on me. She expertly flipped the shiny locks this way and that, showing me how easily they could be arranged and cared for.

I had to admit that things had improved since the seventies. But I still rebelled. I liked to be natural, real, unpretentious. Wigs were so not me. Period.

Just then, an older gentleman came in, wearing a smile, golf togs and a glowing head of white hair. What in the world was he doing here?

"Hi, again," he greeted the shop owner. "I'm ready for a new wig. This one's fine, but I'd like an extra on hand. What have you got in stock?"

Smiling at me, he said, "These little things sure are a bother, but for us chemo patients, they're worth their weight in gold." Chemo patient? Him?

He gave me a thumbs-up. "Don't let it get you down, dear. We're all in this together."

Just then a tall, well-built younger woman breezed in. Her cap of glowing red curls caught my eye, but what really lit up that little shop was her vibrant smile. Perfect picture of health!

"I'm back!" she announced. "I really liked the one I had last year. Got any more in red?" Then to me, "You'll like shopping here. Started chemo already?"

"No, uh, will you be having it too?"

She laughed. "Oh, I'm an old-timer at this. Went through the whole business, lost all my hair. Took a year to grow it back. I was so thrilled to see it again." She wistfully touched one of her curls. "But now they've found a tumor somewhere else. So I'm going on Taxol. Hello, chemo, bye-bye, hair." Laughing, she continued. "Oh, but it is just hair, isn't it? After all, hair can always come back. Life can't."

Tears stung my eyes. "You are so right," I said. "Here, let me help you find what you need." And suddenly we were sisters, laughing and chatting together as I picked a wig out and tried it on her. Perfect!

The storekeeper wrote all three of our names down in a simple spiral-bound notebook, following hundreds of others. "This is my prayer book," she said simply. "I pray for all my customers, in chemo and out. I'll pray for all of you, too, that God will be with you and help you."

That little shop was still crowded, shabby and dark. But suddenly it was filled with light and joy as we all hugged each other. Yes, our newly purchased hairpieces were artificial. But our newfound hope and love as instant friends and supporters was real.

~Bonnie Compton Hanson
Chicken Soup for the Christian Woman's Soul

Woman to Woman

Achieving Your Dream

Don't be afraid to go out on a limb. That's where the fruit is.
~Janie Mines

81

Women Are Persons!

It was we, the people; not we, the white male citizens;
nor yet we, the male citizens;
but we, the whole people, who formed the Union....
Men, their rights and nothing more;
women, their rights and nothing less.
~Susan B. Anthony

Judge Emily Murphy was frustrated. Her last petition had been no more successful than all the others she had sent over the past ten years. It was 1927, and Canadian women were still defined by British common law, which astonishingly stated: "Women are persons in matters of pains and penalties, but not in matters of rights and privileges."

Emily was not at all happy about the outrageous indignity of being told she was "not a person." She had set her sights on becoming Canada's first female senator, but because women were not "persons," no woman was eligible! Emily was determined to change things.

And so it was that between 1921 and 1927, over 500,000 people, men and women, had signed letters and petitions requesting that Judge Murphy be appointed to the Canadian Senate. For most of them, it wasn't about becoming a senator. Like her, they were upset and offended that women were not considered to be persons. Amazingly, despite all her efforts, two prime ministers had still said "no!" But Emily refused to take "no" for an answer and kept up her relentless pressure. Then one day, after ten years of lobbying, she happened upon a new strategy.

Her brother had discovered a legal clause stating that any five citizens acting as a unit could appeal to the Supreme Court to clarify a point in the constitution. So in late 1927, she invited Henrietta Edwards, Louise McKinney, Irene Parlby and Nellie McClung to her Edmonton home. All four of these prominent Alberta women had been active in fighting for women's rights, and all of them were determined that by the end of their efforts, Canada would recognize them and all women as "persons."

That day, the five women signed Emily's petition, and with great hopes and expectations they sent their appeal. Then they sat back and waited. Several months later, Judge Murphy excitedly opened the telegram that arrived from the Supreme Court of Canada.

But her hopes were dashed. "No," read the reply from the learned justices, "Women are not eligible to be summoned to the Senate. Women are not 'persons.'"

Emily and her colleagues were devastated. First two prime ministers, and now the highest court in Canada had formally ruled against them, and they feared they had done irreparable damage to their cause. However, further research revealed one more option. The absolute final court for Canada in those days was still the Privy Council of Great Britain—it could be appealed there. But they were not hopeful. They would have to persuade the Canadian government to appeal the decision, and the rights of women in England were far behind those so far gained in Canada.

Holding her breath, Emily wrote to Prime Minister Mackenzie King, asked for his support, and urged him to appeal this matter to the Privy Council. To her great elation, he responded with his full support, and that of his government, and in addition they would pay for the cost of the appeal!

With their hopes back up, the five women wondered, Should they go to England? Should they write articles for the newspapers? Contact their friends there? No, they were advised, only the merit of the case would be heard. Just wait.

Finally, in October 1929, the five British Lords made their historic decision. When Emily and her friends learned that the new definition of the word "persons" would from that day forward always include both men and women, they were overjoyed! They had won!

As the word spread, women around the world celebrated. The five friends were gratified to know that because of their efforts, every woman in the British Empire would now be recognized as a "person," with all the same rights and privileges as men.

[Editors' Note: On October 18, 2000, a memorial celebrating the Famous 5 and their tremendous accomplishments was unveiled, and our five heroes became the first Canadian women in history to be honoured on Parliament Hill. The monument depicts an imaginary moment when the women received the news of their victory. A joyous Emily stands beside an empty chair and beckons visitors to join the celebration. Today, many come and visit so they can sit in Emily's chair and thank the Famous 5 for what they did. And everyone who does makes a pledge to do their best to participate in the building of a better Canada!]

~Frances Wright
Chicken Soup for the Canadian Soul

$\mathcal{D}$are to $\mathcal{I}$magine

Don't live down to expectations. Go out there and do something remarkable.
~Wendy Wasserstein

When people find out that I competed in the Olympics, they assume I've always been an accomplished athlete. But it isn't true. I was not the strongest, or the fastest, and I didn't learn the quickest. For me, becoming an Olympian was not developing a gift of natural athletic ability, but was, literally, an act of will.

At the 1972 Olympics in Munich, I was a member of the U.S. pentathlon team, but the tragedy of the Israeli athletes and an injury to my ankle combined to make the experience a deeply discouraging one. I didn't quit; instead I kept training, eventually qualifying to go with the U.S. team to Montreal for the 1976 Games. The experience was much more joyous, and I was thrilled to place thirteenth. But still, I felt I could do better.

I arranged to take a leave of absence from my college coaching job the year before the 1980 Olympics. I figured that twelve months of "twenty-four-hour-a-day training" would give me the edge I needed to bring home a medal this time. In the summer of 1979, I started intensively training for the Olympic trials to be held in June of 1980. I felt the exhilaration that comes with single-minded focus and steady progress towards a cherished goal.

But then in November, what appeared to be an insurmountable

obstacle occurred. I was in a car accident and injured my lower back. The doctors weren't sure exactly what was wrong, but I had to stop training because I couldn't move without experiencing excruciating pain. It seemed all too obvious that I would have to give up my dream of going to the Olympics if I couldn't keep training. Everyone felt so sorry for me. Everyone but me.

It was strange, but I never believed this setback would stop me. I trusted that the doctors and physical therapists would get it handled soon, and I would get back to training. I held on to the affirmation: I'm getting better every day and I will place in the top three at the Olympic trials. It went through my head constantly.

But my progress was slow, and the doctors couldn't agree on a course of treatment. Time was passing, and I was still in pain, unable to move. With only a few months remaining, I had to do something or I knew I would never make it. So I started training the only way I could—in my head.

A pentathlon consists of five track and field events: the 100-meter hurdle, the shot put, the high jump, the long jump and the 200-meter sprint. I obtained films of the world-record holders in all five of my events. Sitting in a kitchen chair, I watched the films projected on my kitchen wall over and over. Sometimes, I watched them in slow motion or frame by frame. When I got bored, I watched them backwards, just for fun. I watched for hundreds of hours, studying and absorbing. Other times, I lay on the couch and visualized the experience of competing in minute detail. I know some people thought I was crazy, but I wasn't ready to give up yet. I trained as hard as I could—without ever moving a muscle.

Finally, the doctors diagnosed my problem as a bulging disc. Now I knew why I was in agony when I moved, but I still couldn't train. Later, when I could walk a little, I went to the track and had them set up all five of my events. Even though I couldn't practice, I would stand on the track and envision in my mind the complete physical training routine I would have gone through that day if I had been able. For months, I repeatedly imagined myself competing and qualifying at the trials.

But was visualizing enough? Was it truly possible that I could place in the top three at the Olympic trials? I believed it with all my heart.

By the time the trials actually rolled around, I had healed just enough to compete. Being very careful to keep my muscles and tendons warm, I moved through my five events as if in a dream. Afterwards, as I walked across the field, I heard a voice on the loudspeaker announcing my name.

It took my breath away, even though I had imagined it a thousand times in my mind. I felt a wave of pure joy wash over me as the announcer said, "Second place, 1980 Olympic Pentathlon: Marilyn King."

~Marilyn King as told to Carol Kline
Chicken Soup for the Unsinkable Soul

83

Give It a Try

Shoot for the moon. Even if you miss, you'll land among the stars.
~Les Brown

I love the kids of Hawai'i. I enjoyed being one, and I enjoyed teaching them. So it was fitting that I ended up teaching and coaching at Holy Family Catholic Academy, the same school I attended as a junior high student.

One day in October 1999, two eighth grade girls on my volleyball team, Rachael and Emerisa, came to talk with me. "Coach Angie," they said, "now that the volleyball season is over and this is our last year at Holy Family, we'd really like to try out for the basketball team. But we've never played basketball before, and we'll be embarrassed if the younger players make the team and we don't."

"You're both talented and athletic," I started. "If you don't try, you'll never know." Hoping to convince them, I said, "If you're willing to try, I'll help you prepare for tryouts." I noticed in their faces that they were still reluctant to accept the challenge.

As a coach and teacher, I love to inspire my students to accomplish more than they think they can. So I tried to encourage them with my own story. I told the girls how I'd twice competed and lost in the local and state preliminary pageants to Miss America back when I was just eighteen and nineteen years old. "You win something even if you lose," I told them. "Even though I didn't win the state competitions, I gained self-confidence and honed my communication skills.

I also earned thousands in scholarship assistance. It's always worth it to try." The girls said they'd think about it, and went home.

The next day, Rachael and Emerisa surprisingly agreed to my plan. But there was a catch. "Okay, Coach Angie," they said. "We'll get ready with you for basketball tryouts, only if you'll compete again for Miss America."

"What?" I said in shock. "I was just a teenager then. I've got a job now!"

They looked at each other. "But, you still have one last year to try, just like us! Are you scared?" one asked.

"Don't you want to face and overcome your fear?" asked the other, trying to look angelic and keep a straight face at the same time.

I almost had to laugh. They caught me at my own lesson.

As I went home that night, I thought, How can I talk "the talk" if I don't live it myself? I have to show them I mean what I say.

The next day I went back and agreed to their bargain.

So the girls started practicing basketball, and I once again began honing my public speaking and pageant skills, while continuing to teach and coach at the school.

The night I competed for Miss O'ahu in January 2000, Rachael and Emerisa were in the audience screaming for me. When I was named first runner-up, they both beamed with pride. Even though I was not the winner, I knew I had just displayed courage and taught them that you never know what you can do until you try.

"You came so close!" said Rachael.

"If you try again, I'll bet you can win!" said Emerisa.

Their enthusiasm spurred me to overcome my fears and challenge myself to try one last preliminary pageant—Miss Leeward. It was my very last chance to run in the Miss America system, and this time, I won.

I advanced to the state level and became Miss Hawai'i in June 2000. As one of the fifty-one contestants in the national pageant, a full crew came to Hawai'i to film my students and the youth choir I direct. This became my motivation and my lucky charm. During the actual week of national competition, I didn't have time to be nervous because my focus was just to make the top ten so that my kids would get to see themselves on television! Again, my students had propelled me to do my best and be a role model for them.

Then, on October 14, 2000, I was crowned the first teacher and first Asian to become Miss America in the pageant's eighty-year history.

It was such a blessing to finally realize a dream I thought was once out of reach. I got to travel across the country, talking to thousands of people about my platform of character education in the classrooms, valuing our nation's teachers and about my beautiful Hawai'i.

And the icing on the cake?

Rachael and Emerisa not only made the basketball team; they became team captains.

As my students have taught me, it's always worth it to try.

~Angela Perez Baraquiro
Chicken Soup for the Soul of Hawaii

84

The Song in You

Back in the summer of 1976, in Nashville, Tennessee, I came to a crossroads in my life, and I had a decision to make. Should I stay with my brothers, the Gatlin Brothers, and sing their country music—or follow God's leading in my heart and sing a different song? Although the prospect of stardom lay just ahead for the Gatlins, I could not get away from that tug in my heart. So, after much soul-searching, I chose to sing God's song.

That song has taken me on an incredible journey. It has taken me from the Grand Old Opry to the splendor of the Crystal Cathedral and every place in between. I've sung it in the spotlight with hundreds of people looking on. I've sung it by the nightlight as I sang lullabies to my babies. I've sung it in the halls of corporate powerhouses, and I've sung it in the halls of death row prison blocks. I've found one thing to be true in all those places—people need to hear my song.

Oh sure, the melody and the lyrics change from place to place. Sometimes I sing, "I'm on Top of the World." Other times, however, I sing a far different tune. Like the day that a young female inmate walked up to me in a prison yard and said, "LaDonna, I can remember living in only two places in my entire life—under a bridge in Dallas and behind these prison walls."

I had no idea what to say to that young woman. So I cradled her precious face in my hands and with tears streaming down both our cheeks, I did the only thing I knew how to do—I sang her my song.

"Amazing Grace, how sweet the sound that saved a wretch like me. I once was lost, but now I'm found, was blind but now I see."

I didn't have the power to reverse the young woman's sentence — to sign some document that would set her free. But I did have the opportunity to offer her something that I believe supersedes the constraints of any circumstances — hope — a hope that gave her strength.

My journey has shown me that there's a whole world full of people out there who feel just as imprisoned as that young inmate — imprisoned by their circumstances, their failures, their fears. They have no hope, or so it seems. We all have a God-given song to share, and just as I sang my song to her, we can each sing our songs of hope every day. It may be as simple as a smile, a kind word, a pat on the back or a handwritten note that says, "I'm here for you, I'm praying for you."

None of us should be afraid to sing our songs — we never know who needs to hear the music.

~LaDonna Gatlin
Chicken Soup for the Christian Woman's Soul

85

A Long Hot Summer

Success isn't a result of spontaneous combustion.
You must set yourself on fire.
~Arnold H. Glasow

There are numerous reasons why a middle-aged woman who has been away from the workforce rearing her children decides to go back to work. The obvious might be for money, but that was not my reason.

After my children departed for college, perhaps I was just bored, or possibly I was suffering from the empty nest syndrome, but in actuality I think I decided to return to work because I was just plain hot. Colorado was experiencing an extremely hot, dry summer and my home lacked air conditioning. It was hot, and I was hot. I determined a cool air conditioned office was where I belonged! Years ago my first job was that of a bookkeeper—it was then that I worked for money. While my children were growing up I worked part time in the school system as a teacher's aide.

This time around I wanted to do something different, something new and exciting, and the money wasn't too important, as my husband made a very comfortable living for us. But what should I do? What sort of job should I look for? I knew I needed to be cautious as to what I became involved with. I am not a "quitter" and therefore I hoped to avoid becoming obligated to an employer in a job that might turn out to be a mistake for me.

While I agonized over what to do, I was reminded of a past incident where I needed to replace my original engagement ring as the gold was wearing thin. My husband and I shopped and shopped for one, everywhere we went, even when we were on vacation. Finally this nonstop searching prompted my poor husband to ask, "Just what kind of ring do you want, what exactly are we looking for?"

My reply was, "I honestly don't know, but when I see the correct setting, I will know it." That was the way I felt about the new career I wished to pursue; I didn't have a clue as to what I wanted to do, but knew there was a perfect fit for me, if I would just be patient.

Fortunately, that summer while attending my twenty-fifth high school class reunion, I overheard a former classmate describing what she did for a living. She was a travel agent, and she and her husband had just returned from a trip to Hawaii where they acted as chaperones for a group of travelers. WOW, that sounded like fun, considerably more fun and exciting than being a bookkeeper. Apparently this profession also had some great travel benefits. I innocently pondered the idea of becoming a travel agent. After all, how difficult could it be to write airline tickets and plan vacations? I reasoned if my friend could do it, I probably could, too, and after all, "I love to travel." I later learned uttering the phrase, "I love to travel", is a surefire way to prevent you from being hired when applying for a job in the travel industry. That phrase is definitely a no-no!

BINGO! It was as if fireworks lit up the night sky! Right then and there I knew without a doubt, I had found the perfect fit; I wanted to be a travel agent. Little did I realize travel agents are a specialized group of individuals whose work is both stressful and demanding. Theirs is a profession requiring special education, training and experience to become proficient. There is definitely more to it than meets the eye. There is unquestionably more to it than just generating airline tickets.

I began scanning the "help wanted" ads in my local newspaper and quickly discovered agencies were interested in hiring "experienced only travel agents, or airline personnel." I was neither. However, one agency located near my home (how lucky can you get) had an entry-level position available that involved answering the phone, typing itineraries and packaging tickets. The owner made it very clear this position would never lead to an agent position or agent training, but offered me an interview if I was interested. I was definitely interested! I interviewed and was hired. Bravo, at least I had my foot in the door.

After working on the packaging desk for nine months, I approached the agency owner, and again expressed my desire to become a travel agent. Fortunately, she made an exception and broke her "no experience no training" rules by enrolling me in a United Airlines computer training course. Thus, I realized my dream and became a full-fledged agent.

My confidence and self-worth increased with each error-free reservation and each satisfied customer. I was having a ball! I learned as much as possible about the foreign destinations I booked and got to know my clients well, so their special needs could always be met. I loved my work and took pride in it. I am proud to say, never once did I take the marvelous travel benefits I was receiving for granted. I did keep track of them, however, and received a great deal of satisfaction the year the value of my benefits exceeded my yearly salary. Now that is what I call a job! Way back when I began this career, I could not imagine myself working full time, but just as quickly couldn't visualize myself not working full time, for I was having the time of my life!

What a positive impact those middle-age "hot flashes" had on my life. Ultimately, I became a top-producing corporate international sales agent before my early retirement seventeen years later. I also experienced a world of travel, some shared with family and friends. Most importantly, I proved to myself I could do what I made up my mind to do, no matter how difficult or foreign the task. Yes indeed, life is beautiful and life can begin at forty-plus years of age.

~Carolee Ware
Chicken Soup for the Working Woman's Soul

Over the Wall

I would not have been there except they had lowered the height requirement in the late 1970s to recruit more minorities and women—and I was both a "minority" and a "woman." Their goal was to recruit Asian and Latino men, but it also opened the door for a "little" woman like me to get through. This was my chance—me, Linda Coleman—to become a deputy sheriff.

The day was young and overcast when I arrived at the police academy. But as far as I was concerned, the sun was shining. I'd made it.

It had been a long, grueling year getting to this point. I had taken a written test, a psychological exam and an oral interview, and I had passed all three. Then the background investigation began. They investigated everyone, from my grandmother in Texas, to my next-door neighbors, to the babysitter of my two small children. They knew everything about me from the day I was born.

As part of my qualification process I spent a day at a sheriff station with the captain. I was scrutinized, chastised and down-right ostracized. It was no secret how he felt; he never missed an opportunity to tell me. "Women don't belong on the department, all gays should be taken out and shot, where do 'you people' get off thinking you can do whatever you want nowadays?" If I heard one more story about the "good ole days" when women were women and men were men and "you people" knew your place, I think I would have puked.

But all that was behind me now. I was at the academy, and I was going to be a deputy sheriff. My excitement didn't last long.

My first encounter was with a twenty-year career officer, a sergeant nicknamed "Goliath." He was six-feet-four-inches tall, and 300 pounds of solid muscle, to my five-feet-three-inches and 118 pounds of woman. "Sgt. Goliath" let me know in no uncertain terms he was not happy I was there. Like others in the department, he believed this was a "men only" profession. And it would suit many of them just fine if it were "white men only."

The sergeant never called me by name. It was always "little lady" or "little girl." When he looked at me, he would stare as if he were looking right through me. It was apparent he was not going to make it easy. In fact, his job was to make it as difficult as possible for me to pass the physical agility test, and he did a darn good job.

I had to run the mile, climb through one window and out another, walk a balance beam five feet off the ground, pull a 150-pound mannequin thirty yards and push a police car twenty feet, all in record time. And as the sergeant said before I began, "Look here, Little Lady, if you can't do all of these activities including pushing that police car over here until it touches my kneecaps, I'm gonna have the pleasure of sending you home."

I completed each task, but every bone, muscle and fiber of my body ached. I could hardly catch my breath. Some of the recruits passed out and had to be carried off the course. My vision was blurred, my heart beat a mile a minute, and my ears hummed, but I didn't pass out. In fact, I walked off the course on my own and felt pride welling up inside. I had completed that obstacle course, and I was going to be a deputy sheriff.

But the smirk on the sergeant's face told me I was wrong. That's when I discovered yet another challenge waiting for me. This time even I didn't know if I would be able to make it. My head ached, my legs were as heavy as lead, and my arms felt as if someone had yanked them from their sockets.

The ultimate challenge? Climbing a six-foot, solid concrete wall. If somehow you were able to get through the physical agility test, this would separate the boys from the men—or girls from the women, as it were. Recruit after recruit, both men and women, tackled the six-foot wall only to fall to the ground in defeat. Most of them were taller and bigger than me. I could feel my heart sink and my confidence fade. I saw my career with the sheriff's department slipping away.

Two more recruits, and then it would be my turn. I closed my eyes and tried to envision myself going over the wall. Suddenly, I remembered a song my grandmother used to sing in church, an old Negro spiritual. "I shall, I shall, I shall not be moved." My nerves calmed. I heard my father's voice, "You have to be twice as good and do twice as much just to compete." And I thought, I have been twice as good and I have done twice as much and I have given it my all and now this....

And then I swear I heard the words of my high school track coach. "A lady's strength is in her legs, not in her arms." I had watched the women try to tackle the wall by jumping up like the men and grabbing hold of the wall with their arms in an attempt to pull themselves atop the wall, straddle it and drop to the other side. It hadn't worked for them, and I knew it wouldn't work for me.

I shall not be moved. Be twice as good and do twice as much. A lady's strength is in her legs. It was my turn. The six-foot, solid concrete wall loomed bigger than life—the only thing standing between me and my dream. I closed my eyes and imagined it was a track field.

I took off running as fast as I could, and when my feet hit the concrete I looked up to the heavens. And I ran up that wall! I shall not be moved. Twice as good. A lady's strength. I straddled the top and dropped to the other side.

The whole camp was cheering—everyone, that is, except the sergeant. He never said a word. He turned his back and walked away. Several men made it over that day, but I was the only woman.

Since then, I have gone over a lot of walls, but I learned some valuable lessons at the academy that have helped me. What the

Goliaths think is not nearly as important as what I think about myself. The Goliaths despise change and progress, but there are some things even they can't control.

~Linda Coleman-Willis
Chicken Soup for the African American Soul

Woman to Woman

Taking Time for Yourself

*I love people, I love my family, my children...
but inside myself is a place where I live all alone
and that's where you renew your springs that never dry up.*
~Pearl S. Buck

Calm Mother

As a teenager growing up in the sixties, I knew what I wanted to do with my life and what I didn't want to do. I wanted to travel and see the world. I didn't want to be a mother.

Both desires were a rebellion against my own childhood. I grew up on the flat prairie land of the Midwest and thus yearned to see mountains, clouds and trees. My own parents never treated me well, so I grew up not liking anybody, except for my kind, loving grandmothers.

Every hot, cloudless prairie summer, my family would travel to the tree-lined city to visit both of my grandmothers. Around their own mothers, my parents treated me well. How I loved my grandmothers! Best of all, they loved me back.

Achieving my teenage goals would be easy: After getting a college degree, I planned to travel to the city of my choice and get a job. After two or three years when I began to get bored, I would move on to another ideal city. If I found my true love along the way, I would get married and settle down, but I wouldn't have children.

In my twenties, I graduated from college and went to live in my chosen city. So far, so good. Then one summer I decided to visit the hot, flat prairie town where I grew up. It was fun to chatter away with the adults I had known as a child. For once, I was being treated like an adult among other adults.

One of the couples I visited asked me if I would babysit for their five little boys. I had never babysat for anyone before. How hard can it be? I thought to myself and accepted.

I found out it could be very hard. I didn't know that five boys, aged two to twelve, could be so loud and energetic. They also got very physical, and amazed as I was, I did not try to control them. This made the situation even worse. Just as the parents walked in through the front door, the little two-year-old boy, who was very wound up, hurled himself onto me trying to greet his parents. Without thinking, I turned around and hit him. The whole family froze in shock. I looked bewildered at everybody until the father asked quietly, "Why did you hit my son?"

"He hit me first," I answered, feeling completely justified.

"It was an accident," he replied.

"It was?"

Violence in my own childhood had been intentional and fre quent, never accidental. This new concept had never even occurred to me. I turned toward the little boy and asked, "Did you mean to hit me?"

Still whimpering, he shook his head earnestly, the tears falling down his flushed cheeks. My hardened heart cracked.

"I'm sorry."

The tension relieved, they quickly forgave me and we embraced Their warmth and forgiveness affected me deeply. I saw that simply not having children wouldn't solve the deeper problems inside me The abuse I'd experienced as a child had turned me into a violent adult. I couldn't ignore it anymore, but I honestly didn't know what to do. I didn't want to tell anyone, for fear of ruining what few friend ships I had. After all, I had almost lost one friendship with a loving family—with one unthinking blow.

The following spring I visited my older brother, who had recently married. He and his wife and child lived on an Indian reservation. I attended church with my family, and found it interesting to be in the minority, one of the few whites among so many Native Americans During my visit, I befriended an Indian grandmother.

One day, right after church ended, the grandmother and I were standing together and she remarked, "White man's babies are so noisy." Looking around the room at all the contented Indian babies and then at the crying, whimpering white babies, I realized the truth in her words! My nephew was no exception.

"Why is that?" I asked her in astonishment.

She answered by describing the tradition of her tribe. When a young girl started menstruating, she left the tribe for one day to spend time alone in the wilderness and meditate about what kind of woman she would be when she grew up. Of course, her father followed discreetly to ensure her safety.

Each following month, at the appropriate time, she would spend another day by herself and meditate. As she grew, she meditated about what kind of young man she wanted to attract. After engagement, she meditated about what kind of wife she would be. After her marriage, she meditated about what kind of mother she would be, and so on. Thus, each woman took time each month to be alone and meditate about where her life was going, what kind of person she was becoming and what to do about her problems. The grandmother ended her narrative by saying, "Calm mother makes calm baby."

Listening to her, I felt a surge of warmth and love inside me. I knew I had finally discovered the answer to my curse of violence. I followed her advice exactly, only I meditated once a week to make up for the lost years.

First, I meditated on how to be a better worker at my job and how to be a better friend. In the stillness, answers came. I needed to stop taking offense so easily in both situations. I needed to stop thinking and saying "I" so much and start asking about the other person more.

As I was dating, I meditated about each boyfriend and our relationship. Did I give more than I took? Did we laugh easily? Was I a good listener? Did I like him when I wasn't in love with him?

Eventually, I found my true love. After our marriage, I continued the frequent meditations. The process of two becoming one seemed to bring out issues I thought I had resolved sufficiently when I was single. The questions kept coming. However, I stayed calm and stuck with the plan, meditating week by week, month by month.

It's worked! Our marriage has continued happily, and now we have five wonderful children. All of these "white man's babies" have mostly been calm, and the violence of my childhood has remained a thing of the past.

How grateful I am that an old Indian grandmother whose name I never knew managed to change my life and the lives of my children for the better with her simple wisdom: Calm mother makes calm baby.

~Holly Danneman
Chicken Soup for the Mother's Soul 2

88

It Happened One Autumn

I've been seduced again by the boy next door.

It doesn't happen often, but he does have a way about him. I'm sitting in my office, nose to the grindstone, shoulder pressed to the wheel, struggling to meet deadlines without much success. My brain seems to have slipped into neutral, gone on vacation—oh, you get the idea. So I'm busily shuffling stacks of paper and writing fevered motivational notes to myself: Finish proposal!!!—as if the number of exclamation points will resurrect my will to work.

In the midst of this busy inactivity, I hear a knock on my door. I open it, turn my gaze downward and see Tyler, my young neighbor, and he's holding a football. Somewhat redundantly, he says, "You want to come out and play football with me?"

Tyler is eight, but he knows a playmate when he meets one. The day I moved in, Ty and his brother Jay came over and helped me unload boxes from my U-Haul. After we finished, I bought them each a burger and a root beer. After that, during those first few weeks in my new place, when I needed duct tape or another curtain rod, Ty and Jay were more than willing to accompany me to Wal-Mart and show me the best toys.

Jay is eleven and a cool guy—too cool, actually, to meander over to the lady next door to see if she'll come toss a football with him. Tyler, however, has no such inhibitions. He sees that I have not one, but two bicycles; that I go for walks every day; and that some evenings I sit on my porch and strum on my guitar. So I am, in his eyes, okay.

"Ty," I say, doing my best to be a grown-up, "I really would like to, but I've got to work."

Tyler holds up a piece of white plastic. "Look," he says, as if this piece of conversation will make all the difference: "I got a new tee. I can kick and you can catch."

"Tyler," I repeat slowly, to impress upon him the urgency of my situation. "I have a deadline. That means I have to get this in the mail tomorrow."

"Fifteen minutes," he says steadily, locking my gaze with those cornflower blue eyes.

My children always knew they could do this, too. What kind of signals do I give out, I wonder, that apparently say, "Press on, she can be had?"

I stand in the door, looking at him, considering. Okay, I tell myself, I can go play with Tyler for fifteen minutes and eat dinner at my desk—it's not as if I'm making any progress anyway.

"All right," I respond, wagging a finger. "Let me get my shoes on. But just fifteen minutes. I mean it." Tyler never sees the wagging finger; he's already doing a little end-zone victory dance on my porch.

As I slip on my shoes, my dog enters stage left, positively effervescent. When Bob-Dog sees lace-up shoes come out, he knows the leash is next and then, let the good times roll. So out we go into the front yard—Bob-Dog, Tyler and me. The crystalline air is fresh, cool, filled with the scents of autumn. Leaves crinkle under our feet as Ty kicks off and I dash within the general vicinity of the ball.

"You have to catch it," he says, as if I needed this solemn bit of coaching.

"Thank you, Tyler," I say, as I take up my position down field again.

This time, I catch it and it's my turn to throw. As usual, I toss the football about three feet in front of me. Tyler lopes up beside me in that easy manner of the natural athlete. "The way to do it," he says, picking up the football and demonstrating, "is to twist at the waist before I throw. That way I use more than just my arm."

I try it and I am astounded—I throw the ball halfway across my yard. Not great, but... not utterly pathetic. I try again. Tyler is all over the encouragement thing.

"Way to go!" he says, with absolute sincerity. "Here—throw it all the way down here!"

And so it goes, for about an hour. Finally, my conscience catches up with me. Breathing hard, I tell him it's time to stop.

"Okay," he says, "After you catch one more." He's on very solid turf with that one. He knows I only catch about one out of ten. He tosses. I miss and shag the ball. He tosses, I miss and shag the ball. He tosses and finally I say, "Look, kiddo, I really have to go to work."

He kicks a few leaves and says, "Heck," but then he runs toward the driveway. "Throw long!" he shouts over his shoulder. I do. He misses and I laugh.

Entering the warmth of my house, I remove my jacket—it smells like autumn. My face is cool and I am happy.

Within minutes of sitting down, in a slap-my-forehead, V-8 moment, I suddenly see what my project was missing. Why hadn't I realized that before? Maybe because my body was telling me what my brain didn't want to hear—that recess is important, no matter how old we are or how serious our work becomes.

It's autumn. Front-yard football is best at this time of year and must be savored when in season, just like tomatoes in August or hot cider in December.

I hope I always have a Tyler in my life to remind me that all work and no play make Jill a grumpy girl. I hope that no matter how old I get or how serious I become, that I'll allow myself to be coached—even if the coach is only eight and I can't tell if it's freckles or chocolate milk splattered on his nose.

~K. C. Compton
Chicken Soup to Inspire the Body and Soul

89

The Wonders of Tupperware

Someone to tell it to is one of the fundamental needs of human beings.
~Miles Franklin

Many years ago, in the far distant past of 1966, Tupperware parties were all the rage with stay-at-home moms. Practically all of us "kept house" then, and these parties gave us a pleasant and acceptable way to go out for the evening, usually leaving the dads to handle the kids' bath and bed routine.

We loved actually talking with people older than five, although our conversations mostly centered around those very topics we knew best — kids and housekeeping. While learning the proper way to "burp" a container, we also discussed burping babies. Usually, after about three hours of listening to the demonstrator, playing silly games and filling out our order forms, we would all go home thinking of the wonderful new plastic additions to our already bulging kitchen storage cabinets. We might not see each other again for a month or so until someone else decided to host the next "party."

One day, after a Thursday night Tupperware party at the home of my friend Kay who lived two doors down from me, I was in the backyard hanging out wash (something else we used to do in the olden days, but that's another story). Kay yelled over the back fence that she had some pastries left over and maybe we should gather up some neighbors and finish them off with coffee later that afternoon. This was an unusual idea in our neighborhood. None of us had lived there very long, we all had little ones who took up a lot of our time and we just didn't socialize much except for demonstration parties. I told Kay it sounded good to me, so we called everyone who had been there the night before and made plans to meet at my house at 2:00.

Normally, by 2:00 in the afternoon, most of us had the kids in for a nap, but this time we decided to forgo the naps for just this once and let them play while we ate the pastries and talked. It was raining out, so the little ones had to play in the dining room of my tiny house, out of sight but within hearing distance, while we moms sat talking in the living room. Before we knew it, two hours had gone by and everyone hurried off to start dinner before the men got home from work. But something interesting had happened in those two hours, something that we all knew we wanted to continue.

We continued to meet for three more years, every Friday afternoon at 2:00, bringing the kids along to scatter toys and grind pretzels into the dining room rug of whoever was hosting that week. We didn't mind the mess—we were learning that sometimes all mothers lose their cool with their kids, sometimes every loving husband was an unfeeling oaf. We weren't alone in the world, and we weren't monsters who sometimes lost control in our frustration with trying to be the best wife and mother. Amazingly, we discovered other women were having the same struggles. And quite often, just talking about it with friends who really knew allowed us to handle things better the next time we felt like throwing in the towel or strangling somebody.

Week by week, my sanity was saved and my marriage was strengthened because I found a safe place to vent my frustrations and learn new ways of coping. We moms learned from each other while we developed wonderful friendships among ourselves, and our children learned valuable social skills (such as picking up your own pretzel crumbs) from their tag-along playgroup. And all because of a Tupperware party!

That Tupperware—who knew it could preserve so many things?

Carol Bryant
Chicken Soup for the Mother's Soul 2

90

No More Babies

The moment a child is born, the mother is also born.
She never existed before. The woman existed, but the mother, never.
A mother is something absolutely new.
~Rajneesh

None of the things I have accomplished in my life ever consumed my imagination or yielded the intense gratification that having babies did. And I say this having written books and baked pies, grown vegetables, fixed up houses, rafted rivers, organized political campaigns, acted in plays and built enduring friendships. None of them came close.

This makes things tricky. If what you love best is playing the flute, you can (with luck) play the flute until your dying day. Same with gardening, reading, bird-watching and golfing. What I happen to love best is a game you can play for only so many years. Then you turn in your jersey, clean out your locker and retire from the sport, knowing you're never again going to play it. I will always be the mother of my three children, but the particular thrill (as well as the terror, exhaustion, frustration and loss of self) that comes with conceiving, giving birth and launching a new human being into the world is one I will not know again. There is a measure of relief in that, but regret, too.

Fertility is a great and mysterious gift—our blessing and, as we occasionally call it, our curse. I remember the precise moment I learned my ovaries contained all the eggs I would ever possess—my lifetime's store of potential children. And I remember the moment when I first got my period and realized my body could make a baby. To a thirteen-year-old, it was an awe-inspiring and more-than-slightly terrifying thought. It's been thirty years since that day, but I've never ceased to be amazed by it.

From the time I was very young, I pictured myself a mother. At twenty-four, I became one. I had another baby four years later, and a third, two years after that. Even then I didn't say I would never have another. Five years later, when I was thirty-five, my marriage ended, but I continued to imagine I might have another child with another man. It's embarrassing to admit, but every time I found a man who possessed life-partner potential, my thinking turned toward babies. For me, loving someone was nearly always accompanied by an interest in procreation—and a longing to know one more child of mine. I was forty-three years old when it came to me that the person I needed to know better, after a couple of decades of motherhood, was me.

My moment of closing the door to the baby dream came relatively late. But whether a woman bids goodbye to having babies at menopause or at age twenty-five, because of biology or conscious choice, happily or with great sadness, it is a rite of passage none of us can avoid. It is a moment that ranks—with first menstruation, loss of virginity, marriage, childbirth, death of a parent and divorce—among the landmarks of life.

Throughout adulthood, my fertility symbolized possibility to me. I obviously didn't take advantage of my childbearing potential more than a few times, but I still loved knowing it was there. It's as if I had been carrying an airplane ticket in my purse, destination anyplace. I might not have gotten on the plane, but over the years I took enormous pleasure in thinking about all the places I could go.

Of the adjectives I'd use to describe myself, fertile would be only one, and probably not in the first fifty I'd mention. I was the same me before I had children, and I will be the same me now that I'm done. It was never difficult, even a decade back, to see why the time had come to close the door on the idea of more babies, starting with the fact that I'd had three already. My children have made huge demands on my time, energy and concentration for close to two decades. Without them, I would have written more books, contributed more to my community and planet, cooked more elaborate meals, had a more beautiful home, kept a lusher garden, maintained a flatter stomach. Without children, I would have had more time for friends, more money for trips—and more freedom to take them. Without children, I might now play the piano, run in marathons, dance the tango.

Or not. Because I've also learned over the many years I haven't been doing those things (and occasionally using my children as the excuse) that sometimes it's only when an obstacle prevents you from accomplishing a goal that you acquire the drive to reach it. Before I had children—back when I had all the time and concentration in the world for my own concerns—I wasted a lot of time on very little. I had to lose the freedom of my time to value it sufficiently.

I've finally realized I've been carrying more than one airplane ticket in my purse all these years. One would have taken me back to the land of parenthood. If I had gone there, I would have taken in amazing sights and met unforgettable people—or one, anyway: the child I would have had. If I had gone on that trip, it's doubtful I ever would have said, "I wish I had stayed home."

But there's another trip a woman can take—the one I'm opting for now. This one will take me somewhere I've never been before. Because of that, it's scarier for me than the other journey. It's not an ending, though, for as much as the ability to procreate signals possibilities, the choice to put that aside also signals possibilities—just different ones. Like tango lessons and the freedom to stay out late or sleep in the next morning. And the possibility of having sex on the kitchen floor in the middle of the day or the financial freedom to go on safari in Tanzania.

It's easy to see what a person gives up when she finally acknowledges the hard truth that not one of those remaining eggs in her ovaries is ever going to turn into a person. The rest of that truth is this: Whichever route a woman chooses—to have a child or not—represents both the loss of one gift and the discovery of another. When a woman relinquishes the dream of babies, what she gets, if she is wise enough to recognize it, is her own self back. Maybe a person has to have lost that for a while to recognize how precious it is.

I thought I would feel very old when the day finally came that I knew I was done having babies. That day has come, all right. The funny thing is, it's making me feel very young again. I'm not finished; I'm starting.

~Joyce Maynard
Chicken Soup to Inspire a Woman's Soul

91

Have Freedom, Will Travel

Travel has been my comrade, adventure my inspiration,
accomplishment my recompense.
~Charlotte Cameron

I had a ticket. I had my passport. And he had cold feet. I might have known fairy tales don't come true.

Seven months out of my marriage, I had met the "great love of my life." We dated a year. I'd always longed to see Europe, and, with my divorce final, we planned the trip together. Then two weeks before takeoff, he took off. Having piggybacked two breakups, I felt as if I'd been through a double divorce. Here I was, thirty-nine years old, with two small children, and facing my ultimate fear: a life alone.

Was I ready to spend a month in Europe by myself? I had a hard time going to a movie alone! But it did seem now or never. The kids would be with their dad, the money came as part of my property settlement, and I had a job waiting when I returned. Okay, if I was going to be lonely for the next few years, I might as well start by being lonely in Europe.

The highlight of my journey was to be Paris, the city I'd always wanted to see. But now I was frightened to travel without a companion. I steeled myself and went anyway.

I arrived at the train station in Paris panicked and disoriented. I hadn't used my college French in twenty years. Pulling my red suitcase on wobbly wheels behind me, I was shoved and pushed by perspiring travelers reeking of cigarette smoke, different diets and not nearly enough deodorant. The roar of many languages bombarding me seemed unintelligible—just babble.

On my first Metro ride, I encountered an incompetent, clumsy pickpocket. I melted him with a look, and he eased his hand from my purse to fade into the crowded car. At my stop, I hauled my heavy suitcase up the steep stairs and froze.

Cars zoomed helter-skelter, honking belligerently. Somewhere in this confusing city my hotel was hidden, but the directions I had scrawled suddenly weren't legible.

I stopped two people. Both greeted me with that Parisian countenance that said: "Yes, I speak English, but you'll have to struggle with your French if you want to talk to me." I walked up one street and across another. A wheel broke off my suitcase. When I finally found the hotel, my heart was pounding, I was sweating like a basketball player and my spirits drooped. They flattened altogether when I saw my room.

I couldn't stay. Could I? The wallpaper looked like it had been through a fire. The bedsprings creaked. The bathroom was down the hall, and the window looked out onto the brick wall of another building. Welcome to Paris.

I sincerely wanted to die. I missed my friend. I was entering my third week away from home and my kids, and I had arrived in the most romantic city in the world, alone. Alone and lonely. Alone, lonely and petrified.

The most important thing I did in Paris happened at that moment. I knew that if I didn't go out, right then, and find a place to have dinner, I would hide in this cubicle my entire time in Paris. My dream would be foregone, and I might never learn to enjoy the world as a single individual. So I pulled myself together and went out.

Evening in Paris was light and balmy. When I reached the Tuileries, I strolled along a winding path, listening to birds sing, watching children float toy sailboats in a huge fountain. No one seemed to be in a hurry. Paris was beautiful. And I was here alone but suddenly not lonely. My sense of accomplishment at overcoming my fear and vulnerability had left me feeling free, not abandoned.

I wore out two pairs of shoes during my week's stay in Paris. I did everything there was to do, and it was the greatest week of my European vacation. I returned home a believer in the healing power of solitary travel. Years later, I still urge divorcing or widowed friends to take their solo flight in the form of travel plans.

Those who have gone have returned changed—even by a four-day weekend in Santa Fe, an Amtrak ride up the coast or an organized tour of Civil War battlefields. Traveling alone redeems itself by demanding self-reliance and building the kind of confidence that serves the single life well.

Certainly Paris became my metaphor for addressing life's challenges on my own. Now when I meet an obstacle I just say to myself: If I can go to Paris, I can go anywhere.

~Dawn McKenna
Chicken Soup for the Single's Soul

92

The Piranha

My mother told me never to rock the boat or challenge a male authority figure.

"Men need to save face," she explained. "Conflict isn't worth it."

I took after my father. Opinionated, fearless, ready to crusade for justice.

I struggled with my natural gift of courage versus my desire to please Mom and never be pushy. As a result, I was always conflicted and guilt-ridden if I spoke up.

When my husband and I packed our few possessions and headed west to pursue our dreams of music, I would receive a lesson in assertiveness that would change me forever. Back in the Midwest, I sang local TV commercials. The prospect of finding work in Hollywood was frightening to say the least. For eight months, I mailed out demo tapes, called producers, dropped by studios and basically struck out. One day, I mailed my demo to a new production company.

They called me the very next day.

"We loved your tape!" the producer gushed. "Come to the studio Friday. There's a national TV commercial I want you to sing."

"Wow, that's great," I said.

"We can't pay you regular union rates, and you won't get future royalties, but I can guarantee one day of work a week at one hundred dollars an hour."

So that Friday, I sang the commercial, met the studio musicians and became a national "jingle singer."

Within weeks, I was their regular soloist and even sang backup with the other singers. The fact that we were grossly underpaid and signed agreements to waive all our royalties was okay with me. The hourly rate was more than I had ever earned in my life, and I was doing what I loved, so what did it matter?

Then reality hit.

My paycheck came in the mail every two weeks, and I kept perfect records about every recording session, but somehow the paychecks and my records would never coincide. The checks were always smaller than the amounts I showed being due. I kept "fluffing" it off thinking maybe I hadn't worked as many hours as I thought, figuring it must be my fault. Every two weeks, a check would arrive that was too small, my heart would sink and the same frustration would rise up in me. Finally, I called the accountant and asked her to check it.

"Thanks," I said weakly, "I'm sure it's my mistake, but..."

"No, those are the right amounts," she said.

"But I have down that I worked these days and these hours."

"You did," she said. "What's the problem?"

"At one hundred dollars an hour, that's not right."

"Oh," she laughed. "Well, you're figuring this up at the wrong rate. Why do you think you get a hundred dollars an hour? You make seventy. All the singers do."

"What? Trent guaranteed me one hundred dollars an hour with no future royalties."

"He would never pay a singer that much." She smirked. "He told me to pay you seventy dollars an hour like all the other girls get."

The way she said "girls" made me feel small and stupid. I didn't like that feeling.

"I need to talk to Trent," I said, my heart racing.

She transferred me and he picked up the phone. If I hadn't felt so angry and used, I would never have found the courage to even phone him. I kindly reminded him how much he had promised to pay me. When he laughed, I felt worse.

"Look," he said, "you're scheduled to sing Friday afternoon. Why don't you come over to the business office — we'll straighten out this misunderstanding."

Misunderstanding? That's what he called it?

Friday, I walked into the office complex and saw a new Jaguar parked in Trent's space. The atrium lobby was filled with waterfalls and tropical fish. I had no idea it would be so palatial. I grew more upset as I thought about my small, inaccurate paychecks.

"Trent will see you now," his secretary said.

"Hi! Come on in," he smiled.

I took the seat in front of him. Just then, he reached under his desk and pressed a button. The drapes closed electronically. He pressed another button and the door locked.

"There, that's better," he smiled. "Hold all my calls," he said, leaning into his speakerphone.

The "good girl" who never confronted a man in authority was ready to take this guy on.

"What's the next button you're going to push?" I said folding my arms.

"Does the floor open up and the piranha appear?"

He laughed in a phony sort way and I leaned forward, shouting in my mind not to be intimidated. I came to the point and reminded him what he promised to pay me when he hired me.

"Wow, I just don't remember saying that," he said evasively. "You see, none of the other singers get that and I just don't know why I ever would have promised you that much. Hey, even if I agree now to give you that, how would it look to them? What would I tell them?"

"What you pay other singers is none of my business," I said quickly. "I only know what I need to be paid and I can't work for less than the one hundred an hour you promised me."

"Hope, this is a tough business. You have no idea how much it costs to do this kind of production," he said, staring at me.

Tough business? I thought. Jaguar? Waterfalls?

I felt myself weakening. The old guilt rose up again. What

others needed came before what I needed. I didn't count. I shouldn't inconvenience people.

I was lucky to even have a job. I was just a "woman."

Suddenly, I "woke up."

"I'm an experienced, talented singer," I proclaimed. "Whether you remember or not, we did agree on one hundred dollars an hour. It's way below what other national singers make with royalties, but I chose to work with you in this arrangement. This isn't about what you pay everyone else, it's about what you and I agreed upon."

"I just don't think that would be fair," he repeated.

"I sang those TV station tags." I began. "The ones going to every city."

"So?"

"I've only sung half of them. If you want me to finish them, I will—at one hundred dollars an hour."

Trent put his hands behind his head. "Oh, I get it." He laughed.

Suddenly, he reached under his desk. The door clicked open. The drapes started moving.

"No problem," he said. "A hundred an hour it is, I just thought we should chat a bit."

I walked outside, put on my sunglasses and shouted, "Yes!"

Every two weeks my checks arrived for the right amounts, and I continued an enjoyable career there until I moved to another city.

I had been willing to lose everything in that meeting because I was finally tired of losing myself. I wasn't driving a Jaguar or going to a house filled with waterfalls. But as I drove my little Toyota down the freeway, I felt richer than I had ever felt in my life. I found something I had given up so many times, I thought it was gone forever: my self-respect. And I was never going to lose it again.

~Hope Faith
Chicken Soup to Inspire a Woman's Soul

The Piranha: Taking Time for Yourself 325

93

Message in a Body

Take care of your body. It's the only place you have to live.
~Jim Rohn

ave you completely lost your mind? I asked myself as I walked down the hall to the office of my boss. In my right hand I clutched the resignation letter I had typed the night before.

No, you haven't, the small part of me that wasn't scared to death whispered back. Remember what happened a few months ago?

Oh yes, I remembered it well.

I had worked for the same company for over a decade, my dedication and long hours finally paying off when I was promoted to upper management while still young. I had tons of responsibilities, and there were deadlines and daily crises. The stacks of paper on my desk grew taller as the weeks passed, and phone calls, faxes and e-mails dominated my life. I took great pride in my work, and mailed home some business cards to my parents so they could see the title under my name.

One by one, relationships with friends dwindled as I lived and breathed my job. It had become my whole life, and I gave it 110 percent. I pumped myself up with caffeine during the day and took over-the-counter sleep aids to fall asleep at night. I had five kinds of headache remedies and dozens of antacids in my purse as I pushed myself beyond my limits. I started keeping a pad and pen near my bed so I could take notes during those middle-of-the-night anxiety attacks that started to plague me.

Finally, my body said, No more! I had taken three days off and planned to go to Florida and soak in the tranquility of sun, ocean and beach, but the morning I was scheduled to leave I couldn't even get up. My body refused to move. I was utterly exhausted and drained. I slept all day, getting up only to eat before collapsing back into bed. The next day the same thing happened. I tried to bribe my body by imagining a dazzling mental slide show of our vacation, but my body said, Thanks, but no thanks. I need to be where I am.

By the third day I was scared. After forty-eight hours of almost nonstop sleep I was still exhausted and unwilling to move, so I called my doctor, and his office worked me into their schedule.

I lay on the examining table while a technician ran blood tests. I caught a glimpse of myself in a mirror and was shocked—an older woman stared back at me. Who are you? I wondered. She didn't answer. The doctor came back in and pronounced me the healthiest sick person he had ever seen. "You have hyperstress," he said, and wrote a prescription.

"What am I supposed to take?" I asked. In a barely legible scrawl he had written on the pad: "Get a different job."

That day I made a promise to myself: I will carve out time for myself every day. When the clock says it's 5 P.M., I will leave, no matter what.

The first day back at work I had to force myself to do it, and was actually shocked when the sky didn't fall. What a revelation!

I started walking my dogs again, trying to pay them back for all the times I'd left them. I picked up my journal, blew dust off the cover and began writing. Words came slowly at first, then more freely as my inner voice was finally allowed to speak. During the next three months it said: quit your job, over and over again.

I'd been working since I was seventeen, part-time to put myself though college, and then full-time immediately after graduation. Now I had a strong feeling there was a person under all those diplomas and titles who was literally dying to get out. So, with no firm plans for the future, I gave a thirty-day notice and then spent that month alternating between panic, regret and hysteria. The real shocker—that I was easily replaceable—came when the company filled my position two weeks after my notice. The last day on the job I looked into the bathroom mirror and asked: Who are you?

The silence was deafening.

Suddenly, I had no job on which to hang my identity; I was putting all my trust in the great unknown, and I was truly scared. But there was also a strange, previously unknown faith buoying me up, telling me, Don't be afraid. Everything will work out. Believe in yourself! I clung to that like a frightened child to her mother's hand.

Finally, I was free to embark on my journey of self-discovery. After a while, I realized I'd never really forgotten who I was—I had just covered it up with work, work and more work. As I took long, slow walks in the woods, I rediscovered my inner core. I listened to my body and slept when it was tired, ate when it was hungry. I reconnected with friends, read dozens of books and wrote in my journal.

That faith did not fail me. Two months later, a friend heard of a low-stress job and helped me get an interview. I got the job—and a hefty pay cut as well—but I don't regret it for a second. That eight-week sabbatical changed my life and taught me that a life without balance isn't worth living—it isn't even livable! I felt a profound gratefulness to my body for sending me such a clear message.

I had dipped my hand in the well of restoration, and I will never forget it. I had finally learned to define myself from the inside out, rather than the outside in.

~Kelly L. Stone
Chicken Soup to Inspire the Body and Soul

Woman to Woman

Gratitude

*Help your brother's boat across and
your own will reach the shore.*
~Hindu Proverb

94

First Pick

"We'll each pick a number, starting from oldest to youngest, then we'll each take a pick, in the order of our numbers. You understand?" Louise was fully in charge. We were taking our pick of Mama's quilts.

None of us wanted to fight. Five sisters and one brother were trying valiantly to honor and respect our parents. Louise is the oldest and had the most daily contact with our mother before her quick death from cancer, long quietly taking over her body, but not loud enough to be noticed until too late. Here we sat, on a cold October day, six middle-aged children in the living room of our youth, with eyes red with grief and nervous sweaty hands.

These last six quilts our mother made were something we needed to be fair about and they were all laid out for our choosing. Although not works of art for the most part, they were our heritage. There was a queen-size Dresden plate and two twin-size patchworks, both in good shape. A double-size, double-knit polyester little girl quilt that we remembered from the era of leisure suits and a queen-size log cabin that told its age by the colors: orange and avocado. Then there was the quilt on my mother's bed, a double-size star pattern of Wedgwood blue chintz and cotton. It was gorgeous. And it smelled like Mama.

We reached into the shoebox one at a time for our numbers, and being the baby, I picked last. Fitting, as I got number six, the last to choose from the bed-cover legacy. Libby was the first, and no one was surprised to watch her gather up the Wedgwood blue chintz and fold it into her bag. When my turn came, the double-knit polyester quilt was left, so I took it, remembering Mother handstitching the pitiful thing. So much work for so little beauty! We'll keep it in the car, I thought to myself, for a picnic blanket.

As the holidays approached, our grief stayed with us, mostly hidden, but popping up unannounced as tears over a remembered song or a phone call impossible to make. We all moved our bodies toward Christmas, even as our minds stayed with Mother in her hospital bed before she died, or in her flower garden — or on her sun porch. Christmas would be hard.

Packages began to arrive, though, and I had to notice that the rest of the world didn't stop in the shadow of my sadness. On Christmas Eve, my children have the privilege of opening one package before bed, but on this night they encouraged me to join in. A large box from Ohio had piqued their interest. What could Aunt Libby have sent?

Laughing, I tore open the box, expecting a joke: an inflatable chair or bubble bath buried in yards of newspaper. As I peeked past the wrapping, my hands shook and my vision wavered through a film of sudden tears. Inside the box lay, neatly folded, the coveted chintz quilt from Mama's bed. I buried my face in the folds to take in the lingering scent of my mother, and to add my tears. On top of the quilt was a card:

To my baby sister — my first pick.

~René J. Manley
Chicken Soup for the Soul Celebrates Sisters

95

They Call Me "The Umbrella Lady"

here wasn't a cloud in the sky that warm June morning when my friend Carole and I started out for a day of shopping. We had learned of a quilt shop which showcased the wares of nearby artisans. Carole's heart was set on finding a blue-and-white Dresden plate quilt to put the finishing touch on her guest bedroom.

We parked the car next to the only traffic light in town, armed with fabric swatches and paint chips. But next door, a ladies' boutique lured us inside where we admired the most exquisite collection of rainwear we had ever seen. As I ran my fingers across the vinyl-laminated floral chintz umbrella, I heard myself exclaim: "These are the most gorgeous umbrellas.... Why, they're just like an old-fashioned flower garden."

A sales clerk hastened to my side. "Perhaps you'd like to try one of them out," she suggested. I opened the oversized canopy. Underneath its protective bouquet, I felt wonderfully carefree and sheltered from the whole world.

But with new tires to buy, there was no money for expensive umbrellas. Besides, even if I could afford one, it wouldn't be a practical purchase.

Back in the sixth grade, I'd once eyed a beautiful, pink, frilly umbrella in a department store window. "Safety patrols need nice umbrellas," I'd explained to Mother.

"Safety patrols need serviceable umbrellas, not flimsy parasols," she countered. "Besides, you might lose it." How I'd wanted to own something pretty as well as practical.

"Thanks for showing me the umbrella," I wistfully muttered to the boutique clerk and headed next door to the quilt shop, a few steps ahead of Carole.

When my friend's steps caught up with mine, I noticed a long, slender box underneath her arm. "This is for you," she said softly. "I've never seen you look so longingly at anything before."

"But Carole, it's not Christmas. It's not even my birthday. You were going to buy a quilt today."

"Look, there won't always be sunshine in the sky like today," she answered convincingly. "And when the rain comes, I want you to think happy thoughts of friendship."

I tossed the umbrella's box in the back seat of the car and placed my treasure beside me for the long drive home. It smelled like a brand-new toy, and I felt as cared for as a little girl tucked in bed with her teddy bear. I rolled down the car window, shut my eyes and inhaled the pure mountain air.

I didn't understand it, but in the weeks that followed, I found myself thinking a lot about umbrellas. I couldn't pass a dime-store display without lingering for a second look, and suddenly I noticed all the broken, frayed and faded umbrellas people all around me carried. Sometimes, warm and dry inside my car during a storm, I'd see folks with no umbrella at all. When I spotted a lady dashing to her car with a plastic bag over the top of her head or an elderly man with umbrella spokes that refused to cooperate, it was as if God was saying to me: "Why not start an umbrella ministry, Roberta? You just give the umbrellas away and trust me to do the rest."

"You want me to give away umbrellas?" I asked God one day. "What if someone thinks that I am the one who doesn't have sense enough to come in out of the rain?"

About that time, my comfortable office at work was temporarily moved outdoors to a trailer with no canopied breezeway. During rainstorms, water collected on the roof and poured down in torrents as I came and went, despite the oversized umbrella Carole had given to me. I began to think incessantly about umbrellas.

Gingerly, I purchased only one umbrella at a time to test the waters of this new venture. First, I gave an umbrella to an acquaintance facing surgery. "Into each life some rain must fall. I hope that sunny days are ahead," I explained. As it turned out, her surgery wasn't successful, and I felt utterly foolish. Then she sent me this note: "Thanks for that beautiful umbrella. I can't explain it, but each time I look at it, I feel so loved."

Soon after, a friend whose son had left home telephoned. "Could you just come and spend the evening with me?" she asked. I took her an umbrella, and without saying a word, I prayed that God's son"shine would touch her home and shield her from the storms.

As time went on, I discovered wonderful umbrellas on sale at record low prices. I discreetly stashed some in a hallway closet and tucked others in a sack in the back seat of my car. "Please show people that you are the real source of these umbrellas," I prayed. And, with few words exchanged, the recipients amazingly understood that the umbrellas symbolized both friendship and God's blanket of protection.

It had seemed at first to be the kind of undertaking I could keep hidden, camouflaged in the secret corners of my heart, my closet and my car. I chose my umbrella recipients with precision—people whose paths never crossed, out-of-towners and total strangers; a colleague who had lost her job; a friend who moved to a new city; an innkeeper who operates a bed-and-breakfast establishment; a farmer selling tomatoes at a roadside stand; friends facing a monsoon of difficulty and passersby who seemed to need a bit of encouragement.

But unbeknownst to me, the word of my "umbrella fixation" leaked out. One day, I ran into shelves of lovely umbrellas at a nearby glassware outlet. "I have a feeling you're the umbrella lady," the manager quipped with a curious glance at my armful of finds. "I've heard all about you, and do I have a deal for you! They got us mixed up with another company and sent us their overstock of umbrellas." I scooped up another one, featuring a perky apple motif, sure to charm any teacher.

The following week, a retired teacher from Arizona telephoned me. "I read your recent article on the teacher in one of the crafts magazines," she explained. "I'll be passing through West Virginia and I'd like to meet you."

After we arranged our meeting, I asked a friend, "What do you think about me giving her an umbrella? I just bought that one with red apples splattered all over it."

"I wouldn't do that if I were you," she said. "It doesn't seem very professional. And, besides, you've never even met her before. She'll think you're crazy."

So, dressed in the "proper" clothes and prepared to say the "proper" words, I drove to the restaurant where we were to meet. As I opened my door, the skies opened in a sudden downpour. After I located the teacher in the lobby, she admitted with a lighthearted laugh: "Can you believe I forgot to pack an umbrella? Where I live we haven't had any rain for weeks."

I instantly regretted having no umbrella for her. Why had I not trusted my own instincts? Why had I sought someone else's opinion and allowed another person to put a damper on my umbrella ministry?

The next morning, I wrapped the frivolous apple-print umbrella with practical plain brown paper, tied it up with a piece of heavy, serviceable twine, and addressed it to my new friend. I was certain she, too, could use something pretty as well as practical.

"Another umbrella?" the postmistress queried when I placed it on the counter. By now, she was familiar with the contents of my ubiquitous, long, slender boxes. "Oh, this one's bound for Arizona," she chuckled, as the relentless rain poured outside. "An umbrella headed for the desert... now, that's a new one."

I smiled to myself at the wonder of how an umbrella—such a simple object—when received unexpectedly can brighten just about anyone's day and help people from all walks of life feel cared for and protected. Never again, I promised myself, would I allow anyone to squelch an inner prompting to reach out to someone else, no matter how trivial it seemed. This time it had been a compelling urge to give away umbrellas, but in the future there would be other ideas, other opportunities, and I must never disregard them.

When I turned on the car radio, I heard the weatherman's grim prediction: "More rain expected tomorrow, for the third day in a row."

But I've been growing rather fond of precipitation. For hidden deep in my heart is God's bright forecast: "Continued showers of blessing."

~Roberta L. Messner
Chicken Soup for the Golden Soul

96

The Scar

Everything has beauty, but not everyone sees it.
~Confucius

His thumb softly rubbed the twisted flesh on my cheek. The plastic surgeon, a good fifteen years my senior, was a very attractive man. His masculinity and the intensity of his gaze seemed almost overpowering.

"Hmmm," he said quietly. "Are you a model?"

Is this a joke? Is he kidding? I asked myself, and I searched his handsome face for signs of mockery. No way would anyone ever confuse me with a fashion model. I was ugly. My mother casually referred to my sister as her pretty child. Anyone could see I was homely. After all, I had the scar to prove it.

The accident happened in fourth grade, when a neighbor boy picked up a hunk of concrete and heaved the mass through the side of my face. An emergency room doctor stitched together the shreds of skin, pulling cat-gut through the tattered outside of my face and then suturing the shards of flesh inside my mouth. For the rest of the year, a huge bandage from cheekbone to jaw covered the raised angry welt.

A few weeks after the accident, an eye exam revealed I was near-sighted. Above the ungainly bandage sat a big, thick pair of glasses. Around my head, a short fuzzy glob of curls stood out like mold growing on old bread. To save money, Mom had taken me to a beauty school where a student cut my hair. The overzealous girl hacked away cheerfully. Globs of hair piled up on the floor. By the time her instructor wandered over, the damage was done. A quick conference followed, and we were given a coupon for a free styling on our next visit.

"Well," sighed my father that evening, "you'll always be pretty to me," and he hesitated, "even if you aren't to the rest of the world."

Right. Thanks. As if I couldn't hear the taunts of the other kids at school. As if I couldn't see how different I looked from the little girls whom the teachers fawned over. As if I didn't occasionally catch a glimpse of myself in the bathroom mirror. In a culture that values beauty, an ugly girl is an outcast. My looks caused me no end of pain. I sat in my room and sobbed every time my family watched a beauty pageant or a "talent" search show.

Eventually I decided that if I couldn't be pretty, I would at least be well-groomed. Over the course of years, I learned to style my hair, wear contact lenses and apply make-up. Watching what worked for other women, I learned to dress myself to best advantage. And now, I was engaged to be married. The scar, shrunken and faded with age, stood between me and a new life.

"Of course, I'm not a model," I replied with a small amount of indignation.

The plastic surgeon crossed his arms over his chest and looked at me appraisingly. "Then why are you concerned about this scar? If there is no professional reason to have it removed, what brought you here today?"

Suddenly he represented all the men I'd ever known. The eight boys who turned me down when I invited them to the girls-ask-boys dance. The sporadic dates I'd had in college. The parade of men who had ignored me since then. The man whose ring I wore on my left hand. My hand rose to my face. The scar confirmed it; I was ugly. The room swam before me as my eyes filled with tears.

The doctor pulled a rolling stool up next to me and sat down. His knees almost touched mine. His voice was low and soft.

"Let me tell you what I see. I see a beautiful woman. Not a perfect woman, but a beautiful woman. Lauren Hutton has a gap between her front teeth. Elizabeth Taylor has a tiny, tiny scar on her forehead," he almost whispered. Then he paused and handed me a mirror. "I think to myself how every remarkable woman has an imperfection, and I believe that imperfection makes her beauty more remarkable because it assures us she is human."

He pushed back the stool and stood up. "I won't touch it. Don't let anyone fool with your face. You are delightful just the way you are. Beauty really does come from within a woman. Believe me. It is my business to know."

Then he left.

I turned to the face in the mirror. He was right. Somehow over the years, that ugly child had become a beautiful woman. Since that day in his office, as a woman who makes her living speaking before hundreds of people, I have been told many times by people of both sexes that I am beautiful. And, I know I am.

When I changed how I saw myself, others were forced to change how they saw me. The doctor didn't remove the scar on my face; he removed the scar on my heart.

~Joanna Slan
A Second Chicken Soup for the Woman's Soul

97

Too Young to Understand

I ask not for a lighter burden, but for broader shoulders.
~Jewish Proverb

I sighed and set aside my pen. Writing a letter to a Marine stationed in Cambodia was the last thing I wanted to be doing. Why was Grandma insisting that I be his pen pal?

Posters of Bobby Sherman and David Cassidy adorned the walls of my room, where I was working; my bed behind me was covered with a pink spread. I loved the Partridge Family and stuffed animals—in short, I was a typical, self-absorbed thirteen-year-old American girl. The Vietnam conflict was something my parents and other grown-ups fretted about. I was too young to understand that stuff.

"Dear Corporal Stephen Conboy," I wrote reluctantly. I don't even know this guy, I thought. He won't write back!

I was wrong. Corporal Conboy not only wrote back, but he sent me letters almost every day. Before long, I was hurrying home from school in the afternoons, searching through the mail for an envelope addressed to me in Steve's bold handwriting. When one was there, I'd flush with excitement, tearing open the letter as if there were a million dollars inside. There was no money; it was his words that were worth so much to me.

Opening each of his letters was like opening a window to gaze into a world I never knew existed. Steve described a war-torn

Southeast Asia, completely unlike the safe and sleepy upstate New York town I called home. He told me about his duties there, his friends, his hopes, his concerns. But always, inevitably, Steve's letters turned to the children.

The fierce fighting in Cambodian jungles had orphaned many children, leaving them desperately in need of care. Steve spent much of his free time volunteering at an orphanage run by a group of French nuns, performing various chores and playing with the children. His kindness stirred my awakening conscience.

I filled boxes with chocolate bars and homemade cookies and shipped them to Steve to hand out in the orphanages. (I was only thirteen and a little vague on the nutritional benefits of the care packages I was sending.) But I was sincere. Like Steve, I felt that something about the orphans compelled me to do something—anything—to help.

"Tell me more about the orphans and how they got there," I would beg him in my letters, but no matter how many times I asked, Steve would never write about that.

When his tour of duty ended, Steve was reassigned to another part of the world, and his letters became less frequent, then discontinued altogether. His influence on me, though, had just begun.

Eventually, I abandoned David Cassidy, my pink bedspread and even my stuffed animals. I grew up, married and planned for a family. When, after several years, no children came, my husband and I discussed adoption. Memories of Steve's letters came to my mind. "Let's adopt from overseas," I urged my husband, and so we made a trip to Romania to visit the orphanages. Then I discovered why Steve Conboy had been so drawn to the Cambodian war orphans—and why he was never able to write about their stories.

As we walked through the orphanages, it crushed my spirit to see the neglected children. During our two trips there, we saw them freezing in their cribs in the harsh winters and sweltering in the scorching summers. Many of them were hanging on to life by a thread, with little hope. Their plight moved me beyond words.

Though my husband and I successfully adopted two of the

orphans and brought them home to live in comfort and security, far from the neglect they would have known, I was haunted by the innocent, starving orphans who were still over there. I wanted to do something for them.

I began collecting items for care packages to send to the Romanian orphanages. No chocolate bars this time, but crate after crate of formula, medicine and toys. Our basement began to look like a mini-warehouse for a rescue mission.

One day, while I was labeling another care package to send, my mind drifted to thoughts of the young corporal who had been my pen pal twenty-five years before. I wondered if I could reach him now.

After some investigation, I found his current address. I contemplated the best way to contact him and decided I would rely on the connection we'd already established so many years earlier. Eagerly, I sat down to write him a letter.

I glanced at the pictures on my desk of our two smiling, healthy children. Then I picked up my pen. "I am regularly sending care packages to orphans in Romania," I began. "I don't have to describe to you their situation or how it touches my heart; I know you will remember from your own days in Cambodia." I paused, wondering what to say next. I wanted him to know that he had planted a seed that changed the course of my life. "I do want to tell you what your letters did to open my eyes to the world when I was a little girl," I continued. Then I told him about my children and asked him to write back.

When I received a letter addressed to me in his familiar bold handwriting, I ripped it open eagerly. Steve wrote that he was still a Marine and traveled all over the world. In fact, he had been surprised about my Romanian connection, since not long before he'd received my letter, he had requested an assignment in Romania!

Soon after, Steve accepted my invitation to meet our family. I was nervous, but when I finally saw the man who had given my fledgling conscience wings, something in me felt complete.

Since then, Steve and I have continued our friendship through letters, e-mail and the occasional phone call. I have shared my children's growth and progress with him, for in a very real way, they are his children, too—born of the dream he inspired in me when I was too young to understand but old enough to care.

~Barbara Sue Canale
Chicken Soup for the Veteran's Soul

98

A Boy's Bike

I grew up in the small town of Cazenovia located smack in the middle of New York State. At thirteen, I met Ruth, a girl with a personality like an unbroken mare, wild and unpredictable. We became fast friends.

Ruth had a way of convincing me to do things I normally would not do. For example, when my parents were going to buy me a new bicycle, I had planned to get a regular girl's bike, the one without the top crossbar. Ruth suggested a boy's bike instead. I was scared of that horribly high top bar. I just knew I'd fall flat on my face trying to get my leg over it. Ruth convinced me I could do it, and soon a blue ten-speed boy's bike became my pride and joy.

Ruth and I rode our ten-speeds everywhere—around town, around the lake, into the hills, and over to Syracuse and back. We even bought saddlebags and racks so we could carry gear for overnight trips. For us, there was no greater pleasure than climbing on our bikes and heading off for a twenty-mile jaunt.

One day I heard a story about a group who had ridden from Buffalo to Albany, along the old Erie Canal tow path. The idea of a long-distance bicycle trip captured my imagination. So it was I who talked Ruth into doing something—a five-day tour to Buffalo and back, halfway across the state. We could stay with my grandparents in Rochester and Buffalo.

Plans were made. We got maps, put together gear and set the

date. We were all ready for our trip when, suddenly, Ruth's parents told her she couldn't go. So ended our bike tour before it began.

Grudgingly, I accepted that we were not going on our long-distance bike tour, but in the back of my mind I knew that someday I would.

Years later I got married, moved to San Diego, and had a successful career, a nice car and a wonderful house—everything the yuppie could ever desire. I convinced Brian, my husband, to buy a ten-speed bike, and most Saturday mornings we would go riding somewhere out in the country.

It wasn't too long before memories of that aborted bike trip returned, and my yearning to do it grew. But this time, my ambitions were much higher, a coast-to-coast ride. So one day I said to Brian, "Somehow all this riding doesn't seem worthwhile unless we're going somewhere. What would you think about riding cross-country?"

I couldn't believe it when Brian said, without hesitation, "Sure."

Soon we were selecting routes, buying new bikes, borrowing equipment, arranging time off from work, and training, training, training. We were excited, yet at the same time, we were somewhat apprehensive.

How would we do? Could we handle sitting on the seat of a bicycle day after day, mile after mile? Would we get injured or sick? Could we tolerate whatever Mother Nature could throw at us? What about those infamous headwinds of the plains? Would they force us to quit? Is two months long enough? And would we still be talking to each other at the end?

On August 5, 1988, after months of preparation, we turned our first pedal and our journey of four thousand miles began with just one push.

Two months later, on October 2, we arrived in Bar Harbor, Maine—safe, pooped and still very much in love. In fact, on that first day out of Bellingham, while riding on a quiet road along the Skagit River, Brian had made a prediction: "This could be addictive." And it was.

By the time we reached Bar Harbor, we were hooked. As we

pushed our bikes down to the water's edge to dip the wheels in the Atlantic Ocean, I kept repeating, "I wish we could take a week rest and then keep on going." Jobs, a new house, car payments and one cat awaited us in San Diego. We had to go back. But a new dream had begun to form for both of us—a worldwide bike journey.

For the next eight years, we continued taking short bicycle trips, a few weeks each year. Yet our dream of a worldwide bike tour persisted. We knew that riding around the world at a pace that would allow us to explore would take many years.

Could we gather the money to allow us this amount of time? How much would it take? While bicycling can be cheap—basic food and camping is about all that's required—it does take some capital. So we started saving.

We sold our house, all our furniture and our cars—almost everything we owned. It was heart-wrenching. We gave away or sold everything that had defined our lives for nearly fifteen years. But we had our goal: We knew what we wanted to do and that kept us going.

I often felt frustrated, angry and depressed, questioning if we would ever be able to do it. I had heard that if you have a goal, you need to place some item that represents that goal, in a place where you see it each and every day. Otherwise it can easily get lost in the shuffle of day-to-day life. So, in my office, right in front of me, I hung a poster of a bike tourist riding up the Going-to-the-Sun Highway in Glacier National Park. This poster was my reminder. I'd look at it, say to myself, Soon. It's not far off, regain my composure and get back to the job at hand.

On August 3, 1995, in sweltering heat just outside Denver, Colorado, we climbed aboard our loaded bicycles and took off on a journey around the world.

Two years later, on October 9, 1997, after riding through Mexico, Belize and Guatemala, and up the East Coast, we rode into the small town of Cazenovia, New York.

There, after so many years, I pulled up at Ruth's house, on my "boy's bike."

As I walked up to the door, I recounted all the miles I had clocked since that bike trip she and I never took. I could feel tears welling up inside me as I rang the bell and awaited the familiar face of my childhood friend and the opportunity to thank her for pointing me in the right direction.

~Caryl Bergeron
Chicken Soup for the Traveler's Soul

99

My Family Was Separated

Is solace anywhere more comforting than in the arms of a sister.
~Alice Walker

My family was separated and placed into foster care when I was five years old. We grew up living in separate homes, never knowing each other. As I grew older, the only memory that remained of my family was of a tall, slender woman always being there to comfort me. In my mind, this woman was my mother. I believed that someday she would return and life would be normal again. She was in my prayers throughout my childhood.

On Thanksgiving Day, which was also my forty-fifth birthday, there wasn't much to celebrate. My son was moving to another state, and I was feeling not only older but also sad to be losing the closeness of the only family I knew. A card arrived in the mail with a return name and address of someone I didn't recognize. Opening it, I found a Thanksgiving wish with a short note reading, "I was thinking of you on your birthday, Mom." The memories of the tall, slender woman flashed through my mind. My feelings felt like a roller coaster going from anger to extreme happiness in moments. If this was my mother, why had she abandoned us? Why didn't she ever come to get me? Why would she be writing now, after all these years? At the same time, I wanted to hear her voice and feel her warmth.

For two weeks, the card lay on the table tearing at my heart. Finally, summing up the courage to call information, I got her number.

Holding my breath and trying to calm my heart, I dialed. On the fifth ring, I felt relief that no one was answering. Then, just as I was about to hang up, a voice from the past said, "Hello." Unsure of what to say, I asked to whom I was speaking. It turned out to be my older sister who was cleaning out our mother's apartment. Two weeks after sending the card, Mom had died.

As we talked, reacquainting ourselves, I asked what my mom looked like. My sister was surprised that I didn't remember. She told me Mom was a very short, stocky lady. Then who was the tall, slender woman that I remember?

As we continued our conversation, our family and our life began returning to me.

My older sister was seven when our mother left us. For two years, she was the one caring for us, keeping us safe, cooking our meals and drying our tears. She was the one holding me at night when nightmares woke me, singing me songs, wiping my tears when I was scared. It was my sister who told me to run and lock myself in the bathroom as she tried to keep foster care from taking us away.

We talked for hours that night, reminiscing about the past. She had found our brother and baby sister, and we made plans to reunite after forty years of separation. Neither one of us wanted the night to end, but as dawn approached we finally gave in. "By the way," I asked before hanging up, "how tall are you?"

She answered, "Five-foot-nine, why?"

"Because you were the tall, slender woman who made the difference in my life." She was crying as I said, "Good night, I love you."

~Nora Steuber-Tamblin
Chicken Soup for the Sister's Soul

100

Tearing Down the Wall

Forgiveness does not change the past, but it does enlarge the future.
~Paul Boese

There was a moment, a day, when I first discovered that my father was famous. I was about five years old, and my parents had taken me to Disneyland. We were waiting to get on the Teacup ride when dozens of people realized that Ronald Reagan, the host of General Electric Theater, was there. We were suddenly surrounded by eager, smiling faces and arms begging for my father's autograph.

I remember looking up at my handsome father and feeling frightened that he was being taken from me, claimed by strangers, swallowed by the crowd.

Daughters lean toward their fathers in ways that they never do with mothers: tenderly, with unrequited longing. If that father is famous, the longing for him cuts deeper until it is a river running through your life, drowning every other relationship.

I was fourteen when my father was elected governor of California; I knew there would be no turning back. Politics is a demanding mistress and for eight years, California was my father's other child. I was consumed with sibling rivalry; I was angry, petulant. I wanted more of him, his time, his attention. I lashed out bitterly, tearfully, hurting him with my defiance, all the while loving him desperately. My real fury was at the life of public service I believed had taken him from me.

When he was elected president in 1981, America was now the favored child, or so I believed. During his two terms in office, I felt that when I reached for him, all I could grasp was his shadow.

I got my revenge with other men. I frequently chose ones whose lives had no opening for me, oftentimes, married men. Or I would set my sights on men who had no ambition, no future. Either way, they were stand-ins for the man who once taught me to ride a horse and swim in the ocean, who climbed hills with me on windy days to fly a kite and who could find Pegasus in a sky full of stars. I used other men to act out my rage, but the two who really suffered were my father and me.

The problem was that I hadn't separated the private man from the public figure. I had been looking at my father's chosen profession and goals as a type of larceny; they were stealing him from me. It took me many years to understand that the shadow people cast in the world is a part of them.

All the while I thought my father had abandoned me. The truth was that I had abandoned him.

I returned as he was starting to leave, pulled away not by his duty or his country, but by a disease. I have returned with a reverence for the life he lived: for the persistence of his dreams and the unfailing faith that let him burn past his history as a poor kid from a dusty Midwest town, past those who scoffed about an actor becoming president, past those who said his passion was just pretense. He proved them all wrong, and his absence left a hole in the world now that he is gone.

History will immortalize Ronald Reagan as the president who helped end the Cold War, who stood in front of the Berlin Wall and said, "Mr. Gorbachev, tear down this wall." As his daughter, I immortalize him in the quiet passages of my heart. By instructing me in the rhythms of nature, my father taught me about life. By waiting for me, the prodigal child, to come back, he taught me patience. I live my life differently for having known him. As dramatically as the Berlin Wall came down, the walls between us crumbled and I stood on open ground, wondering why I had ever put up walls at all.

After the anger, after the ranting and acting out, we finally grow up and we realize it's a gift to be born to someone who dreams big and reaches far. It inspires us to do the same, because their blood runs through us, and the lessons they pass on to us are powerful.

~Patti Davis
Chicken Soup for the Father & Daughter Soul

Twins Entwined

"Diane! Marsha! You girls get on in here. Supper's on the table!"

My sister and I glanced up, quickly and silently signaling each other for a race to the back door. My grandmother stood there, one hand on her hip and the other shielding her eyes from the summer sun. She was heaven in a housedress. She smelled of Jergen's Lotion, chocolate-covered cherries and TubeRose snuff. We worshipped her.

I won the race, almost tackling Nannie in the doorway.

"My Lord, hon, look at you!" she scolded as she pulled me back for inspection. Then her gaze turned to Marsha, who had finally reached the steps. "Now look at your sister. How come she looks like a little lady?"

As we sat down at the dinner table, I shot a look at Marsha. We were twins, joined at the soul from the moment we took our first breaths. We were supposed to be the same, but we weren't—not by a long shot. Marsha loved lace, velvet, patent leather shoes and all of the things girls were supposed to like. She could sit for hours drawing paper dolls, designing their elaborate wardrobes and cutting out all of the patterns with precision.

I was a tomboy. I had a passion for trees and had conquered each and every one in our neighborhood. No boy could climb higher or faster.

I closed my eyes and started to pray that Marsha might be more like me. But then it occurred to me that we were okay with who we each were. I made the mud pies, and she decorated them with pebbles and rose petals. We found ways to work around our differences.

Years passed. We both grew up, married and took on the trappings of responsibility. No more climbed trees or paper dolls.

Somehow during those years, my sweet, prim, spotless sister became a gardener. The child who would never jump into a rain puddle or pat out a mud pie now reveled in the earth. But I, the one who had practically eaten the outdoors every day, shunned it. I was an adult now, after all.

I would shake my head in disbelief when I saw her bury her hands in the soil. When she rattled off the names of her roses, I'd roll my eyes. "I'll never relate to this, Marsha. A rose is a rose!"

So many other things taxed our childhood connection. Finally a time came when it seemed as though our special bond could never be repaired or regained. I had been divorced for years, struggling to raise my son on my own and bouncing from one relationship to the next. My sister was a counselor on a community hotline for battered women. She saw the signs in my life way before I did. She told me—but I didn't want to hear. By the time I realized that she spoke the truth, I had made her the enemy. I ignored the fact that the man that I was living with was methodically and systematically chipping away at my self, at my own identity.

Things got worse. Each day, my only goal was survival. My soul went underground. Finally, one morning while I was getting ready for work, I looked into the mirror and didn't recognize the person staring back at me. Something inside of me snapped. I had to find a way out or die. I called my sister. Although we only lived a few blocks from one another, it had been four years since we had last spoken.

Marsha came to me without hesitation. We agreed that I had to move out, yet I was nearly penniless. I started spending every spare moment looking for a place to live, all the while worrying how I could afford it.

One particular night, after I'd just finished another disappointing search through the real estate ads, my sister called.

"Get dressed, kiddo. I'm coming to get you."

As we drove off in the darkness, I asked Tony, her husband, "What gives? Where are we going?"

All he said was, "Just wait, Diane, you'll see."

We turned down a street and pulled up in front of a house that looked just like the house my grandmother had once owned. It was in disrepair and looked as if it had been vacant for years. The yard was barren—just like my life, I thought. But the place called to me. I knew it was meant to be mine.

Tony worked with someone who knew the owner and persuaded him to rent the property to me, cheap. Marsha's only request was that I let the garden be hers. No problem. I had no interest in it.

On the move-in day, Marsha arrived with a plan showing the beds of the garden, but she said that the choice of plants would be mine.

"I don't know a daffodil from a clump of crab grass," I told her. "You figure it out."

"No," she replied. "This is your playground. The plants have to suit you, not me." I thought she was nuts, but I went along.

We started the garden just days after I moved in. I went to the nursery with her and tried picking by color. I'd point to something and Marsha would shake her head and pass it by, or smile and put it in the cart. It amazed me that you had to buy soil! I was totally ignorant of the process. I thought that things just grew!

Together, we loaded everything in the car and headed for home. We chatted about our purchases and joked about my gardening ignorance. As we pulled into the driveway of my "new" home, I suddenly realized I had not been frightened or unhappy that day—not once.

And then something more happened. There is a moment for each of us that transforms us—a moment just as mundane as any other, but a moment that will forever be etched in your mind just the same. Mine came as I tugged the huge bag of soil over to Marsha. She was on her knees, weeding out a bed we were planting.

"Open it and dump it right here," she demanded.

"The whole thing?" I asked.

"Yep," she said. "The whole darn thing."

I took off my shoes and stood in the midst of the flower bed we were constructing. Then I slit the bag and let the soil cascade down my legs and bury my feet. As the sensation of the warm dirt traveled across my skin, something clicked in my memory: all of those days when I had gone barefoot as a child, and how much I had loved to feel mud squish between my toes. Suddenly I plopped down in the middle of all that dirt and looked directly at my sister.

She knew something had happened. As our eyes held, I reached down and picked up a handful of earth and made a perfect little pie. With tears in her eyes, she looked down beside her, picked up a small pebble and placed it right in the middle of my creation.

We sat there in the warm earth, two grown women streaked with dirt and tears, awed by the love that had never really left us. At that moment, we knew without words that we had come full circle. Nothing on this earth would ever separate us again.

Now as I weed in the fragrant peace of my garden, I realize that there is still a lot of work to be done—in my garden and in my life. But thanks to a sister who wouldn't let go, we're growing just fine, both my garden and I.

~Diane C. Daniels
Chicken Soup for the Gardener's Soul

More

Chicken Soup
for the Soul.

Chicken Soup for the Soul

Share with Us

We would like to know how these stories affected you and which ones were your favorites. Please write to us and let us know.

We also would like to share your stories with future readers. You may be able to help another reader, and become a published author at the same time. Please send us your own stories and poems for our future books. Some of our past contributors have launched writing and speaking careers from the publication of their stories in our books!

The best way to submit your stories is through our web site, at:

www.chickensoup.com

If you do not have access to the Internet,
you may submit your stories by mail or by facsimile.

Chicken Soup for the Soul
P.O. Box 700
Cos Cob, CT 06807-0700
Fax 203-861-7194

Chicken Soup for the Soul®

Enjoy these additional fine books for Women:

Chicken Soup for the Woman's Soul
Chicken Soup for the Mother's Soul
A Second Chicken Soup for the Woman's Soul
Chicken Soup for the Parent's Soul
Chicken Soup for the Expectant Mother's Soul
Chicken Soup for the Christian Family Soul
Chicken Soup for the Mother's Soul 2
Chicken Soup for the Grandparent's Soul
Chicken Soup for the Christian Woman's Soul
Chicken Soup for the Mother & Daughter Soul
Chicken Soup for Every Mom's Soul
Chicken Soup for the Grandma's Soul
Chicken Soup for the Single Parent's Soul
Chicken Soup for the Mother and Son Soul
Chicken Soup for the Working Mom's Soul
Chicken Soup for the Soul: Celebrating Mothers and Daughters
Chicken Soup for the New Mom's Soul
Chicken Soup for the Soul: A Tribute to Moms

There is a special bond between mothers and their sons and it never goes away. This new book contains the 101 best stories and poems from Chicken Soup's library honoring that lifelong relationship between mothers and their male offspring. These heartfelt stories written by mothers, grandmothers, and sons, about each other, span generations and show how the mother-son bond transcends time. Some of these stories will make readers laugh and some will make them cry, but they all will warm their hearts and remind them of the things they love about each other.

978-1-935096-16-0

$\mathscr{C}$heck out the other books in th

How often have you seen a teenage girl pretend to be perturbed, but secretly smile, when she is told that she acts or looks just like her mother? This new collection from Chicken Soup represents the best 101 stories from Chicken Soup's library on the special bond between mothers and daughters, and the magical, mysterious similarities between them. Mothers and daughters of all ages will laugh, cry, and find inspiration in these stories that remind them how much they appreciate each other.

978-1-935096-07-8

Mom will know where it is…what to say…how to fix it." This Chicken Soup book focuses on the pervasive wisdom of mothers everywhere, and includes the 101 best stories from Chicken Soup's library on our perceptive, understanding, and insightful mothers. These stories celebrate the special bond between mothers and children, our mothers' unerring wisdom about everything from the mundane to the life-changing, and the hard work that goes into being a mother every day.

978-1-935096-02-3

Books
for Moms Series

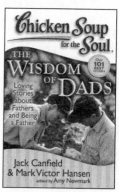

The Wisdom of Dads

Stories about Fathers and Being a Father

978-1-935096-18-4

Children view their fathers with awe from the day they are born. Fathers are big and strong and seem to know everything, except for a few teenage years when fathers are perceived to know nothing! This book represents a new theme for Chicken Soup – 101 stories selected from forty past books, all stories focusing on the wisdom of dads. Stories are written by sons and daughters about their fathers, and by fathers relating stories about their children.

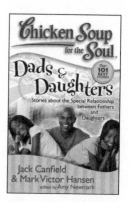

Dads & Daughters

Stories about the Special Relationship between Fathers and Daughters

978-1-935096-19-1

The day a girl is born she starts a special relationship with her father. It doesn't matter whether she is ten years old or fifty – she will always be his little girl. And daughters take care of their dads too, whether it is a tea party for two at age five or loving care fifty years later. This wide-ranging exploration of the relationship between fathers and daughters provides an entirely new reading experience for Chicken Soup fans, with selections from forty past Chicken Soup books. Stories were written by fathers about their daughters and by daughters about their fathers, celebrating the special bond between fathers and daughters as they move through life's phases, from birth to childhood, to those sometimes difficult teen years, to marriage and grandchildren, and to end of life issues.

Books for Families

On Being a Parent
Inspirational, Humorous, and Heartwarming
Stories about Parenthood
978-1-935096-20-7

Parenting is the hardest and most rewarding job in the world. This upbeat and compelling new book includes the best selections on parenting from Chicken Soup's rich history, with 101 stories carefully selected to appeal to both mothers and fathers. This is a great book for couples to share, whether they are just embarking on their new adventure as parents or reflecting on their lifetime experience.

Grand and Great
Grandparents and Grandchildren Share Their
Stories of Love and Wisdom
978-1-935096-09-2

A parent becomes a new person the day the first grandchild is born. Formerly serious and responsible adults go on shopping sprees for toys and baby clothing, smile incessantly, pull out photo albums that they "just happen to have" with them, and proudly display baby seats in their cars. Grandparents dote on their grandchildren, and grandchildren love them back with all their hearts. This new book includes the best stories on being a grandparent from 33 past Chicken Soup books, representing a new reading experience for even the most devoted Chicken Soup fan.

Chicken Soup for the Soul

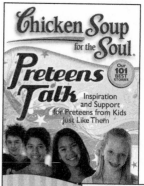

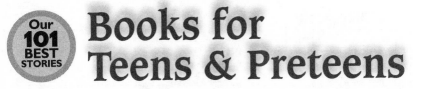

Books for Teens & Preteens

Chicken Soup for the Soul: Preteens Talk
Inspiration and Support for Preteens from Kids Just Like Them
978-1-935096-00-9

Chicken Soup for the Soul: Teens Talk Growing Up
Stories about Growing Up, Meeting Challenges, and Learning from Life
978-1-935096-01-6

Chicken Soup for the Soul: Teens Talk Tough Times
Stories about the Hardest Parts of Being a Teenager
978-1-935096-03-0

Chicken Soup for the Soul: Teens Talk Relationships
Stories about Family, Friends, and Love
978-1-935096-06-1

Chicken Soup for the Soul: Christian Teen Talk
Christian Teens Share Their Stories of Support, Inspiration and Growing Up
978-1-935096-12-2

Chicken Soup for the Soul: Christian Kids
Stories to Inspire, Amuse, and Warm the Hearts of Christian Kids and
Their Parents
978-1-935096-13-9

Chicken Soup for the Soul®
Loving Our **Dogs**
Our 101 BEST STORIES
Heartwarming and Humorous Stories about Our Companions and Best Friends
Jack Canfield & Mark Victor Hansen
edited by Amy Newmark

Chicken Soup for the Soul®
Loving Our **Cats**
Our 101 BEST STORIES
Heartwarming and Humorous Stories about Our Feline Family Members
Jack Canfield & Mark Victor Hansen
edited by Amy Newmark

Chicken Soup for the Soul®
Woman to **Women**
Our 101 BEST STORIES
Women Sharing Their Stories of Hope, Humor, and Inspiration
Jack Canfield & Mark Victor Hansen
edited by

Chicken Soup for the Soul®
Older & **Wiser**
Our 101 BEST STORIES
Stories of Inspiration, Humor, and Wisdom about Life at a Certain Age
Jack Canfield & Mark Victor Hansen
edited by Amy Newmark

Chicken Soup for the Soul®
Happily Ever After
Our 101 BEST STORIES
Fun and Heartwarming Stories about Finding and Enjoying Your M...
Jack Canfield & Mark Victor Hansen
edited b...

Chicken Soup for the Soul®
Tales OF Golf AND Sport
Our 101 BEST STORIES
The Joy, Frustration, and Humor of Golf and Sport
Jack Canfield & Mark Victor Hansen
edited by Amy Newmark

Chicken Soup for the Soul®
Christmas Cheer
Our 101 BEST STORIES
Stories about the Love, Inspiration, and Joy of Christmas
Jack Canfield & Mark Victor Hansen
edited by Amy Newmark

Chicken Soup for the Soul®
Stories of Faith
Our 101 BEST STORIES
Inspirational Stories of Hope, Devotion, Faith, and Miracles
Jack Canfield & Mark Victor Hansen
edited by Amy Newmark

More Great  Books

Chicken Soup for the Soul: Loving Our Dogs
Heartwarming and Humorous Stories about our Companions and
Best Friends
978-1-935096-05-4

Chicken Soup for the Soul: Loving Our Cats
Heartwarming and Humorous Stories about our Feline Family Members
978-1-935096-08-5

Chicken Soup for the Soul: Older & Wiser
Stories of Inspiration, Humor, and Wisdom about Life at a Certain Age
978-1-935096-17-7

Chicken Soup for the Soul: Happily Ever After
Fun and Heartwarming Stories about Finding and Enjoying Your Mate
978-1-935096-10-8

Chicken Soup for the Soul: Tales of Golf and Sport
The Joy, Frustration, and Humor of Golf and Sport
978-1-935096-11-5

Chicken Soup for the Soul: Christmas Cheer
Stories about the Love, Inspiration, and Joy of Christmas
978-1-935096-15-3

Chicken Soup for the Soul: Stories of Faith
Inspirational Stories of Hope, Devotion, Faith and Miracles
978-1-935096-14-6

Chicken Soup
for the Soul

Who Is
Jack Canfield?

ack Canfield is the co-creator and editor of the *Chicken Soup for the Soul* series, which *Time* magazine has called "the publishing phenomenon of the decade." Jack is also the co-author of eight other bestselling books including *The Success Principles™: How to Get from Where You Are to Where You Want to Be*, *Dare to Win*, *The Aladdin Factor*, *You've Got to Read This Book*, and *The Power of Focus: How to Hit Your Business and Personal and Financial Targets with Absolute Certainty*.

Jack has recently developed a telephone coaching program and an online coaching program based on his most recent book *The Success Principles*. He also offers a seven-day *Breakthrough to Success* seminar every summer, which attracts 400 people from fifteen countries around the world.

Jack is the CEO of the Canfield Training Group in Santa Barbara, California, and founder of the Foundation for Self-Esteem in Culver City, California. He has conducted intensive personal and professional development seminars on the principles of success for over a million people in twenty-three countries. Jack is a dynamic keynote speaker and he has spoken to hundreds of thousands of others at more than 1,000 corporations, universities, professional conferences and conventions, and has been seen by millions more on national television shows such as *The Today Show*, *Fox and Friends*, *Inside Edition*, *Hard Copy*, *CNN's Talk Back Live*, *20/20*, *Eye to Eye*, and the *NBC Nightly News* and the *CBS Evening News*.

Jack is the recipient of many awards and honors, including three honorary doctorates and a *Guinness World Records Certificate* for having seven books from the *Chicken Soup for the Soul* series appearing on the *New York Times* bestseller list on May 24, 1998.

To write to Jack or for inquiries about Jack as a speaker, his coaching programs, trainings or seminars, use the following contact information:

Jack Canfield
The Canfield Companies
P.O. Box 30880 • Santa Barbara, CA 93130
phone: 805-563-2935 • fax: 805-563-2945
E-mail: info@jackcanfield.com
www.jackcanfield.com

Who Is
Mark Victor Hansen?

Mark Victor Hansen is the co-founder of *Chicken Soup for the Soul*, along with Jack Canfield. He is also a sought-after keynote speaker, bestselling author, and marketing maven.

For more than thirty years, Mark has focused solely on helping people from all walks of life reshape their personal vision of what's possible. His powerful messages of possibility, opportunity, and action have created powerful change in thousands of organizations and millions of individuals worldwide.

Mark's credentials include a lifetime of entrepreneurial success. He is a prolific writer with many bestselling books, such as *The One Minute Millionaire, Cracking the Millionaire Code, How to Make the Rest of Your Life the Best of Your Life, The Power of Focus, The Aladdin Factor,* and *Dare to Win,* in addition to the *Chicken Soup for the Soul* series. Mark has had a profound influence in the field of human potential through his library of audios, videos, and articles in the areas of big thinking, sales achievement, wealth building, publishing success, and personal and professional development.

Mark is the founder of the *MEGA Seminar Series. MEGA Book Marketing University* and *Building Your MEGA Speaking Empire* are annual conferences where Mark coaches and teaches new and aspiring authors, speakers, and experts on building lucrative publishing and speaking careers. Other MEGA events include *MEGA Info-Marketing* and *My MEGA Life.*

He has appeared on *Oprah*, *CNN*, and *The Today Show*. He has been quoted in *Time*, *U.S. News & World Report*, *USA Today*, *New York Times*, and *Entrepreneur* and has had countless radio interviews, assuring our planet's people that "You can easily create the life you deserve."

As a philanthropist and humanitarian, Mark works tirelessly for organizations such as Habitat for Humanity, American Red Cross, March of Dimes, Childhelp USA, and many others. He is the recipient of numerous awards that honor his entrepreneurial spirit, philanthropic heart, and business acumen. He is a lifetime member of the Horatio Alger Association of Distinguished Americans, an organization that honored Mark with the prestigious Horatio Alger Award for his extraordinary life achievements.

Mark Victor Hansen is an enthusiastic crusader of what's possible and is driven to make the world a better place.

Mark Victor Hansen & Associates, Inc.
P.O. Box 7665 • Newport Beach, CA 92658
phone: 949-764-2640 • fax: 949-722-6912
www.markvictorhansen.com

Who Is
Amy Newmark?

A my Newmark was recently named Publisher of Chicken Soup for the Soul, after a thirty-year career as a writer, speaker, financial analyst, and business executive in the worlds of finance and telecommunications.

Amy is a graduate of Harvard College, where she majored in Portuguese, minored in French, and traveled extensively. She is also the mother of two children in college and has two grown stepchildren.

After a long career writing books on telecommunications, voluminous financial reports, business plans, and corporate press releases, Chicken Soup for the Soul is a breath of fresh air for Amy. She has fallen in love with Chicken Soup for the Soul and its life-changing books, and found it a true pleasure to conceptualize, compile, and edit the "101 Best Stories" books for our readers.

The best way to contact Chicken Soup for the Soul is through our web site, at www.chickensoup.com. This will always get the fastest attention.

If you do not have access to the Internet, please contact us by mail or by facsimile.

Chicken Soup for the Soul
P.O. Box 700
Cos Cob, CT 06807-0700
Fax 203-861-7194

Chicken Soup for the Soul

Thank You!

Our first thanks go to our loyal readers who have inspired the entire Chicken Soup team for the past fifteen years. Your appreciative letters and emails have reminded us why we work so hard on these books.

We owe huge thanks to all of our contributors as well. We know that you pour your hearts and souls into the stories and poems that you share with us, and ultimately with each other. We appreciate your willingness to open up your lives to other Chicken Soup readers.

We can only publish a small percentage of the stories that are submitted, but we read every single one and even the ones that do not appear in a book have an influence on us and on the final manuscripts.

As always, we would like to thank the entire staff of Chicken Soup for the Soul for their help on this project and the 101 Best series in general.

Among our California staff, we would especially like to single out the following people:

- D'ette Corona, who is the heart and soul of the Chicken Soup publishing operation, and who put together the first draft of this manuscript

- Barbara LoMonaco for invaluable assistance in obtaining the fabulous quotations that add depth and meaning to this book

- Patty Hansen for her extra special help with the permissions for these fabulous stories and for her amazing knowledge of the Chicken Soup library

- Patti Clement for her help with permissions and other organizational matters.

In our Connecticut office, we would like to thank our able editorial assistants, Valerie Howlett and Madeline Clapps, for their assistance in setting up our new offices, editing, and helping us put together the best possible books.

We would also like to thank our master of design, Creative Director and book producer Brian Taylor at Pneuma Books LLC, for his brilliant vision for our covers and interiors.

Finally, none of this would be possible without the business and creative leadership of our CEO, Bill Rouhana, and our president, Bob Jacobs.

Chicken Soup for the Soul

www.chickensoup.com